CELEBRATING

50 YEARS

Texas A&M University Press

publishing since 1974

Farm-to-Freedom

Gideon Lincecum Nature and Environment Series
Sponsored by Jerry B. Lincecum and Peggy A. Redshaw

Farm-to-Freedom

In Our Garden, After the War

Two More Papayas

I see them first.
Two green thumbs
that will grow into
orange-yellow delights
smelling of summer.
Middle sweet
between a mango and a pear.
Soft as a yam
gliding down
after three easy,
thrilling chews.

—Thanhha Lai, from *Inside and Out and Back Again*

And we might, in our lives, have many thresholds, many houses to walk out from and view the stars, or to turn and go back to for warmth and company. But the real one—the actual house not of beams and nails but of existence itself—is all of earth, with no door, no address separate from oceans or stars, or from pleasure or wretchedness either, or hope, or weakness, or greed.

—Mary Oliver, from *Upstream: Selected Essays*

Interstitial spaces and identities can become points of connection and belonging. Of course, they could also be points of contention and rootlessness. However, home gardens of herbs, fruit trees, and vegetables have birth meaningful and appreciable in-between spaces for Vietnamese Americans. Furthermore, they have transplanted them as refugee Americans, a term indeed marked with two distinct identities—as refugees and as Americans—merging into a singular complex identity of in-between*ness* and both*ness*. As refugee Americans, they could not simply erase their traumas of war, refuge, resettlement; nor could they remain silent, choosing instead to stake their belonging as Americans, particularly when they transformed this land into beautiful food gardens of various portions and purposes.

Immigrants and refugees help build much of America, not only to create a better future and country here in the United States, but also to remember the past; the past that they lost in time, as well as in familial and cultural connections that are essential to home. This is the price that immigrants and refugees pay: the lost time and the disconnection to their family, homeland, and past. This is their price of admission to the United States. Upon planting roots in America, they would have to restart their lives; endure painful toil and hard labor; partake low-paying and often denigrating menial jobs; experience a loss of identity; be constantly reminded to prove their self-worth; and a host of other challenges for them and their offspring. However, in memory and post-memory, refugees and immigrants do retain and reconnect a part of their past, and cultivating a home garden helps them establish cultural continuities and find a way home. For Vietnamese refugees and immigrants, home gardens surround their houses with the possibility of reclaiming a homeland on a foreign soil. Of equal significance is finding emancipatory foodways through food sovereignty, culinary citizenship, and homeland duality; in this way home gardens lend themselves to Vietnamese foodways, creating essential stories and memories that can heal, feed, suture, root, and embolden Vietnamese American lives. Such home gardens help Vietnamese diasporans answer the question: How do we make a foreign place smell, taste, look, and feel safer and more familiar as we cope with (dis)placement and (be)longing on this multi-American land? So, on these positive, interstitial spaces—and in-between two homelands—lay green gardens that bear herbs, vegetables, and fruit trees where Vietnamese American home gardeners could smell, taste, see, and feel more at home.

If you follow the foodways, from Việt Nam to desperate refugee camps across Southeast Asia, to the new frontiers of Vietnamese America, produce cherished and grown by Vietnamese can be found memorialized on old South Vietnamese stamps (figure 0.1), in home gardens, in makeshift or traditional kitchens, and at dinner

Figure 0.1 Postage Stamps from South Việt Nam. (Collection of Vietnamese stamps and currency. MS-SEA052, Box 1, Folder 3. Special Collections and Archives, UC Irvine Libraries, Irvine, California.)

tables where homegrown produce is finally to be consumed together in family meals. We all cherish fresh, wholesome, affordable, and accessible food because it nourishes our souls, minds, and bodies. Akin to other cultures, food is embodied in Vietnamese heritage, and when Vietnamese American home gardeners dig the soil and plant, raise, and nurture familiar crops, they speak an unspoken language with the land they cultivate. I like to believe that the diacritical marks in the Vietnamese language are the herbs, fruits, and greens in Vietnamese cooking. Without them, it could dramatically alter the flavor of a dish, just as if one were to remove even one diacritical mark the entire meaning of a Vietnamese word is altered. Hence, commonly grown produce—papayas, water spinach, luffas, lemongrass, mint, and chili peppers—is essential to Vietnamese foodways, just as diacritical marks are to the Vietnamese language.

A garden is often scribed as a literary metaphor, a religious allegory or civilization marker, or as a place of sanctuary, peace, and prosperity. Home gardens encompass more than just herbs, vegetables, and fruit trees for Vietnamese American gardeners to nurture their bodies and to be consumed with their meals. Their home gardens not only produce food, but they also provide Vietnamese Americans a memory and piece of *home*, transporting them figuratively back to their homeland of Việt Nam, feeding their bodies, nurturing and healing their refugee souls, and reminding them of what it is to be Vietnamese. Laboring on the land of their backyards (and sometimes even their front yards) Vietnamese diasporans root themselves here and make a home in the United States, while also rooting themselves elsewhere, cultivating their Việt Nam to remember and reminisce through home gardening. This simultaneous duality of home becomes a positive way to reflect and rewrite their traumas of war, uprootedness, relocation, and marginalization, which could easily overwhelm them in a bitter cycle and entrapment of perpetual statelessness, of neither belonging here (United States) nor there (Việt Nam); sentiments that too often echo and resonate among refugees and immigrants alike. However, home gardens offer Vietnamese Americans spaces that become places of their own, where they may root, grow, and nurture their belonging to one homeland, while longing for another. In essence, through cultural continuities and political acts such as home gardening, refugees and immigrants seek to regain an old homeland while eking out a life in a new homeland. As a result, they are choosing a duality as active agents of history by challenging perpetual statelessness, even as they operate their lives in continuous in-betweenness, constantly searching and craving for a home they have lost.

In comparison to war, exile, relocation, and resettlement, what has been recreated may first appear minuscule, inconsequential, and irrelevant. However, seeds, soil, sun, and water, mixed with physical labor, persistence, ingenuity, and pursuit of life's rich rewards, have, without a doubt, helped connect Vietnamese Americans to their old homeland of Việt Nam. The products of their labor—a cornucopia of vegetables, fruits, and herbs—reward the growers with an opportunity to provide a lifetime of repasts that are shared among family, relatives, and friends. These meals bind loved ones, communities, and generations. Hence, they regain some of their lost time and place, a disruptive experience that has separated immigrants and refugees from their loved ones and beloved homeland.

For Vietnamese diasporic gardeners, their home gardens are places of sanctuary and healing as well. They heal the mind, body, and soul, giving them peace, solace, and joy. What grows in Việt Nam continues to be grown in the home gardens of Vietnamese Americans, creating a transnational link via shared foodways. Such strong personal ties to food have survived through wars, exodus, and uprootedness, opening a gateway to memories of a bygone era and the ghost country that is South Việt Nam,[1] a transhistorical cord to a nation that has ceased to exist since April 30, 1975.

From a farming culture and country rich in agricultural and culinary history, it is not at all surprising to witness a plethora of home gardens across Vietnamese America. From the small, tight spaces of dense working-class neighborhoods where condominiums are colloquially known as "villages," to the large, lush gardens in the front and backyards of two-story brick homes in middle class, suburban neighborhoods, Vietnamese Americans display their ability to transform negative spaces of cultural disconnect and statelessness into food gardens of their own. What is also amazing is the refugee resilience that was shown in camps, where thousands of post-war Vietnamese and other Southeast Asian refugees sought and waited for months, even years, to gain political asylum to a willing host country. Despite the squalid, overcrowded living conditions and the scant resources while they existed in a state of legal status purgatory and chronic uncertainty,[2] Vietnamese refugees discovered opportunities to cultivate the empty lots of refugee camps, converting them to more comforting places of normalcy and familiarity. As they awaited their fates, dictated by more powerful, unknown forces in the bodies of United Nations High Commissioner for Refugees (UNHCR) agents and local government officials, they relied on their farming abilities and resourcefulness to cultivate small garden plots. From refugee camps in Indonesia, Thailand, and others, Vietnamese refugees used their agricultural knowledge in hopes of momentarily relieving themselves from the daily stresses of living in political limbo, unsure of whether or not they would be forcefully repatriated to Việt Nam, remain in refugee camps for months (even years) on end, or, if lucky, finally gain approval and clearance for political asylum to migrate to another nation.

For Vietnamese refugees and immigrants who were "fortunate" to have gained asylum to resettle in another country such as the United States, they had to confront the practical and personal issues of resettling and taking care of their families and loved ones while also experiencing the trauma of loss, whether it was those they left behind in Việt Nam, those they lost at sea, or those they befriended in refugee camps. Upon resettlement in America, home gardens, no matter how big or small, diverse or homogeneous, provided Vietnamese refugees and immigrants a place of sanctuary, peace, recovery, nurture, and memory. These home gardens are more than just food or kitchen gardens: they are cultural and personal gardens that provide daily healing, memories, and hope through the collaborative harmony of nature and honest labor, feeding their bodies, minds, and spirits. Vietnamese American home gardeners seek and follow their traditional foodways to help regain their freedom—freedom from despair, hopelessness, and foreignness—as they unearth a new freedom and strive to cultivate two homelands.

This book attempts to capture their freedom from war, destruction, destitution, and rootlessness through their cultivation and production of home gardens. My intended audience includes (but not limited to) Việt Nam War and food historians, Asian Pacific American history and critical refugee studies scholars, undergraduate and graduate students, horticulturists, small farmers and gardeners, and, most of all, Vietnamese Americans themselves. My research encompasses interviews, newspaper articles, cookbooks, recipe books, memos, photographs, maps, census data, and other primary sources from the Southeast Asian Archive and Special Collections at the University of California–Irvine Libraries, Special Collections at the University of Houston Libraries, Houston Asian American Archive Chao Center for Asian Studies at Rice University, Houston Metropolitan Research Center, Foodways Texas Greater Oral History Project, Manzanar National Historic Site Collection, Gerald R. Ford Presidential Library and Museum at the University of Michigan, and the Sam Johnson Việt Nam Archive at Texas Tech University. I also incorporate and cite secondary sources such as published articles from academic journals, literary novels, and poetry collections.

The book aims to historicize Vietnamese Americans and their home gardens with an emphasis on Vietnamese Texans and their struggles for food sovereignty, homeland duality, and culinary citizenship through the act of gardening and the produce they cultivate. From war-torn Việt Nam to Southeast Asian refugee camps and to resettlement in Texas, home gardens give Vietnamese Texans some peace, solace, and freedom by retaining their food heritage. The epilogue delves into Vietnamese Texan home gardeners' culinary citizenship connections with contemporary Syrian refugees living in makeshift refugee camps in the deserts of Jordan and Lebanon, and also Congolese refugees who have resettled their lives in southwest Houston. Chapter 6 ("Conclusion") houses the manuscript's thesis: historically marginalized populations in US history (i.e., African Americans, Latinx, and Native Americans) create their own distinctive food gardens to find and gain emancipatory foodways, to preserve their food heritage, to survive and even thrive in spite of the oppression, racism, and marginalization they endure as they transform negative spaces into more positive places built by their own hands. In the process, marginalized gardeners advance the growing foodways of America and its future generations.

In the first chapter, I discuss traditional home gardening in Việt Nam, before and during the Việt Nam War and in refuge. I describe home gardens planted and raised by Vietnamese farmers and gardeners from the French colonial period to the Việt Nam War and to the undesirable refugee camps, in an attempt to survive, nurture themselves at home, and supplement their diet and/or income during colonialism, war, and refuge. For Vietnamese refugees who hurriedly and unexpectedly left Việt Nam near the war's end and after, they attempted to craft some sense of normalcy. A majority ended up living in squalor conditions of far-flung refugee camps located throughout Southeast Asia; such camps existed from the mid-1970s to the late 1990s. Nevertheless, despite subpar or impoverished camp conditions, Vietnamese refugees somehow managed to grow and harvest vegetables, herbs, and fruit trees to survive, nourish their health, pass the time, bond with fellow citizens, and maintain their food heritage by producing astonishing food gardens with limited spaces and resources.

For Vietnamese refugees who escaped from Communist Việt Nam and survived the perilous sailings across the South China Sea, fraught with harrowing ordeals and far too often deadly encounters, there was the arduous and often humiliating ordeal of residing in overcrowded camps while waiting in chronic uncertainty to resolve their political asylum cases. Should they win their cases, Vietnamese refugees then endured the ostracization, marginalization, and acculturation pains of resettling as refugees and strangers in host countries such as the United States. Even though they would experience the unpleasant moments of displacement, they carried with them their home gardening traditions and foodways to a new homeland. Vietnamese refugees were able not only to cultivate vegetables, herbs, and fruits commonly grown in Việt Nam, but also to consume what they were accustomed to eating. Furthermore, the food they produced was essential to the recipes required to make traditional meals made with and served to with family members, relatives, and friends. Only when necessary would Vietnamese American home cooks substitute greens that they were accustomed to consuming in Việt Nam but were difficult to find in the United States, as was more common during their first years of resettlement in the 1970s and early 1980s.

In chapter 2, to historicize the Vietnamese diaspora in the United States, I shift to the American shores, whose land between the "shining" seas is replete with displaced, colonized, and racialized populations eking out a living in the foreign wilderness of America and rendered invisible on the margins of American society. I discuss the Japanese American internment gardeners during World War II and introduce other Asian Pacific Americans and immigrants who cultivated gardens of their own. I look back into US history, retelling the excruciating years of Chinese exclusion, to study and determine how marginalized and racialized Asian Pacific Americans managed to develop garden plots of their own despite the constant threat of racial terror. I also reflect on the impact of the Hart-Cellar Immigration Act of 1965 and investigate how Asian Pacific American populations were transformed by this monumental immigration policy—passed in the midst of the transformative and historic modern civil rights movement—that finally removed the restrictive and racist national origins quota system.

From there, I reintroduce the Vietnamese refugees and elaborate on their resettlement in the United States, particularly in Texas, and examine how and why they decided to relocate to the Lone Star state. I delve into the community formation strategies and their personal lives to elaborate on their own resettlement pains and struggles, and how starting home gardens helped them start the process of healing, remembering, and living as Vietnamese Americans. I argue that, like their Asian Pacific American predecessors, Vietnamese Americans in Texas would actively seek to create new food spaces and determine how to live their own lives. The Vietnamese diasporic communities in North Texas, Houston, and along the Gulf Coast would regrow, retain, protect, and expand their food heritage. Finally, I postulate that Vietnamese foodways not only contribute to the rich culinary history of Asian Pacific American foodways, but they also enhance the cultural visibility and sustainability of what it means to be Asian Pacific American. How could we simply bypass the social construct of the Asian Pacific American identity, when we have not had the opportunity to fully formulate and speak of their own identity, especially with the constant marginalization, racialization, and perpetual foreignness bestowed upon them? Only once they are given their deserved right to explore their identity to the fullest extent, can they fully embrace their American*ness*—an identity that they must construct and develop for themselves. In this sense, we have barely scratched the surface of Asian Pacific Americanism. As a Vietnamese American, I am part of Asian Pacific Americanism and therefore, I identify with their struggles, challenges, and resistance.

In chapter 3, I dedicate attention to Vietnamese Texans and their home gardens and argue that, for Vietnamese diasporic home gardeners, the act of gardening and cultivating fruit trees, herbs, and vegetables help them remember their homes and lives in Việt Nam. Gardening also serves as a leisure activity to maintain their health and wellness, a way to reminisce about their youthful days, forge an escapism from the nightmares and pains of war, loss, and resettlement, and stake a claim in the Texas soil that has become their new plot of homeland in America, giving them an opportunity to cultivate their own unique homeland duality as refugee Americans. Such home gardens are places of sanctuary, where Vietnamese refugees root themselves and overcome the insidious and ever present undertones of rootlessness; a rootlessness that resurfaces with every ugly reminder of a war that summons and rekindles fears they can never forget. But with these home gardens, they become Vietnamese refugee Americans, and their roots grow in every embattled inch of land they sow.

Chapter 3 also showcases stories and articles on Vietnamese Texans cultivating home gardens to produce a wide array of food to nurture the body with healthy, affordable, and accessible greens, sooth the mind, mend the heart, and heal the soul. Here, Vietnamese Texans demonstrate their farming and gardening skills to reconstruct a sustainable life and transform their own yards and neighborhood lots into beautiful, colorful, and healthy garden landscapes; even in the concrete, urban, tired, and worn working class residential quarters. Preparing and cultivating food gardens leads to stronger bonds between loved ones, families, relatives, friends, and neighbors. They share a common practice of laboring the land with their hands, tools, and ingenuity, toiling for hours and days in the sun and rain. Consequently, the more they dig, the deeper their roots are bound to this adopted homeland of America, reviving their connections to their home country of Việt Nam, and thus gradually eroding their (dis)placements and sentiments of statelessness.

Chapter 3 also examines Vietnamese refugees' entry into working-class America. Stateless and nearly penniless, an overwhelming majority of Vietnamese refugees resettled in the United States, struggling to survive and adapt, while often forced to accept low-wage, menial jobs in the fast food, domestic service, and sanitation industries. Yet, here again, they demonstrate their resourcefulness, resilience, gardening efficacy, and innate desire to produce familiar crops and regain some food sovereignty. Vietnamese American home gardeners and cooks also share and exchange their food items and recipes with each other. In giving their fruits, vegetables, and herbs to neighbors, friends, and relatives, Vietnamese American home gardeners perform a communal act that further strengthens their community. In Texas, Vietnamese diasporic home gardeners and cooks provide and exchange recipes and advice on food preparation, which lends to communalism and bonds them to their unique community. They share their recipes, seeds, gardening tips, and food they produce with others, which constitutes a distinctive communal act. Furthermore, Vietnamese Texans create makeshift home gardens to transform their limited living quarters into positive green spaces that beautify their modest surroundings, particularly in the working-class residential complexes of southeast Houston.

Chapter 4 unearths a bit of the cooking magic that Vietnamese American home gardeners perform when they use what they produce to create recipes and meals in their kitchens, including outdoor and makeshift kitchens, for familial dinners, showcasing the importance of cooking and sharing a homemade meal together as a family unit. Dining together as a family exemplifies an essential social practice that is central to the Vietnamese household and secures family unity, stability, and tradition. By procuring quintessential ingredients from their home gardens to create recipes and meals in their own kitchens, Vietnamese American home cooks demonstrate the significance of retaining their food heritage. Even makeshift indoor and outdoor kitchens exhibit their traditional food preparations, harking back to their days of living in Việt Nam. For Vietnamese diasporic home cooks, it is not uncommon for the kitchen to be separate from their living quarters. The kitchen may be a shed in the backyard, equipped with a cooking station; or a patio or garage that could be closed off from the rest of the house when cooking; or an added room that extends from the original house. In Vietnamese, a kitchen is called nhà bếp, which literally translates into "kitchen house." Therefore, the primary kitchen for cooking is not always considered as a room inside the house or as part of the living quarters. One major reason is that some Vietnamese American home cooks prefer not to have the lingering smell of cooked food inside the house. To them, the smell of cooked food inside their homes would be considered as adulterating the air. In other words, the aroma from the cooking would actually be considered an unsavory smell if permeating throughout the living quarters of the house.[3]

Furthermore, dining together as a family is an important tradition for Vietnamese American families. Dinnertime is an opportunity for a family to sit down and share a four-course meal, and thus is considered their most important meal of the day. A family that dines together, grows together. This dining ritual traces back to their familial practice in Việt Nam. Vietnamese parents do their utmost diligence to ensure that the entire family living under one roof—which often includes grandparents and extended family members in some households—eats a daily meal together.

I also assert that Vietnamese American home gardeners establish foodways that reconnect them to Việt Nam, and that they also help further diversify American cuisine, particularly Texan and Southern foodways. One path to preserve their food heritage is through home gardening. Vietnamese American home gardeners cultivate fruits, herbs, and vegetables that remind them of their former homeland. They also produce home gardens that include okra and mustard greens, vegetables that are typically cultivated in the US South, as well as popularly consumed by American Southerners. Thus, transnational and regional linkages and foodways are forged and combined by Vietnamese Americans home gardeners. Subsequently, Viet-Tex, Viet-Cajun, and Viet-Southern dishes are created in the restaurant kitchens of Vietnamese Texan chefs, as well as in makeshift kitchens of Vietnamese diasporic homes.

Additionally, Southern, Texas Mexican, Cajun, and Texan influences on Vietnamese gastronomy and vice versa have led to stronger cross-cultural influences and regional ties that are made via the food produced by Vietnamese Texan home gardeners. Plus, Vietnamese Americans bring their Global South food heritage to American Southern foodways; a region and culture imbued with a terribly violent and racist past that continues to haunt the Southern populace today. Yet, Vietnamese refugees and marginalized "others" continue to transform the US South to (re)claim the Southern soil as their own land; a land reclamation that could actually and finally usher in the New(er) South. This makes them culturally connected to the American South and the Texas Gulf Coast, yet also more cognizant that their new homeland is geographically and historically juxtaposed to the terribly violent saga of colonization, slavery, Jim Crowism, and ongoing racial and socioeconomic inequities that plague much of the region (and country).

Chapter 5 shifts the attention to Vietnamese American identity formation through their home gardens and foods they produce, with an emphasis on what I call the tenets of emancipatory foodways: food sovereignty, culinary citizenship, and homeland duality. Here, the exceptional hybridity of their identity is a clear reflection of the perceived perpetual sojourner that is the Vietnamese American. The thousands of Vietnamese refugees who fled their homeland after the fall of Sài Gòn and collapse of South Việt Nam that ended the massively destructive Việt Nam War sought another country to resettle. Such a troubled history of war and exile have left the Vietnamese diaspora bereft of a single, intact homeland. In addition to their marginalization as foreigners in the United States and the racial, class, and gender castes that have historically devastated our country, Vietnamese in America pursue ways to retain their culture and construct their own unique American identity. Furthermore, a history of racial segregation laws, praxis, and violence toward African Americans, Latinx, and Native Americans in the region preceded Vietnamese Americans' arrival in Texas. Ghosts of racial segregation and violence remain to linger and torment Southerners as reminders of the region's troubled past. Vietnamese refugees had their fair share of violent encounters with the Ku Klux Klan during the late 1970s and early 1980s, especially across the Gulf Coast region. Nonetheless, along their journey of finding a home, Vietnamese Americans made attempts to maintain their culture, creating and adding a new hybrid identity to the American mosaic society through home gardens and foodways that firmly plant and root them in this nation through their food sovereignty, culinary citizenship, and homeland duality.

This chapter delves into how Vietnamese Texans achieve emancipatory foodways by protecting and practicing their gardening culture while establishing their own American identity through what they cultivate. I also assert that a form of resistance is in full display by what they produce in their yards, how they prepare their meals, what meals they cook, and how they consume their meals. I argue that Vietnamese Americans grow and utilize their gardens to develop a coping mechanism from their experienced traumas, nurture their spirits and health, further preserve their food heritage, construct an identity, foster a community of like-minded gardeners, resist the gradual erosion of Vietnamese culture in the United States, and achieve homeland duality, food sovereignty, and culinary citizenship—all part of their survival traits (learned and instinctive) from war, refuge, displacement, and racialization. Food sovereignty is about having control over some healthy food sources. If space and resources are available, no matter how limited, refugees and immigrants will usually cultivate produce to gain access to fresh, affordable food, which leads to better overall diet, health, and food security. Immigrants and refugees typically cultivate crops familiar to their daily food consumption from their home country, preserving their food heritage. By preserving their food heritage, they demonstrate food resistance to unhealthy food options that are often ubiquitous in refugee/immigrant working class neighborhoods. To overcome the marginalization of their food heritage, they become agents of food justice, using herbs, fruits, and vegetables from their own farms and gardens to make culinary dishes that remind them of home.

Regarding culinary citizenship, Vietnamese American home gardeners establish roots and a stronger sense of belonging to their Vietnamese homeland by cultivating familiar produce and preserving food heritage. Plus, they establish their roots and rights of belonging here in the United States via gardening familiar crops. In addition, they grow fruit trees, herbs, and vegetables to make and prepare Vietnamese culinary dishes—both traditional and new. While it is not legal citizenship per se, Vietnamese American home gardeners establish culinary citizenship by forging a strong awareness of belonging and connection to two homelands that they cultivate, literally and figuratively. Consequently, they firmly ascertain their rights to belong to the multi-American landscape here in the United States through years of intense labor on the land and sustainable urban gardening.

As for homeland duality, Vietnamese diasporic home gardeners maintain their Vietnamese food heritage and roots via gardening, which in turn gives them the opportunity to establish their American roots. Thus, a symbiotic and interdependent lifestyle is created wherein Vietnamese American home gardeners mold a purpose of belonging to two homelands. Consequently, they avert a double dislocation via seeking and gaining the emancipatory foodways of not only homeland duality, but also food sovereignty and culinary citizenship. Furthermore, they help diversify the culinary and cultural landscapes of Texas with their garden produce and homemade cuisine.

So much of Việt Nam's history has been anchored and moored by the Việt Nam War and for the Vietnamese diaspora. To add to the burgeoning Việt Nam War historiography, critical refugee studies, and ethnic studies that often intertwine and intersect, we need to look further into the Vietnamese American experience and what they have produced in the United States, specifically here in Texas, despite the trau-matic experiences of war, exile, relocation, and being treated as perpetual foreigners. Vietnamese American home gardeners transform their yards into gardens that tran-sition into a positive platiality or place-making.[4]

These chapters cover the gamut of the farm-to-freedom concept and the human desire and embodiment of freedom—freedom from war, tyranny, destruction, oppression, and rootlessness. For many Vietnamese Americans, their food gardens become an essential grounding connection to their lost homeland, more specifi-cally, their ghost country of South Việt Nam. Such gardens and the fruit trees, vege-tables, and herbs they produce are not only small reminders of their Việt Nam, but they also evoke the roots they want to plant in their new home country that is the United States. While some of these home gardens may eventually fade and escape from memory, they nevertheless help nurture and heal the minds, bodies, and spir-its of Vietnamese American gardeners, particularly for those living in Texas.

In their postwar resettlement, and for many, an eventual secondary migration to Texas, what is practiced by generation after generation becomes habitual, a com-mon ground of knowledge and part of the culture—even long after their homeland of South Việt Nam was gone. For them, homeland is neither completely Việt Nam nor completely the United States. For Vietnamese Texans, the common gardening practices entail foodways such as the food they remember, grow, prepare, consume, share, and cherish. Such transnational foodways become significant cultural praxis, resulting in a palatable portal to past memories of taste, smell, sight, and touch—powerful and enduring memories from the war, as well as before the war. Now, these memories—little, but not insignificant fragments of their homeland—are planted and raised in the Texas soil by Vietnamese American home gardeners. When they harvest, give, and consume the bounty they produce from their home gardens, they share a sliver of their homeland. They unearth and maintain a sanctuary from the experiences of war, exile, relocation, and acculturation, and they create a home-land duality, gaining culinary citizenship and food sovereignty in the process of rehabilitation and resilience via gardening.

By replanting their roots and raising bountiful home gardens here in the Texas soil, Vietnamese Texans cultivate ties to a Việt Nam they remember, so that future generations may enjoy the fruits of their labor. Whether purposefully or not, with their hands digging the earth, they have cultivated a farm-to-freedom movement, freeing a part of themselves and others to seek and gain emancipatory foodways that have them further removed from the devastating Việt Nam War and its terrible con-sequences. In addition, they have planted the seeds for future generations to partake the opportunity to expand and strengthen Vietnamese place-making here in the United States and thus have the support, courage, willingness, and grounded history to embrace their two rooted homelands. As a result, they have transitioned themselves to commit to a sense of (be)longing: remembering and re-establishing their Vietnamese food heritage to gain their right to belong here in Texas and the United States. Moreover, they overcame the challenges of (dis)placement caused by a violent and grotesque war, and then being (mis)placed in a foreign land, as Vietnamese diasporans were widely dispersed throughout the United States by the federal government. For Vietnamese home gardeners, their gardens and produce help them cope with the difficulties of (dis)placement, giving them an opportunity to maintain their food heritage and gain cultural sustainability.

Starting with chapter 4 and through the remainder of the book, I transition to using the Vietnamese word first followed by its English translation to further demonstrate the transitional lives of Vietnamese Americans of feeling safer, more comfortable, and proud of their Vietnamese roots.

CHAPTER 1

Kitchen and Food Gardens in War and Refuge

garlic = bawang puteh
onion = bawang kechil

—author unknown, from a pocket diary of
a Vietnamese oceanic refugee, 1979

I believe that one of the most dignified ways we are capable of, to assert and then reassert our dignity in the face of poverty and war's fears and pains, is to nourish ourselves with all possible skill, delicacy, and ever-increasing enjoyment. And with our gastronomical growth will come, inevitably, knowledge and perception of a hundred other things, but mainly of ourselves. Then Fate, even tangled as it is with cold wars as well as hot, cannot harm us.

—MFK Fisher, from *How to Cook a Wolf*

Garlic and onion are two essential ingredients for cooking. For the unknown Vietnamese boat refugee, or "oceanic refugee,"[1] which is the more appropriate term used by Pulitzer Prize-winning author Việt Thanh Nguyễn, these were important. Although he traveled for months and chronicled his arduous journey, filled with Herculean challenges, he made a concerted effort to note the significance of garlic and onion on the final pages of his red pocket diary;[2] he eventually learned those sacred cooking ingredients in the Indonesian language, as Indonesia was the last known place of refuge for him and his family. He scribbled those words, "garlic" and "onion," near the end of his pocket diary—a diary replete with heartaches, setbacks, fierce determination, and desperate hope, matched with words of wisdom and poise and hand-drawn maps. The size and condition of the minuscule red diary, with unsmooth and soiled pages, do not nearly match the value of the author's words—written in English, Vietnamese, and French—as he inscribed their morale and living conditions on the unsteady boat, which slowly lurched across the perilous seas, wave by wave, prayer by prayer. Yet, toward the end of their journey, and the end of his diary, the author scribbled "garlic" and "onion" and their Indonesian translations. Why would garlic and onion be so vital for a Vietnamese refugee and his family? If finally procured, what comfort and value could they possibly bring? For the legendary gastronomy writer, MFK Fisher, that would be our dignified selves. In the most calamitous of situations, to eat to survive *and* to eat what we need and want, that could feed, nourish, and comfort the most broken of souls. Michael Pollan, critically acclaimed author on the human history of food consumption and production, imagines the garden as a mirror that we hold ourselves to reflect on who we really are.

Throughout Vietnamese history, a number of herbs, fruits, and vegetables used in traditional, home-cooked meals have historically become indispensable and necessary for Vietnamese consumers. The wide and beautiful array of greens and fruits are considered natural to accompany or complete a traditional Vietnamese meal. As early 1836, several crops, along with species for meat consumption and natural landscapes, were memorialized on enormous bronze urns. Emperor Minh Mạng "had all of his realm's renowned resources cast in relief on nine enormous bronze urns at the dynastic temple in Hue. Along with natural features such as mountains, rivers, and forests, the urns include a grand feast's worth of animal and agricultural products."[3] Across nine bronze urns, such agricultural products included jackfruit, onions, rambai fruit, garlic, mango, scallions, areca palm, cabbage, peach, cardamom, longan, ginger, pear tree, perilla herb, lychee, mandragora, and garlic chives.[4]

During the Việt Nam War, the government of the Republic of Việt Nam (RVN), commonly referred to as South Việt Nam,[5] issued postage stamps of fruits and vegetables that were widely grown and consumed throughout the country. The beloved trái khổ qua or bitter melon was depicted on the 1.50 piastres (đồng) stamp.[6] The soursop (măng cầu) was canonized on a 3.00 piastres stamp and the cashew apple (trái điều) on the 0.50 piastre stamp.[7] Such produce, immortalized on stamps, are still grown half-a-world away by Vietnamese Americans. For the Vietnamese diaspora, both the Việt Nam War, whose end approaches a half century ago, and the sudden exodus remain a distant nightmare and a painful, raw memory; a reminder of what was destroyed . . . and yet can be recreated. So, in their own home gardens, after the war, they carved out a sliver of the old homeland to mix with the new, as they sought freedom from war, violence, destitution, and rootlessness.

The Communist victory over South Việt Nam in 1975 led to a massive exodus of Vietnamese refugees who braved the seas or walked on unknown lands, seeking a host country where they could finally be accepted as political refugees. Over time, Vietnamese exiles would come to the realization that they had become natives of a ghost country, a nonexistent nation-state whose governance, existence, and ideals still transcended place, time, and generations. The South Vietnamese flag, history, and nation remain strong and real in the hearts and minds of those who left its shores. These people have performed a transhistorical act by keeping a nonexistent nation alive, altering their own course of diaspora history forever. One important part of remembering South Việt Nam would be the creation of home gardens in the Vietnamese diasporic world.

This chapter covers traditional food gardening in Việt Nam, before and during the Việt Nam War, and in exile. Here, I use the terms food and kitchen gardens. Because Việt Nam was naturally the homeland of Vietnamese refugees before their exile, the phrase "home gardens" does not possess a double meaning during the Việt Nam War. Thus, it may be considered redundant and inaccurate to call their kitchen gardens home gardens before their exile, particularly because the word "home" was not culturally approached, developed, and engrained as a double entendre for Vietnamese forced to flee from Việt Nam in the days and years after the war. Home gardens really only apply to Vietnamese diasporic home gardeners.

I utilize the more common term "kitchen gardens" to describe Vietnamese who grew gardens next to their homes before and during the Việt Nam War. However, for Vietnamese refugees in exilic transit I choose to use the phrase "food gardens" because they became stateless in flight, with their legal status in limbo as they awaited their fates in makeshift refugee camps. Without doubt, such food gardens gave them nutritional immediacy and accessibility necessary for their physical survival, in addition to maintaining a modicum of sanity and normalcy. For the Vietnamese diaspora, I assert the term "home gardens" because those exiled Vietnamese actually live in a host country, making a home for themselves by replanting the old in order to add to the new homeland. Even as their gardens may appear paltry and inconsequential, they are certainly not insignificant places of cultural remembrances of their old homeland. Henceforth, home gardens provide a double meaning of "home"—literally and figuratively—which is appropriate to describe and analyze the value and contributions of such gardens to Vietnamese diasporic gardeners and their communities. Thus, the value and contributions of such gardens—and what they symbolize and represent to their caretakers—change and evolve over time.

Kitchen gardens were commonly grown by Vietnamese homeowners to subsist and nurture themselves in times of war, and temporary makeshift gardens were quickly established in times of refuge to cultivate some sense of normalcy and stability. From the late 1970s through the mid-1990s, thousands of Vietnamese refugees were situated in unsanitary, overcrowded living conditions in far-flung refugee camps throughout Southeast Asia.

Despite their dire and dreadful conditions, Vietnamese refugees planted vegetables, herbs, and fruits commonly grown and consumed in Việt Nam, and produced essential ingredients for recipes they needed to make meals and dishes that they were familiar enough to prepare, cook, and consume. Vietnamese refugees who managed to escape from Communist Việt Nam and survived a harrowing and life-threatening journey, whether sailing the South China Sea or traveling on foot to refugee camps in Thailand, also had to survive the arduous ordeal of residing in camp squalor. Additionally, they did know whether if they would be forced to repatriate, remain on camp for a prolonged period of time, or if fortuitous, gain political asylum in a willing host nation. Even gaining refuge in another country would lead to struggles with marginalization and resettlement as foreigners. Yet, upon their arrival in the United States, Vietnamese refugees sought to bring their gardening traditions to new lands. They would introduce innovative and resourceful gardening techniques, as well as vegetables, herbs, and fruit trees not commonly grown in the United States. Meanwhile, utilizing the produce from the home gardens, they maintained traditional meals and dishes while creating new recipes, which helped them sustain *and* elevate Vietnamese foodways. Thus, Vietnamese refugees not only transformed the physical landscapes they resettled, but they also dramatically changed American foodways by adding their unique culinary customs and ways of farming, gardening, and cooking meals, allowing their Vietnamese heritage to shine more visibly, and their foodways to be discovered, embraced, and appreciated by others. Vietnamese food would intertwine with Texan, Texas-Mexican, Cajun, and Southern cuisines. Significantly, the retention and expansion of Vietnamese foodways start with their gardening traditions.

Vietnamese Kitchen Gardens before the Việt Nam War

Food historian Vũ Hồng Liên elucidates the significance of studying food history. "Each individual or group has a different way of dealing with the need for sustenance, so the treatment of food can be a door through which to catch a glimpse into a people's culture, their view of life and afterlife, and their expectations, hopes and despair," states Vũ. "To know what a people eat is to understand how its society works, why it goes to war or sues for peace. To understand how a group of people eat is to acknowledge how they both differ from and are similar to oneself."[8] She appropriately positions food history to the center of the table for all of us to view and acknowledge its presence, at the very least.

In hopes of adding to the rich repast of food history, I delve into a study on the ever-evolving kitchen/food/home gardens of the Vietnamese. These gardens provide essential vegetables, herbs, and fruits that are staples not only in the Vietnamese diet, but also important ingredients that accentuate or accompany numerous Vietnamese dishes. Renowned cooking instructor, 2018 James Beard Award recipient, and author of notable Vietnamese cookbooks, Andrea Nguyễn, emphasizes the Vietnamese desire to have vegetables and herbs on the dining table and how such produce complements and enhances meals: "Vegetables are woven throughout the Vietnamese table. A plate of vegetables and herbs arrives with a bowl of noodle soup; cucumbers, jicama, and greens join meats and seafood in rice-paper rolls; and everyday soups (*canh*) usually include a vegetable for flavor, texture, and color."[9] Nguyễn also examines the importance of vegetables in Vietnamese cuisine, asserting that vegetables are served as "one of the four components of the classic Vietnamese four-dish meal of a soup, a meat or seafood dish, a vegetable dish, and rice."[10] She shifts our attention to the Vietnamese version of a healthy and balanced meal, with vegetables playing a prominent role on the dining table.

Historically, religion has played a transformative role in the Vietnamese daily diet, particularly the necessity to cultivate fruit trees, herbs, and vegetables to cook vegetarian dishes. With the introduction and spread of Buddhism in Việt Nam, vegetarian cooking became increasingly more prominent and essential. Vũ studies the effects of Buddhism on Vietnamese food choices and consumption, with vegetarian diet gaining traction under the Ly dynasty, as the influence of Buddhist teachings and practices spread throughout the region. For instance, "the killing of living things is forbidden in the Buddha's teachings, so Vietnamese vegetarian food is strictly vegan and is seasoned with salt and soy sauce, rather than the traditional fish sauce. With many temples being built throughout the country, and the rise of devout

Buddhism as a virtue for all, vegetarian cooking quickly became the norm, from humble temple to royal table."[11] No doubt, the popularity of Buddhism placed a greater importance on having vegetables, fruits, and herbs accessible and available for consumption for the burgeoning Vietnamese Buddhist populace. Thus, to a significant degree, kitchen gardens helped make vegetarian consumption more feasible for Việt Nam's Buddhist majority population.

VIỆT NAM UNDER FRENCH COLONIALISM

Although French missionaries first arrived in Southeast Asia in the second half of the seventeenth century, the French colonial period officially began in 1887 and effectively ended with the defeat of French military forces at the hands of Vietnamese nationalist and Communist forces at the Battle of Điện Biên Phủ in 1954. At the dawn of French colonialism, three regions—Tonkin (north), Annam (central), and Cochinchina (south)—were declared French protectorates to makeup a Francophone Việt Nam. Along with the colonization of Việt Nam under French rule, the three protectorates were merged with Cambodia and Laos to complete the French Indochinese Union or Indochina colony. French colonial rule dramatically and traumatically dictated new national and cultural identities. Although a strident anti-foreign sentiment was not uncommon throughout Vietnamese history, French attempts to assimilate the local population into Francophiles would ironically start a chain of events that would birth another Vietnamese national identity, one that was anticolonial. The bordering of three distinct regions into French protectorates that made up Việt Nam and as part of French Indochina, would help galvanize the native intelligentsia that included anticolonialists Phan Bội Châu and Nguyễn Ái Quốc (later known as Hồ Chí Minh) to construct a new Vietnamese national identity and independence, one that was on their own terms and accord. After turning to communism, Nguyễn Ái Quốc ultimately succeeded in welding the ideals of Marxism-Leninism with Vietnamese patriotism to create a formidable political group that fought for independence against the French.

The growing momentum of Vietnamese nationalism in the French colonial period spawned a powerful nationalist organization known as the Việt Minh. From its inception in 1941, the Việt Minh, which included several patriotic political organizations, led the struggle for Vietnamese nationhood against the French. Distinguished Việt Nam War historian George C. Herring asserts that "displaying an organization and discipline far superior to those of competing nationalist groups, many of which spent as much time fighting each other as the French, the Việt Minh established itself as the voice of Vietnamese nationalism."[12] Nguyễn Ái Quốc changed his name to Hồ Chí Minh as Vietnamese Communists spearheaded the nationalist movement toward independence from the French colonial administration and Japanese occupation during World War II.

The year 1945 was momentous for Vietnamese nationalists because it manifested the beginning of the end of French colonial rule and national independence. During the period known as the "Japanese Interlude," Japanese policymakers decidedly took over Indochina in March 1945 and removed the final vestiges of the Vichy French government from power. Japanese forces abolished French colonial authority and granted the unification of Việt Nam under Emperor Bảo Đại, who was nothing more than an appointed puppet leader under Japanese authority.[13] In the August Revolution of 1945, Hồ Chí Minh managed to fuse Vietnamese patriotism and anti-colonialism to create a successful nationalist movement for full sovereignty; a movement fronted by Minh and the Vietnamese Communists. Hồ Chí Minh's 1945 August Revolution also marked a tumultuous turning point for the Vietnamese. Huỳnh Kim Khánh contends that the August Revolution "marked the end of direct foreign domination in internal Vietnamese affairs, formally abolished the centuries-old monarchical-mandarinate political system, brought large numbers of Vietnamese into the political process, and finally fulfilled the Vietnamese wish to make independent Vietnam a part of the global political configuration."[14] Esteemed Việt Nam War scholar William Duiker explains that by the end of 1945, "Vietnam was divided into a communist north and a non-communist south, with French forces trying to restore control over all of Indochina."[15] Already, a recognizable anti-communist sentiment had been brewing in South Việt Nam by the end of this watershed year, albeit those who embraced such a sentiment were still very much under French colonial influence and control, whether they approved or not.

Even after World War II and Hồ Chí Minh Minh's August Revolution, the French had no intention of relinquishing Việt Nam. Unfortunately, for the anti-communist South Vietnamese nationalists, what became more troubling and apparent would be the nationalist limitations of legitimacy for the French-created and colonial dominance of the Republic of Cochin China and its lack of sovereignty. Realistically and rightfully, only the complete French withdrawal from Việt Nam would provide nationalist legitimacy to the anti-communist Vietnamese contingent in South Việt Nam. However, Cold War geopolitics dictated otherwise.

As for the French colonialists, they made a halfhearted effort to give anti-communist South Vietnamese forces a small degree of autonomy, and therefore South Việt Nam was left with little nationalist legitimacy. French policymakers, with reluctance, established the Associated State of Việt Nam (ASV) under former Emperor Bảo Đại in the hopes of appeasing Vietnamese non-communist nationalists in the south and making it more palatable for diplomatic recognition from critics abroad, especially US policymakers. Unfortunately, the ASV lacked the political legitimacy and authority that Bảo Đại's government needed in order to rally a skeptical Vietnamese public and properly govern the foreign-created, non-communist Vietnamese state as a viable alternative to the more popular Communist-governed north under Hồ Chí Minh. Ironically, the French reluctance to hand over greater political power to Bảo Đại and the ASV drastically undermined its efforts to provide a reliable political alternative capable of competing with Hồ Chí Minh and his Communist and nationalist supporters. French refusal to grant the ASV complete independence and full sovereignty quickened the demise of France's colonial enterprise in Southeast Asia and its created non-communist Vietnamese state. US policymakers weighed in their options, as a French withdrawal appeared more imminent despite the increasing US military and economic aid to French efforts in the First Indochina War (1945–54). However, US policymakers were also reluctant to give Bảo Đại's government full reign over the ASV. Consequently, ASV's legitimacy was questionable from the start, even as it changed to the Republic of Việt Nam[16] under US guidance, influence, and control in 1955.

VIETNAMESE KITCHEN GARDENS DURING FRENCH COLONIALISM

Unsurprisingly, Vietnamese kitchen gardens were not uncommon before and during the Việt Nam War, and they remain prevalent in twenty-first century Việt Nam and Vietnamese diasporic communities. In times of colonization, war, refuge, and resettlement, such gardens with their produce become even more vital for the Vietnamese to grow, consume, and survive. A rich agricultural region and culture centered on rice cultivation, Việt Nam and the Vietnamese people have a long history of relying on farming and gardening to sustain themselves. As Andrea Nguyễn notes, the classic Vietnamese four-dish meal includes a vegetable dish, so having fresh, accessible produce was essential and customary in their daily diet. Kitchen gardens therefore are important spaces for Vietnamese to raise vegetables, herbs, and fruit trees for daily access.

Under French colonial rule, Vietnamese kitchen gardens were quite a common sight in the late nineteenth century. During the early French colonial period, in times of food paucity, Vietnamese villagers "no longer went out to the fields to plant and bring in the harvest: instead [*sic*] they gardened only right next to their own houses."[17] As a result, such gardens became critical to Vietnamese villagers and increased their chances of survival, particularly when food was scarce under French occupation.

An expert on Vietnamese food history, historian Erica Peters remarks that the significance of a village location in Việt Nam that would have a profound impact as to what foods villagers cultivated and the availability of such produce.[18] Peters lists the available produce in southern villages in great detail: "In the south, villagers had many tropical fruits, such as mangrove apple (eaten green or ripe), star gooseberry tree, prickly pear, guava, durian, jackfruit, mango, mangosteen, papaya star fruit (carabole), coconuts, pineapple, lychees, custard apples, longans, pomegranates, persimmons, and many kinds of bananas."[19] Peters also affirms the prominent relationship between kitchen gardens and village farming, remarking on the fields of corn, sugarcane, and peanuts cultivated between villages, while household gardens were used to raise other vegetables.[20] She further elaborates on the produce typically cultivated in villages and how villagers would utilize, prepare, and consume their home-grown vegetables, herbs, and fruit trees:

> Chinese cabbage and mustard greens were very common, along with water spinach (rau muống), water primrose, water lilies, water mimosas, water chestnuts, and other aquatic plants. Water lily seeds were eaten green or ripe, and the roots were boiled. Gardens were also likely to have various kinds of gourds. Villagers picked bitter melons before they were ripe and boiled them to alleviate their bitterness. . . . Manioc was also grown in gardens; villagers roasted it for a flour that they used in several kinds of cakes. Among the most common herbs in village gardens were Vietnamese coriander (rau răm), turmeric (nghệ), fish mint (giấp cá), anise basil (rau húng quế), as well as lemongrass, fennel, mint, green onions, and garlic. Onions flourished in the north, while cilantro grew better in southern gardens. Cilantro's leaves were used as an herb and its seeds were used in pastries.[21]

Even under the duress of French colonialism, Vietnamese villagers made a concerted effort to find the time and space to plant and raise kitchen gardens and maintain their traditional foodways. After the collapse of French colonialism and final humiliating defeat of French military forces at Điện Biên Phủ, in what would be oft-referred to as the First Indochina War, Vietnamese villagers continued to raise kitchen gardens and grow herbs, vegetables, and fruit trees because they were still

living in constant turmoil and uncertainty. They did so to maintain some food security and gain immediate access and control over produce essential to their diet and
livelihood. They would continue to cultivate food gardens in times of another
destructive war. Under the heavy strain of a war that ultimately resulted in millions
of Vietnamese lives lost, Vietnamese kitchen gardeners would seek and find some
semblance of normalcy and control over their own lives by nurturing small plots of
land to grow crops for consumption and preserve their traditional foodways.

1954: The End of French Colonial Rule and the Division of Việt Nam by Foreign Powers

In 1954, Hồ Chí Minh and the Việt Minh defeated the French military forces at the
Battle of Điện Biên Phủ, marking the military end of French colonial rule. The last
vestiges of French colonialism officially ended with the signing of the 1954 Geneva
Accords, which resulted in an agreement that all French forces would leave Việt
Nam that year. After the Việt Minh's victory at Điện Biên Phủ, negotiations in
Geneva called for the temporary partition of Việt Nam and for it to be reunited
under the victor's party in the 1956 national election. Other aspects of the Geneva
Accords divided Việt Nam into two zones—North Việt Nam, led by Hồ Chí Minh
and the Communist forces; and South Việt Nam, a non-communist state under Ngô
Đình Diệm that would be financially funded and militarily backed by the United
States.

Yet, such a division of Việt Nam was problematic, as eminent Việt Nam War
historian Robert Buzzanco noted: "Vietnam was historically a single country, with
the southern half, the RVN, artificially created at the Geneva Conference in 1954 by
the United States. From that point on, the struggle in Vietnam revolved around the
very issue of who constituted the legitimate government of that country. Thus, to
call the southern section 'South Vietnam' conveys the status of nationhood where it
is not established."[22] Scholar Frances FitzGerald declares: "In neither of the two
documents (armistice and the Final Declaration of the Geneva Accords) was there
any mention of a second state in Vietnam: it was the French who were to administer
their regroupment zone in the south during the period of the armistice."[23] With Hồ
Chí Minh's popularity, Vietnamese Communists would have handily won the election over Hồ's main rival, Ngô Đình Diệm, a US-backed Vietnamese leader who was
vital to American policymakers' Cold War calculations to "rescue" Việt Nam from
falling to communism. Consequently, by 1955, with growing US diplomatic and
financial involvement (and direct military intervention later), Việt Nam remained a

divided nation at the seventeenth parallel, with North Việt Nam led by Hồ Chí
Minh and Vietnamese Communists, and South Việt Nam under the reign of Ngô
Đình Diệm and the US-backed anti-communist regime. South Việt Nam would
exist as a non-independent republic for twenty years.

Although the Geneva Accords did not explicitly establish the permanency
of two separate Việt Nams, much less create an independent South Việt Nam,
the agreement planted the seeds of South Vietnamese nationalism in the non-
communist zone. Only after the terms of the Geneva Accords were finalized did
South Vietnamese nationalism start taking root. Although anti-communist sentiments began when communism was first introduced in Việt Nam, South Vietnamese
nationalism did not fully formulate until Ngô Đình Diệm was ushered in as the first
president of the RVN, and the 1954 Geneva Accords were signed. Prominent historian Gabriel Kolko asserts that "Diệm was by 1954 one of the very few unequivo-
cally anti-French and anti-communist politicians of any note to whom the United
States could turn to."[24] Here lies the historical connection between the Cold War
anti-communist narrative and South Vietnamese nationalism, and the conundrum
of an untenable marriage between Diệm and the US government.

However, Diệm did not have the political astuteness, wherewithal, or fortuity
to establish a stable democratic government. He failed to display the leadership and
organizational skills to properly govern and manage the RVN. Though he was clearly
an anticolonial and anti-communist nationalist, Diệm failed miserably to galvanize
the non-communist populace in South Việt Nam. He alienated many South
Vietnamese, thousands of whom would help form the National Liberation Front
(NLF) and join the Communist war for liberation of South Việt Nam. Diệm's
regime sorely lacked political maturity and sophistication, and therefore could
never gain traction for nationalist legitimacy. In fact, over time, Diệm's government
appeared more as the heir to the French-controlled ASV under former Emperor
Bảo Đại. FitzGerald argues, "What was most strange was that Diem, this proud
nationalist, did not even symbolically dissociate his regime from the government he
so despised as a 'French puppet'. . . . The Republic of Vietnam had the same flag and
the same anthem as the Bao Dai government, and Diem himself lived in the gover-
nor's palace."[25] The history of the flag pre-dates the existence of the RVN and its
subsequent development of South Vietnamese nationalism. Furthermore, Fitz-
Gerald states that the flag is historically linked to the French-controlled ASV under
Bảo Đại. The flag she refers to is the South Vietnamese flag that remains ubiquitous
in Vietnamese diasporic communities around the world today. The flag, with three
horizontal red stripes stretched across the yellow background, from one end to the

other, in perfect symmetry, is widely considered as *the* official national flag of Việt Nam by the Vietnamese diaspora.

The South Vietnamese populace was confronted with three traumatic, concurrent struggles throughout the turbulent and deadly years of the Việt Nam War (sometimes cited as the Second Indochina War, or the American War): (1) the struggle for the reunification and control of a single Việt Nam between the communist north and US-backed South Việt Nam; (2) the struggle between the NLF and South Vietnamese forces for hegemony over South Việt Nam itself; and (3) the struggle to gain political legitimacy for South Việt Nam among anti-communist South Vietnamese nationalists. Throughout its existence, if we are to acknowledge the existence of the RVN, the republic was, sadly, in a constant state of anarchy and disorder, beset by tremendous social unrest, political turmoil, economic upheaval, and foreign dependency, even as the RVN government and military officials attempted to create a constitutional, parliamentary government in the post-Diệm years.

Vietnamese Kitchen Gardens during the Việt Nam War

During the Cold War, Việt Nam was mired in a war within a war. The United States supported a pro–United States but inept and corrupt leader in Ngô Đình Diệm and South Việt Nam, and the Soviet Union supported the more popular and effective leader in the anti-colonialist-turned-Communist Hồ Chí Minh and North Việt Nam. But even throughout the horrific and violent Việt Nam War, kitchen gardens remained commonly cultivated by Vietnamese villagers. On his extensive study on the Khánh Hậu village in the Mê Kông Delta and near Sài Gòn, Gerald Cannon Hickey offers an extensive and in-depth study on village life and the challenges and changes endured by Khánh Hậu villagers under South Việt Nam, from 1959–64: "Most families have a few fruit trees, and some cultivate fruit groves to produce an ancillary cash crop. Kitchen gardens are common but not universal."[26] Analyzing the farmsteads in Khánh Hậu in rural South Việt Nam during the war, Hickey describes that "A kitchen garden commonly is found to one side of the house, and most villagers cultivate a variety of fruit trees. If there is sufficient space the fruit trees may be planted in a grove, but in most instances [*sic*] they grow in pleasantly disorganized profusion."[27]

As for what were typically grown in Vietnamese kitchen gardens during the war, according to Hickey, "Many garden arbors contain the prickly balsam pear [bitter melon], and it can either be served in soup or stuffed with ground meat and steamed; although extremely bitter, it is very popular and is thought to have the medicinal effect of 'refreshing' the stomach and intestines. Red chili peppers crushed or sliced are eaten with most meals, and mint is served with meat dishes. Carrots are pickled in brine and customarily added to fish sauce as a condiment . . . Several varieties of onion are widely cultivated, and green leafy vegetables are consumed almost daily by villagers."[28] Hickey adds that Vietnamese villagers also grew medicinal plants in their kitchen gardens and village grounds, especially chili peppers, which are grown in every garden. Chili peppers, in addition to being a popular spicy ingredient and condiment, are considered as a preventive medicine against worms.[29]

Vietnamese villagers established kitchen gardens to supplement their income as well. Hickey notes that "In 1959 several families also began cultivating vegetables as a cash crop. One family living near the Ban Chin Dao Cao Dais temple in Ap Dinh-A planted a large vegetable garden in a section of their paddy land, and with the aid of kin and friends dug a deep reservoir for irrigating the garden and their rice seedbeds as well. The produce of the garden was destined for the Tan An market."[30] Hickey also points out the villagers' garden techniques and methods vary with different types of plants.[31] He concludes that although there were some noticeable variations in garden cultivation, the differences were not great, and in fact, a common collection of vegetables were grown in every garden.[32]

ETHNIC MINORITIES AND THEIR FOOD GARDENS DURING THE VIỆT NAM WAR

For centuries, a number of ethnic minorities have resided in what are the geopolitical borders of the nation-state of the Socialist Republic of Việt Nam today. Before the end of the Việt Nam War, two notable minority groups were the ethnic Chinese, many of whom once resided in Chợ Lớn (Big Market) or Chinatown District of Sài Gòn, and the Hmong of the Montagnard tribes, who dwelled in the mountainous regions of the Central Highlands bordering Laos and Việt Nam. The former would make up a significant percentage of refugees from the second wave of exodus from Việt Nam, particularly when the ethnic Chinese in Việt Nam were persecuted by the Communist government when Việt Nam–China relations soured into an outbreak of war between the two nations in 1979. As for the Hmong, they began to depart from Laos and Việt Nam in subsequent waves immediately after the fall of Sài Gòn on April 30, 1975. The primary reason is that the "Lao, Hmong, and other ethnic minorities who collaborated with the United States were ostracized and had to seek refuge elsewhere after the communist regime came into power in 1975."[33] However, their stories of migration and refuge also began before the war ended in 1975. Hmong and other Montagnard tribes were displaced from their homes in Laos and Việt Nam, abandoning their villages in search of safe havens during the war.

The Việt Nam War (and practically in every war) resulted in internal mass migrations by wartime refugees. Even before the outbreak of war, soon after the 1954 Geneva Accords, nearly one million Vietnamese Catholics, gravely concerned about living under Hồ Chí Minh's Communist regime, moved to anti-communist and pro-US South Việt Nam. Conversely, thousands of South Vietnamese migrated to the communist north. During the Việt Nam War, a lesser-known instance of wartime migration was the displacement of thousands of the Montagnard, an ethnic minority from the central Vietnamese highlands, who sought refuge in the Quảng Ngãi province, and after resettlement, cultivated kitchen gardens of their own.[34] By 1960, the Hre Montagnard refugee population numbered approximate twenty-seven thousand in Quảng Ngãi.[35] According to a Research and Development Corporation (RAND) report: "Gardens are plentiful in Hre villages. The plants include yams, corn, green beans, red peppers, onions, spinach, varieties of watermelons and pumpkins, pineapples, tea, manioc and tobacco. Also around the villages there may be some sugar cane, mango, banana, and papaya trees. There are some jack fruit trees, and most families cultivate areca palms around which betel vines grow."[36]

As for the Bru Montagnard refugees—another tribal people forcefully relocated, many of whom resettled in the Khe Sanh area during the war—they used large permanent gardens to cultivate "corn yams, manioc, beans, peas, a variety of squash, melons, and in small gardens near the house they grow lettuce, red peppers and tobacco. Some villagers also grow coffee trees, the produce of which they sell. Papaya, coconut, orange, mango and banana trees grow in most villages, and there are occasional avocado trees. Jack fruit trees also grow in some villages."[37]

Hickey reports on the wartime refugee resettlements in Giá Vực, Hương An, and Hương Vĩnh. Regarding Giá Vực refugees, he writes, "Most refugees in the vicinity of Giá Vuc are from villages in the surrounding valleys while a small number appear to have come from the more remote, higher areas. Currently they number 2,989, of which 1,744 are located in two refugee hamlets while the remainder are resettled in eleven already existing villages. There are an estimated 1,000 hectares of cultivated land in the surrounding area—90 percent of which is in the paddy while the remaining 10 percent is in kitchen gardens."[38] Hickey also mentions the Khe Sanh district chief's report on the status of refugee settlements of Hương An and Hương Vĩnh,[39]

"Each family was given a small plot for their house site and kitchen garden. In addition [sic] the residents have large gardens in which they grow manioc, yams, and tobacco [according to the Khe Sanh district chief]."[40] Despite their migration to these refugee hamlets that were supposedly safe havens from Vietnamese Communist insurgents, they could never completely escape from the dangers and terrors of war. In addition, they were foreigners in South Việt Nam and perceived as foreigners by the RVN government; they were far removed from their ancestral village homes and forced to relocate to the refugee hamlets. Yet, despite the overwhelming challenges and duress, these wartime refugees managed to create their own kitchen gardens to subsist, survive, and remember what they lost when they were forced to evacuate from their home villages to resettle in so-called safe havens of South Việt Nam. Their kitchen gardens provided a temporary respite and a sliver of land that reminded them of their ancestral villages.

COLLAPSE OF THE REPUBLIC OF VIỆT NAM AND END OF THE VIỆT NAM WAR

The American intervention in Việt Nam was part of US policymakers' Cold War geopolitical strategy to halt the spread of communism throughout Asia. Unfortunately for the United States and its Vietnamese allies, the American intervention devolved into a tragic quagmire of death and destruction, devoid of a tangible purpose. Further problems arose in Ngô Đình Diệm's South Vietnamese government as the struggling Southern Republic was embroiled in political corruption, bureaucratic ineptitude, brazen nepotism, and state-sanctioned violence and murder, resulting in widespread protests and demands for social and political reforms. Sociologist Y Thiên Nguyễn asserts that "The Diệm administration instituted anticommunism as a nationalist and state doctrine, which legitimized the massive persecution, surveillance, torture, and execution of those deemed communists by the South Vietnamese state."[41] Nguyễn astutely notes that "To be anti-communist or to be part of the anti-communist state in the Republican era meant opportunities for social mobility and access to occupational privilege, state support, and politically legitimate voice." According to Nguyễn, "South Vietnamese anticommunism thus was perpetuated by the dual mechanisms of political violence and political reward."[42]

Diệm, a devout Catholic in power over a Buddhist majority populace, also violently cracked down on Buddhist demonstrations and protests against his government, resulting in Buddhist monks conducting self-immolation in protest. On November 2, 1963, Diệm himself would be assassinated during a coup d'état by

RVN generals. More coup d'états and chaos would soon follow. Some stability of the RVN government occurred under President Nguyễn Văn Thiệu after he was elected into office in 1967. Unfortunately, the Southern Republic's stability sputtered throughout Nguyễn's presidency, despite the US policy of escalation and steady increase of American soldiers in Việt Nam. Although a military setback, the Vietnamese Communists' Tet Offensive in January 1968 was widespread and shocking to US forces and their South Vietnamese allies. The Tet Offensive demonstrated the war was nowhere near its end, as President Lyndon B. Johnson had earlier proclaimed. Consequently, Johnson announced his resignation when his term ended. His successor, President Richard M. Nixon, fared no better with his Vietnamization policy and expansion of the war into Cambodia and Laos. The war crawled toward its murderous conclusion with the US withdrawal under President Nixon's "peace with honor" and the signing of the Paris Peace Accords in January 1973. After the signing of the 1973 Paris Peace Accords and the subsequent US official withdrawal arranged by US secretary of state Henry Kissinger and North Việt Nam's diplomat Lê Đức Thọ, it was only a matter of time before the incompetent, inefficient, and unstable South Việt Nam government collapsed during a military offensive campaign by Vietnamese Communists forces.

In quick and stunning fashion, Vietnamese Communist forces defeated the remaining remnants of the RVN forces in the final weeks of the war, with many RVN soldiers finally relinquishing their futile hopes of prolonging the war. They unsurprisingly and understandably refused to continue to sacrifice their lives for the much-maligned RVN government, especially when their wartime heroes and leaders—like Nguyễn Cao Kỳ and President Nguyễn Văn Thiệu—essentially abandoned RVN forces and the republic's populace even before the capitulation of their capital city, Sài Gòn. In light of this abandonment, RVN soldiers, pilots, and sailors made heroic and concerted efforts to save and rescue as many of their family members, relatives, and friends from approaching Communist forces and flee their beloved homeland while the last US government officials made their evacuation from the US embassy in Sài Gòn. Finally, on April 30, 1975, Sài Gòn fell to Vietnamese Communists forces, marking the official end of the devastating Việt Nam War. The Republic of Việt Nam was no more.

The final days of the war were embroiled with chaos, heartbreak, confusion, betrayal, turmoil, and the tragic separation of loved ones; these separations would bring pain and heartache that lasted for years, and in some cases indefinitely. The brutal war and its consequential aftermath resulted in millions of Vietnamese lives lost, as well as the death of hundreds of thousands of Cambodians, Laotians,

Hmong, and tribal peoples, in addition to over fifty-eight thousand American soldiers killed in combat. The historic tragedy continued on after its end, as hundreds
of thousands of South Vietnamese and other Southeast Asian refugees fled from
Communist Việt Nam. The war would follow them in exile . . . and so they carried
with them—among important personal objects, practices, and memories—their
traditional foodways.

However, the fall of Sài Gòn did not exactly end the war. Wars do not end neatly,
and the Việt Nam War did not end without consequences. The war shattered and
ruined much of the country, crippling the nation and the people. The Vietnamese
victors faced the daunting and impossible task of reunifying the two broken and bat-
tered halves of Việt Nam (an artificial split from the beginning), healing the wounds
of war, recovering the nation's war-torn economy, and rebuilding a new society. The
Communists' complete victory over South Việt Nam resulted a massive exodus of
Vietnamese refugees who braved the high seas, seeking refuge and political asylum.
With the Communist takeover of Sài Gòn, approximately 130,000 Vietnamese refugees fled from their home country, and then in subsequent waves, from the late of
1970s to the mid-1990s, hundreds of thousands more risked their lives to escape
from Communist Việt Nam. Many left their beloved homeland in hopes of gaining
political asylum in a host country or third country that would be willing to accept
them. Thousands of Vietnamese oceanic refugees perished in the seas, as well as land
refugees who died during their dangerous journeys to refugee camps in Thailand, in
their desperate attempts to leave, most of these during the second wave of refugees
during the late 1970s and early 1980s. Yet, upon resettlement in a host nation,
Vietnamese exiles would come to the realization that they were now natives of a
ghost country; a nonexistant nation-state that remained very real in their hearts and
minds. For the Vietnamese diaspora, planting home gardens and re-establishing their
traditional foodways not only provided an opportunity to heal, nurture, and subsist,
but by cultivating their own fruit trees, herbs, and vegetables they were able to sustain
their memory of a bygone Việt Nam, allowing them to maintain their roots while
being uprooted, and then rooted, in a new homeland.

DESPERATE PLACES, DETERMINED LIVES: VIETNAMESE REFUGEES AND THEIR CAMP GARDENS

For the remainder of the chapter, I hope to convey a coherent and intelligible explanation as to why these refugee detention camps that once sheltered and detained
thousands of Vietnamese refugees[43] in Indonesia, Malaysia, the Philippines, Thailand,

and other places are historic sites of sentimental importance and tangible value. I wish to reevaluate our representation of home by considering these refugee detention camps, which were hastily constructed as temporary (for some, permanent) shelters of Vietnamese refugees and asylum seekers, as "in-between or interstitial home spaces" that they managed to carve into existence. In the cases of the second, third, and fourth waves of Vietnamese and other Southeast Asian refugees, many of them miraculously grew small camp gardens to subsist off of fresh greens, create a sense of normalcy, gain some hegemony over their daily lives, preserve their food heritage, and pass the time that appeared painfully endless while they waited with "chronic uncertainty,"[44] that is, in constant fear, turmoil, and anxiety of the unknown. In other words, they had already started to establish emancipatory foodways, seeking liberation and freedom from the strains of war, refuge, relocation, and ostracization by cultivating such small camp gardens, even before their resettlement in the United States and other host nations. Historian Jana K. Lipman argues that "By magnifying the places in between, the camps are no longer marginal, but rather a key stage where Vietnamese, Guamanian, Malaysian, Filipino, Hong Kong Chinese, and international actors fought over who would or would not be a refugee.... The camps were potent sites, because they could be conduits to resettlement or they could be used to deter, detain, and turn people back. Vietnamese in the camps and in the diaspora understood the stakes and organized."[45] I agree with Lipman's assertion that these camps were not just marginal places but also contested spaces where Vietnamese refugees were actively engaged with camp officials, local governments, and international governing bodies. In addition, they did their best to restore their livelihood and raise food gardens in subpar camp conditions. These in-between or liminal spaces of contestations for political asylum were also temporary, interstitial homelands cultivated by Vietnamese refugees trying to regain some normalcy and control over their own lives.

Furthermore, by viewing the Vietnamese refugees through the lens of political and daily activism, resilience, and food resistance, I reevaluate their camp days and years as when they constructed a temporary in-between homeland of small gardens, churches, temples, bakeries, restaurants, murals, paintings, sculptures, cemeteries, and memorials. They were active and alive, not entirely helpless, nor were they in constant need of saving and rescue by international governing bodies and foreign governments. *Farm-to-Freedom* attempts to contribute to critical refugee studies and "challenge the assumptions of refugee gratitude" as Lipman states in her book.[46] The leading scholar of critical refugee studies, Yến Lê Espiritu, opposes the rescue narrative that exacerbates "the United States as the savior and the Vietnamese refugee as the 'saved.'"[47] As refugees, political asylees, and diasporans the overseas Vietnamese—or Người Việt Hải Ngoại, as Vietnamese natives would name these postwar expatriates—were in need of assistance at camps and asylum in third countries for sure, but they also forged their own paths to freedom, survival, and success. They even sought to protect, maintain, and expand their traditional foodways throughout refuge and resettlement, foodways that include cultivating vegetable gardens in far-flung refugee camps with subpar conditions.

VIETNAMESE REFUGEES AND SEEKING A NEW HOME

The first wave of Vietnamese refugees and political asylees who abruptly departed their homeland in April 1975 or immediately after the fall of Sài Gòn were considered to be the lucky ones; the latter waves of Vietnamese and other Southeast Asian refugees were to face even greater obstacles during their harrowing sea voyages and land treks to escape Việt Nam. Despite their own challenges and distress, the majority of the 130,000 Vietnamese refugees in 1975 survived their arduous journeys, and they were among the first who were temporarily resettled in US military bases abroad: Subic Bay, the Philippines, Guam, and Hawaii. Under Operation New Life, they were then flown to mainland United States to resettle in temporary, makeshift refugee camps: Camp Pendleton, California; Fort Chaffee, Arkansas; Fort Indiantown Gap, Pennsylvania; and Eglin Air Force Base, Florida. At these camps, Vietnamese refugees were housed in military barracks, fed American food, given English language lessons, and tutorials on American culture and practical skills, such as following auto traffic laws and shopping in US supermarkets. In the meantime, they waited for their documents to be processed by US government officials, who coordinated with voluntary agencies (VOLAGs) and nongovernment organizations (NGOs) to find sponsors for thousands of refugees. Eventually, thousands of Vietnamese refugees were assigned to sponsors across the United States, and by the federal government's design, were widely dispersed throughout the lower forty-eight states. However, within a few short years, many Vietnamese refugees made a secondary migration to reunite with family members, seek better job opportunities, and reside in warmer climes. Thus, the largest concentration of Vietnamese refugees ended up resettling in states like California, Texas, Louisiana, and Virginia, with sizable communities also located in Massachusetts and Washington. The distinct advantage for the first wave of Vietnamese refugees over the latter waves is that they experienced relatively greater acceptance from President Gerald R Ford's administration and a more receptive Congress as they entered and resettled in the

United States. However, by the late 1970s, as another exodus of Vietnamese and Southeast Asian refugees developed in the thousands, the US government and society were more opposed to granting them political asylum and welcoming them into America.

In Việt Nam, the immediate postwar years were abysmal and near apocalyptic. With the war-devastated, undemocratic, and impoverished state that was the Democratic Republic of Việt Nam (DRV), millions of Vietnamese suffered in abject poverty, particularly as the DRV would be dragged into more wars, one with Communist China in 1979, and another with Pol Pot and the Khmer Rouge in Cambodia in the late 1970s. To add insult to injury, the US government imposed inhumane economic sanctions on Việt Nam that ultimately and severely punished Vietnamese civilians and had little effect on the DRV government leaders and bureaucrats.

Vietnamese refugees and asylum seekers left their native land in search of a better life outside a Communist-governed nation that was obliterated and wrecked by a terrifying war that took away more than two million Vietnamese lives, fifty-eight thousand American lives, and the lives of thousands of Laotians, Cambodians, Hmong, and others. Consequently, the Vietnamese Communist regime immediately faced severe postwar shortages and infrastructure challenges. They fought to rebuild the country amid a ravaged economy worsened by the DRV's disastrous economic reforms, the retribution and reeducation of former South Vietnamese military personnel and government officials, the crippling US trade embargo on Việt Nam, and the DRV's conflicts with China and Pol Pot's Khmer Rouge. Thousands of Vietnamese barely subsisted via an informal economy of peddling and selling whatever homemade goods and foods that they could muster and produce.

Predictably, by the late 1970s, hundreds of thousands of Vietnamese desperately sought to leave their homeland and made high-risk ventures to secretly escape from the government's watchful eyes. The flood of escapees started to crest in 1978, with thousands of Vietnamese seeking refuge from the wars with China and the Khmer Rouge in Cambodia, harsh reeducation and labor camps, worsened postwar economic conditions, and a retributive and incompetent Communist regime. They took their chances and risked their lives, often on more than one occasion, to flee from the deteriorating political, social, and economic conditions of Việt Nam. Under great duress and secrecy, they bribed boat captains and owners with their life savings to sojourn across the dangerous seas, praying to make it to Indonesia, Hong Kong, the Philippines, Singapore, or Malaysia. Thousands of others trekked on foot in hopes of reaching Thailand. As thousands of Vietnamese and other Southeast Asian refugees poured into the aforementioned countries and places, refugee camps were hastily and poorly organized, and frequently lacked adequate resources to offer decent living conditions for the refugees.

This second wave of Vietnamese refugees were often referred to as the *boat people*, a term of derision with a negative connotation that distinguished them from prior refugees. Lipman succinctly pinpoints the growing animosity from governments of first asylum nations and third countries who viewed the second Vietnamese exodus less favorably. "In the late 1970s, the Malaysian, Thai, Indonesian, and Philippine governments rarely defined Vietnamese as 'refugees,'" asserts Lipman. "Instead they were 'boat people,' unlawful aliens, or 'illegal immigrants.'"[48] The boat people started leaving Việt Nam in mass exodus in 1978 and 1979. A few thousand Vietnamese escaped between 1976 and 1978. James M. Freeman breaks down the figures: "In 1976, the number of escapees jumped to 5,247; in 1977, 15,690 people escaped. In 1978 and 1979, the numbers skyrocketed to 85,213 and 185,826, respectively: between May 1975 and July 21, 1979, 292,315 Vietnamese successfully escaped by boat."[49] Consequently, with the mass exodus of Vietnamese refugees in 1978–79, refugee camps were hastily organized in places where many refugees and their vessels safely and finally reached shore, at destinations such as Hong Kong, Malaysia, Singapore, Indonesia, and the Philippines. Government officials from aforementioned places and the UNHCR workers had tremendous difficulties in providing the overwhelming influx of Vietnamese refugees with basic and proper necessities at their makeshift detention camps. Freeman asserts that "the voyages of the Vietnamese boat people fleeing from persecution were as remarkable as they were often tragic. One of the greatest feats of navigation ever recorded was that of a Vietnamese fishing boat containing fifty-six people which landed in Australia after a journey of some 5,000 miles."[50]

Freeman also discusses the risks and perils taken and endured by Vietnamese refugees: "Thousands of people failed in their attempts to escape, missing rendezvous, being cheated by people who claimed to be organizing escapes, and being caught by security forces while trying to flee Vietnam. Since, according to Vietnamese law, leaving the country without permission was a crime, those who were caught were placed in jail, women and children in one room, the men in another. . . . Despite failures, refugees made repeated attempts to escape."[51] Freeman mentions the grave, tragic endings and ongoing violence many Vietnamese refugees would experience and reports that at least 10 percent of the asylum seekers lost their lives while attempting to leave Việt Nam, although he notes that some estimates are much higher. In addition, of the surviving boats, one-third of them were intercepted by pirates who robbed the Vietnamese refugees. Of those boats carrying refugees that were stopped by pirates, one-third of them were further subjected to rape and murder.[52]

Refugee camp life was also a dire and grim experience for most Vietnamese refugees. In 1979, Elmer B. Staats, the Comptroller General of the United States, reports: "By the end of February 1979, there were about 143,000 land refugees in thirteen camps in Thailand and over seventy-five thousand boat refugees—twenty-nine thousand in one small Malaysian island camp with virtually no health or sanitary facilities."[53] Altogether, Staats provides the approximate number of Southeast Asian refugees seeking asylum and the alarming refugee crisis: "Although the United States, France, and other countries responded to the crisis by accepting refugees for resettlement, the flow of people into asylum countries far exceeded the numbers able to be permanently resettled outside their countries of origin. This has resulted in a current camp population (as of February 1979) of about 218,000 Indochinese refugees in temporary asylum."[54]

The majority of the second wave of Vietnamese refugees would remain stuck for months and even years in overcrowded camps throughout Southeast Asia; and these camps also happened to be where many would grow food gardens to subsist and supplement their food rations. Staats specifies some of the reasons for refugee-raised-and-planted food gardens: "Although the food situation was not critical in the camps we visited, most refugees reported that they received less food than standard amounts and that the food received was often spoiled. Many refugees had to buy additional food."[55] He further explains that food rations were determined by the refugee camp population rolls taken two months before such rations were finally delivered. During the two-month interval, refugee camp populations increased to where the food ration distributions turned out to be insufficient and substandard for each refugee.[56] Furthermore, to compound their difficulties, compassion fatigue for Vietnamese and Southeast Asian refugees had set in by the late 1980s.

DEATH IN THE CAMPS

For the second and latter waves of Vietnamese refugees, their troubles continued beyond food shortages, as they realized that their political asylum status would be questioned and thus, they faced repatriation to Việt Nam or a prolonged stay in sub-par camp conditions, living in a perpetuated cycle of statelessness and chronic uncertainty, which resulted in a disturbing and appalling number of refugee suicides. In the postapocalyptic aftermath from a war of attrition, Vietnamese suicides in refugee camps are heartbreaking tales of lives ending prematurely. Deeply dejected and desperate, some Vietnamese resorted to suicide as their final act of surrender—and resistance. Though they ended their own lives, their suicides haunt us long after they fell silent. Tragically, suicide was not an uncommon occurrence among Vietnamese refugees protesting repatriation to Communist Việt Nam and harsh refugee policies. Between the late 1970s and mid-1990s, countless Vietnamese refugees protested against what they perceived as unfair screening policies from UNHCR officials, physical violence and abuse from local law enforcement agents, and a lack of compassion from local government employees. Their pleas to the rest of the world exhibited a heartfelt, devoted, and persistent request to be resettled to a welcoming third country and not return to Việt Nam, where they would likely be persecuted, imprisoned, and/or ostracized. Their numerous protests included hunger strikes, marches, petitions, and letter-writing campaigns. Sadly, for one too many, they resorted to suicide via self-immolation, consuming toxic chemicals or slicing their own stomachs with a sharp object. Throughout the turbulent years of Hong Kong refugee detention centers (1979–97), Vietnamese refugees protested for fair treatment and screening, and opposed unjust refugee policies and mistreatment by local and international authorities. As a final resort, some chose to end their lives in hopes of casting a light far and wide that would demonstrate the life-and-death struggles of Vietnamese refugees to the masses.

The Vietnamese suicides did not just occur in Hong Kong; Vietnamese refugees resisted repatriation and protested unjust refugee policies in detention camps in Thailand, Indonesia, and Malaysia. In these disparate locales, the desperate cries for help were from the second and third wave of postwar Vietnamese refugees, those who needed even more assistance and attention than the first wave of Vietnamese refugees, whose tragic tales of fleeing their homeland after the fall of Sài Gòn are better documented, albeit still unfinished or untold. Overall, the latter waves of postwar Vietnamese refugees suffered greater inequities in refugee camps and worse odds of being resettled in a host country. Despite personal losses of loved ones, physical pain, mental anguish, and fear of repatriation, UNHCR and local officials considered a majority of Vietnamese refugees at the time to be "economic migrants," a political term employed to minimize their real plight and therefore pejoratively and wrongfully categorize and contextualize them as people who only wanted to improve their own economic standing (as if abject poverty is not a good enough reason for refuge). In addition, such a term completely ignored the refugees' strong desire for greater political freedom and their fear of repatriation that would likely result in persecution, reprisal, marginalization, and even imprisonment by the Vietnamese Communist government.

At the Whitehead Detention Camp in Hong Kong, thousands of displaced Vietnamese oceanic refugees were gathered in temporary, crowded barracks, as local and UNHCR officials attempted to assess, interview, and determine whether the detainees were refugees or economic migrants. On February 18, 1992, Nguyễn Văn Hải, who was twenty-seven years of age, hanged himself.[57] Mr. Nguyễn was discovered dangling in a public toilet room by a fellow detainee. He left a suicide note stating, "I am killing myself to protest against the screening policing of the Hong-kong [sic] government, which is too strict and unfair."[58] A Boat People SOS memo confirmed the tragic end of Mr. Nguyễn and the grim scenario at the refugee camp: "Mr. Hải's [Nguyễn's] death is the first reported by the Hongkong [sic] Correctional Service Department in a series of suicide attempts at the Whitehead detention center that houses twenty thousand Vietnamese freedom seekers."

On December 11, 1992, at the Sikhiu Camp in Thailand, Hoàng Thị Thu Cuc, age twenty-six, hanged herself to death after being denied refugee status.[59] Three years earlier, Ms. Hoàng and four of her brothers escaped on boat to Thailand. After three years of waiting at Sikhiu Camp, in hopes of gaining political asylum and freedom to resettle in a third country, Ms. Hoàng and her brothers were categorized as economic migrants and faced the likelihood of repatriation to Việt Nam.[60] A fellow oceanic refugee in the Sikhiu Camp wrote a letter in response to Ms. Hoàng's suicide and agonizingly remarks, "Her suicide fervently expressed the yearning for freedom by the Vietnamese who have come to despise the communist regime. Petitions, hunger strikes, and suicides are the only ways they know how to inform the world of their ordeal and to awaken the world's compassion."[61]

The story of Trịnh Kim Hương is another tragic story. Just twenty-eight years old, Ms. Trịnh was an asylum seeker in Galang Camp in Indonesia.[62] On August 30, 1991, in protest of camp officials' denial of her refugee status, she set herself on fire at 3:30 A.M.[63] More individuals committed suicide in Galang Camp. In response, Vietnamese diasporans responded collectively and formed the nonprofit Boat People SOS, an organization with headquarters in Washington, DC, and several chapters now established throughout the United States. The organization is created and led by Vietnamese Americans who made determined and painstaking efforts to rescue Vietnamese refugees. In addition, they wanted to shine a light on the refugees' plight and fight for their legal status, hoping to have them declared as political asylees seeking resettlement in a willing host nation. Boat People SOS also documented several Vietnamese refugees who committed suicide at the Galang Camp, after they were denied refugee status. In one case, the Vietnamese diasporic organization reported that "twenty-one-year-old Trinh Anh Huy, son of artillery lieutenant Trịnh Văn Diệp, doused himself with kerosene and set himself on fire in front of the UNHCR's office. . . . While the flame engulfed him, he repeatedly screamed out to the UNHCR officials present, 'We are not economic migrants, we are refugees.'"[64] Mr. Trịnh passed away in late August of 1992.

At the Sungei Besi Camp in Malaysia, Nguyễn Ngọc Dũng, took his own life on March 5, 1993 after being denied refugee status.[65] Mr. Nguyễn Ngọc Dũng stabbed himself in the heart in front of the office of the Sungei Besi Task Force after hearing that they had rejected his refugee status. He died on the way to the hospital.[66] Earlier that year, on February 14, Lưu Thị Hồng Hạnh attempted suicide by setting herself on fire. Ms. Lưu was taken to Pinang Hospital where she died four days later.

In these suicide tragedies and many more, Vietnamese refugees chose to end their own lives as a desperate plea for help and to protest against the unjust asylum screening decisions that denied them and/or their family refugee status. In Hong Kong, Thailand, Indonesia, and Malaysia a significant number of Vietnamese refugees residing in unacceptable camp conditions with meager rations and little hope, resorted to destroying what only they could control: their own bodies. In addition, their protests placed significance on their desire to be declared human refugees, a term unfortunately often politicized and mislabeled with derision. Yet, in the context of their political persecution, social ostracization, and economic desperation, seeking refugee status was understandably and justifiably sought by thousands of Vietnamese who risked their lives to resettle in a host country in search of a better life than the one they left behind.

Another tragic tale out of many for post–Việt Nam War refugees from Southeast Asia pertains to the selling of cooked food at a market. James M. Freeman provides explicit details of one Vietnamese refugee's account at a Thailand detention camp: "The most brutal of the camps were on the tense, unsettled border of Thailand and Cambodia. Mrs. Do Thanh Huệ, a Vietnamese refugee now living in California, described to me her life in one of those border camps, known as Site 2 . . . [Mrs. Do Thanh Huệ:] 'But the greatest danger for us came from the Thai camp guards. . . . And I was there when they stopped a Cambodian woman from selling fried bananas in the market. She was not permitted to do that, so the guards took the boiling oil from her pan and poured it on her head. Her two eyes blew up and she died instantly, right in front of her two small children. . . . With the never-ending hunger, the shelling [from Vietnamese troops occupying Cambodia at that time], the Cambodian bandits, the Thai guards, the continuous fear of death and torture at any moment, the dirt, the lack of privacy, the exhaustion, the disease, and the uncertainty of what was to happen to us [sic] . . . we were always in a panic."[67]

The Việt Nam War continues to cast a long shadow, crossing over to new generations of the Vietnamese diaspora. Wars perpetuate a tragic history of violence, even after the war, as they did for thousands of Vietnamese refugees who died in their attempts to leave their home country, for the many who lost their lives in refugee camps, and for those who survived the unforgettable postwar traumas. Yet, such history must be remembered, for memory and storytelling could lead to enlightenment, inspiration, healing, and compassion. Home gardens offer a refuge for recovery, restoration, and empowerment for the refugees who were fortunate enough to survive but must also live their remaining years coping with the war, displacement, resettlement, and racialization that resulted from it.

NOT ALL IS LOST: A GARDEN GROWS IN A REFUGEE CAMP

In the midst of such violence, misery, hopelessness, and tragedy, food gardens help refugees land their feet on *terra firma* despite living on the *terra incognita* of refugee camps. Here, they would dig the land, rummage the soil with their hands, and plant a life, a memory, and a taste of the past, no matter how temporary their stay would be. Vietnamese refugees camped in far-flung, isolated outposts in Thailand, Malaysia, Indonesia, and the Philippines, as well as near large population centers like Singapore and Hong Kong; there they cultivated what little spaces they could control, and transformed them into food gardens of their own. These food gardens were more than a necessity for survival, they offered what little nutrition refugees could access to maintain their health. Through gardening, Vietnamese refugees attempted to establish their food sovereignty, justice, and resistance to remain alive. Thus, Vietnamese exiles living in refugee camps were more than just innocent bystanders. They were certainly victimized, neglected, and abused, but they were more than mere victims. Today, Vietnamese refugees are more than just survivors, even as they continue to cope and heal from the traumas of war, exile, relocation, and marginalization. They are the progenitors of how to subsist, survive, and overcome untenable living conditions. Vietnamese and other Southeast Asian refugees demonstrated incredible perseverance, and their food gardens in refugee camps provide evidence of their determination, and adaptability.

Why did they grow such food gardens, aside from sustaining themselves and passing time, if their stay at refugee camps would be temporary, even if they remained for months and years, and in some cases, permanently? What was the significance of having food sovereignty over the vegetables, herbs, and fruit trees they cultivated, when they had such little control over their own future and lives? What could Vietnamese refugees possibly have gained from growing these food gardens? Such food gardens gave them daily exercise and peaceful activity to improve their physical and mental health. Also, an everyday routine of gardening broke the monotony, frustration, and boredom that came with the constant waiting and distress in seeking political asylum. Food gardens also helped them retain a part of their food heritage and culture, providing refugees a sense of normalcy and dignity as they endured the humiliating process of waiting patiently for months and years for their fates to be determined by UNHCR officials and government agencies. In spite of their poor, overcrowded camp conditions, food gardens provide evidence of Vietnamese refugees making a concerted effort to live their lives, demonstrating their resilience, ingenuity, and resourcefulness, while also challenging the paternalistic and patronizing notion that they were just helpless victims who were incapable of surviving. Living in chronic uncertainty, Vietnamese refugees nonetheless sought ways to survive and improve their camp life. Whether apparent or not, Vietnamese refugees committed themselves to the political act of cultivating food gardens in camps in Thailand, Malaysia, Indonesia, Singapore, the Philippines, and Hong Kong, showcasing their incredible ability to adapt and survive in *terra incognita* and seek their own *terra firma* to survive, live . . . and wait.

Although the Vietnamese oceanic refugees who fled from their country by sea on overcrowded and rickety vessels dominated the headlines and narrative of the second, third, and fourth waves of refugees, thousands more were land refugees, fleeing on foot to Thailand where a number of refugee camps were hastily and shoddily constructed. Refugees from Việt Nam were not the only residents in Thailand's refugee camps. Laotians, Cambodians, and ethnic Vietnamese from Laos were also land refugees who fled on foot to Thailand.[68]

Like their oceanic refugee counterparts, land refugees also cultivated small food gardens with limited spaces and resources. According to a 1979 US congressional report, the findings show that "In many instances, refugees tend gardens to supplement official food supplies."[69] For example, at Aranyaprathet refugee camp in Thailand, a predominantly Cambodian refugee camp, some refugees resorted to cultivating food or family gardens to subsist and survive. One photo depicts a family gardening project at the Aranyaprathet camp, and what appears to be a father and son overlooking their food garden, smiling slightly for the camera, and perhaps a little proud of their small yet monumental achievement under such ominous conditions.[70] Elmer B. Staats reports that family gardening was evident but fairly limited by refugee camp circumstances. "One project common to most camps was family gardening. This had enjoyed the most success, but poor soil, lack of water, and

Figure 1.1   Vietnamese refugees cultivate their own gardens, as they remain in Pulau Bidong Refugee Camp, Malaysia, waiting and hoping to gain political asylum. (Photo copyright @ 2012–2014 Refuge Camps. info. All Rights Reserved.)

reluctance of the Thai Government to permit the use of land has hampered efforts."[71] At the Sikhiu refugee camp in Thailand, a Vietnamese refugee camp, food gardens were cultivated and utilized. Several photos provide ample evidence of gardening at the Sikhiu Vietnamese refugee camp.[72] Such food gardens created by Southeast Asian refugees in refugee camps across Thailand demonstrate their hard work ethic, perseverance, ingenuity, and resourcefulness. These food gardens became temporary, consumable, and vital "historic artifacts," displaying their attempts to regain some food sovereignty over their traditional foodways.

In his report to US Congress, Staats confirms that Vietnamese refugees made a concerted attempt to grow food gardens at one Malaysian refugee camp. Staats also declares that, at the Pulau Besar refugee camp in Malaysia, the camp "had enough wells with lots of good water—even enough to irrigate the dozens of small family vegetable gardens."[73] At Pulau Bidong, another Vietnamese refugee camp in Malaysia, Vietnamese refugees cultivated their own food gardens, while hoping to gain political asylum eventually (figure 1.1). In one photo, a Vietnamese male refugee stands by his food garden in Pulau Bidong, posing for a photo while holding a hoe (figure 1.2). Another archival photo showcases a community food garden or micro-

Figure 1.2 A Vietnamese male refugee cultivates his garden in Pulau Bidong Refugee Camp, Malaysia. (Photo copyright @ 2012–2014 Refuge Camps.info. All Rights Reserved.)

farm, showing how Vietnamese refugees in Pulau Bidong worked together to cultivate crops of their own in spite of their prolonged and stressful statelessness while they waited to gain political asylum.[74]

Food gardens were also evidently abundant at refugee camps in Indonesia, the Philippines, and Hong Kong. For instance, at Galang, Indonesia, Vietnamese refugees cultivated many individual food gardens. In fact, a number of photos provide spectacular proof of food gardens grown and raised by refugees. In refugee camps in the Philippines as well, Vietnamese refugee created and tended their own beautiful food gardens. At Palawan, Philippines, numerous photos show evidence of Vietnamese refugees cultivating their food gardens (figure 1.3). At one refugee camp in Hong Kong, a food garden was set up. At the Shek Kong Detention Centre, one of several refugee camps arranged in Hong Kong, a small vegetable and herb farm, or vườn rau, was raised with the assistance of NGO workers in 1991 (figure 1.4). The vườn rau shown in the photos appears to be a microfarm organized and cultivated via a collaboration between Vietnamese refugees and NGO workers. The vườn rau served as an emancipatory plot of cultivated land, particularly for Vietnamese refugees who wanted and desired to grow herbs, fruits, and vegetables in an effort to regain their traditional foodways and food sovereignty; this act liberated them, at least for brief moments, from the traumas of war and refuge, chronic uncertainty, lack of control, and helplessness.

Such food gardens grown and raised in refugee camps throughout Southeast Asia became essential for many Vietnamese refugees, particularly as their stay in detention camps was prolonged into endless months and years; and for some of those whose asylum cases were rejected by a host nation and who refused repatriation to Việt Nam, their stay became permanent. Thus, food gardens sustained the refugees, helping the Vietnamese cope with the countless troubles they endured seeking political asylum. More than just herbs, vegetables, and fruits to sustain their

Figure 1.3   Philippines Palawan minigarden, Philippines Palawan Refugee Camp, 1991. (James M. Freeman Collection, MS-SEA033, Box 7, Folder 8, Number 6, Special Collections and Archives, UC Irvine Libraries, Irvine, California. Photo courtesy of James M. Freeman.)

Figure 1.4   Hong Kong Shek Kong Detention Centre, Hong Kong Refugee Camp, 1991. (James M. Freeman Collection, MS-SEA033, Box 7, Folder 7, Number 2, Special Collections and Archives, UC Irvine Libraries, Irvine, California. Photo courtesy of James M. Freeman.)

health and supplement their diet, these food gardens provided survival food that lifted the refugees' spirits and made living conditions more bearable, allowing them to regain some of their food sovereignty and heritage. In the unsettling and traumatic environment of refugee camps, such essential food gardens became their own "victory" gardens, giving Vietnamese refugees some peace, joy, solace, and dignity, while carrying forth their traditional foodways. These food gardens opened a portal to their Việt Nam past, preserving their food heritage and sovereignty, no matter how temporary. They also humanized the refugees—as we all should with refugees, political asylees, and documented and undocumented immigrants—demonstrating their resilience to survive, adjust, and live for another day.

Therefore, I argue that, by cultivating these food gardens, Vietnamese refugees and political asylees transformed negative camp spaces into positive places of green gardens by their own volition. On these small plots of land, Vietnamese refugees could plan, organize, operate, observe, nurture, and consume the produce they grew. As a result, with these food gardens and microfarms, they asserted greater control over the fate of their produce—and consequently, a little bit more of their own fate, which goes a long way in their path to freedom. These victory gardens aided them in overcoming daunting challenges on their arduous journeys, buoying their hopes of gaining political asylum and refuge in host countries like the United States. Such food gardens and produce lend a possible path forward for Vietnamese to partake and embrace emancipatory foodways.

THE THINGS THEY STILL CARRIED: POSTWAR MEMORIES OF VIETNAMESE KITCHEN GARDENS AND FOODWAYS

> They carried the land itself—Vietnam, the place, the soil—a powdery orange-red dust that covered their boots and fatigues and faces. They carried the sky. The whole atmosphere, they carried it, the humidity, the monsoons, the stink of fungus and decay, all of it, they carried gravity…They carried their own lives.
>
> —Tim O'Brien, *The Things They Carried*

In harrowing and deadly escapes, for many Vietnamese refugees, including the anonymous oceanic refugee's diary entry at the beginning of this chapter, the things they carried included the clothes they wore and perhaps a few more clothing items that they rushed to bring; a handful of coins and paper bills that amount to little money; perhaps a few valuables and trinkets of jewelry carried for sentimental reasons or luck, or to bribe the boat's captain and government officials or bargain with pirates to spare their lives and their family's lives; a small family photo or two to remind them who they are and what they left behind; and traces of food, some seeds, and fresh water that they managed to procure right before or during their precarious journey to seek freedom and a new homeland. The latter, of course, would prove as elusive as the former. Like Tim O'Brien's American soldiers,[75] for Vietnamese refugees, they too carried the land of Việt Nam: the country's humid air and monsoon rains, the heavenly mountains and muddy rivers, the lush forests and dreamlike mists, the hard-working water buffaloes and land-shaped dragons, even the red dirt and flooded rice paddies that fed and nurtured them. They carried with them their ancestral homeland; the memories persisted, and no matter how faded, they mattered like the onion and garlic scripted neatly in a tiny, red pocket diary from an unknown Vietnamese refugee. Memories of loved ones lost and left behind, before, during, and after the Việt Nam War, whose lives will never be erased, forgotten, or unseen. And the stories that haunt and guide them as they carried on to a distant place—hoping for a new home yet still so far from being at home.

Before their exodus, many Vietnamese refugees had their own kitchen gardens in Việt Nam and were taught how to garden by their parents and/or grandparents, cultivating the vegetables, herbs, and fruit trees that were immortalized in South Việt Nam's postage stamps; such gardens and produce were not uncommon in Việt Nam. After the war and various migrations, thousands of Vietnamese refugees resettled in host countries, living in exile, as strangers and foreigners, foraging *and* forging a new homeland. Most would end up in the United States. Despite years of struggling and making difficult adjustments to adhere to American mainstream culture and cuisine, Vietnamese refugees still preserved their own foodways of growing produce, utilizing ingredients, exchanging seeds, offering and taking gardening tips, cooking meals, and consuming food more closely familiar to their food traditions. In other words, Vietnamese diasporans never abandoned their unique foodways. Overcoming unimaginable hardships, they transplanted their food heritage in the United States, and even expanded and reinvented their traditional foodways to adapt to the multicultural and medley palates in America.

Figure 1.5 A small food garden at a home in Quảng Ngãi, Việt Nam. The food garden contains a trellis with a variety of gourds, including luffas. (Photo courtesy of Ngọc Vũ.)

For Vietnamese American home gardeners, long after the Việt Nam War, they still fondly remember their kitchen gardens cultivated back when they were living in Việt Nam (figure 1.5). For instance, regarding seasonal crops grown, Andrea Nguyễn recalls the growing seasons of Việt Nam and the delicate care taken by her paternal grandmother (bà nội) in growing cabbages: "Because cool-season crops such as cabbage and cauliflower are difficult to grow in Vietnam, they enjoy a special status. In fact, my dad remembers how his mother carefully tended the cabbage heads in the family garden, covering each one with a cooking pot to encourage the leaves to curl."[76]

In her cookbook, *ăn: to eat*, which she coauthored with her daughter, Jacqueline An, Executive Chef Helene An mentions how important it is to have fresh ingredients when cooking Vietnamese food.[77] On the desire of having fresh herbs and vegetables readily accessible, the renowned chef recalls that "Growing up, we had kitchen gardens and also chicken and fish farms, ponds for raising shrimp, and a family fishing boat. Using our natural resources was not only about self-reliance and sustainability, but it was also the healthiest way to cook and eat. There is nothing like fresh produce or fresh protein in a dish . . . Starting with the freshest, locally grown or produced ingredients you can find can elevate even the simplest dish into a masterpiece."[78] Helene also observes, "We have always grown our own herbs and vegetables—from our family's large plantations in Vietnam to kitchen gardens at our restaurants."[79] She further explains, "I grew up with kitchen gardens, orchards, a chicken farm, a fish farm, a shrimp pond—all right in my backyard."[80]

Refugees learned how to tend vegetables, herbs, and fruit trees at a young age. They were taught how to garden by their own parents and grandparents. Gardening was certainly a common activity filled with joy, passion, purpose, and spirituality. Vietnamese American home gardeners, including Vietnamese Texans, recall their gardening practices while growing up in Việt Nam and learning from their parents. For instance, Nguyễn Văn Nam,[81] a retired University of Houston Vietnamese language professor, learned how to garden while growing up in Việt Nam, helping his mother in their front and backyards.[82] Mr. Nguyễn reflects, "Back home in North Việt Nam, when I was little, my father was the only one working. My mother stayed home, taking care of the house, watching the children, going to the market nearby to get food, preparing the meals and working in the garden when she had time. . . . We had a big backyard with fruit trees and a bigger front yard for vegetables. . . . When my sister and I came home from school, we tried to do our homework and study our lessons first. If we still had time, we went to the front yard to help mom. I learned from mom how to use the shovel, hoe, and rake. I also learned how to plant different kinds of vegetables and how to take care of them."[83]

Other Vietnamese Texans also remember their gardening days in Việt Nam. My father, Vũ Kiến An Quân, who learned to garden from his parents while in Việt Nam,[84] informs me that "In Việt Nam, people work hard with their hands, watching vegetables and fruits and [the] weather."[85] At the tail end of the second wave of Vietnamese exodus, Hoàng Quang and his wife, Nguyễn Lan, resettled in the United States in 1985.[86] Mr. Hoàng Quang learned to garden as a four-year-old child growing up in Việt Nam.[87] Their eldest son and offspring, Son Hoàng, remarks, "My dad inherited my grandfather and great-grandfather's love of working on the land."[88] Bạch Tuyết Phạm of Fort Worth, Texas, recalls that she was born in the South Việt Nam countryside, where it was natural and common knowledge to learn how to garden and plant trees by traditional practices.[89] Growing up in Việt Nam, Ms. Tammy Đình recollects her childhood home in Huế, where they lived in a spacious residence with a huge garden and an abundance of farm animals. She recalls, "My parents' home was like a zoo. . . . They cultivated a big garden. . . . They had a farm full of animals: chickens, pigs, ducks, rabbits and more."[90] She also mentions the various fruit trees her parents would plant and nurture in their yard, producing a bounty of delicious fruits: papayas (đu đủ), small sweet bananas (quả chuối moc), and sweetsops or sugar apples (mãng cầu). Unfortunately, the Việt Nam War would come to them as well, and her big family, which included twelve other siblings (ten brothers and two sisters), had to leave their home in Huế and relocate to Sài Gòn, where her father worked for the South Vietnamese government under Ngô Đình Diệm. She met her future husband, Nicholas Đình, who graduated from the Đà Lạt Military Academy and served in the South Vietnamese army, earning a rank of captain. They were married in Sài Gòn on December 29, 1974, a few months before the war's end, and lived near Tân Sơn Nhất International Airport.

For Vietnamese American home gardeners, digging into the soil, planting seeds, and nurturing plants are acts of healing that also help them remember their homeland and preserve their cherished foodways. Scholar Wenying Xu writes, "The desire for home generates its re-vision and idealization, motivating an endless search for and invention of the origin. . . . Foodways nevertheless continue to be the bloodline that keeps alive ethnic identity and the bittersweet longing for home. Yet the foodways also set the exile apart as an 'alien,' an abject and threatening presence in the midst of 'natives.'"[91] Xu poignantly observes that foodways are tangible connections and strong emotional pulls that aid exiles (and refugees) to seek and find home, a home they longed for and one they must be moored to in order to remain afloat and steady themselves from the gale-like storms of war, loss, abandonment, survivor guilt, refuge, and displacement. Simultaneously, refugees and exiles are strangers, outsiders, and foreigners to the natives, and their foodways are alien to the natives' palates. Xu further declares: "For the exile, his or her culture's foodways must function as a cushion from displacement and homelessness, as comfort food that momentarily transports the exile to the ever-elusive home. It is often through the palate and notes that the exile awakens the memories of his or her home and loved ones."[92] Here, Xu reinforces the significance and substance of foodways to nurture and heal the exilic. Not surprisingly, for Vietnamese refugees, political asylees, and exiles their foodways lead to home. Thus, their "home" gardens take on more than one meaning. The garden produce provides not only a healthy sustenance of fresh herbs, vegetables, and fruits, but it also reminds them of

their homeland of Việt Nam while they attempt to establish a new home in a foreign land.

Gardening sustained many Vietnamese, even while living in overcrowded, subpar refugee camps. In addition, their gardens brought back memories of home,
reminders of their passion, joy, purpose, and spirituality—sentiments that they
carried with them throughout their postwar journey, immediately and well after the
war, for war never leaves the survivors. There is no guarantee of an end to the haunt-
ing Việt Nam War nightmare for survivors. However, what may also never leave
Vietnamese refugees is the longing and yearning for home . . . and the gardens and
their produce help bring them closer to home.

Vũ Hồng Liên addresses the import and retention of Vietnamese foodways, as
hundreds of thousands of Vietnamese refugees in a span encompassing three
decades eventually resettled in the United States, Australia, and other nations after
the Việt Nam War. She thoughtfully articulates how Vietnamese refugees, who left
their home country and sought refuge and resettlement in the West and Australia,
carried with them a part of Việt Nam they refused to completely abandon, and that
is "their tastes of home and, once resettled, tried to re-create those tastes wherever
they found themselves."[93] Most Vietnamese refugees and political asylees eventually
resettled in the United States, which "admitted one hundred thousand Southeast Asian
in 1981, sixty-four thousand in 1983, and fifty thousand in 1984 through the 1980
Refugee Act."[94] Vũ astutely explains that in order to survive, subsist, and save what
little capital they had, in addition to missing and yearning their own Vietnamese
food, many resorted to home cooking.[95] Here, this generation of Vietnamese exiles
would learn how to recreate and prepare their own favorite Vietnamese dishes and
become skilled home cooks, whereas, had they remained in Việt Nam where
Vietnamese food was ubiquitous, they would not have resorted to developing and
mastering their home cooking skills. Living in the United States, Vietnamese home
cooks would take advantage of the abundant availability of good ingredients and
labor-saving technology, and when familiar herbs were not available in grocery
stores nearby, then they resorted to cultivating home gardens to grow such herbs in
their front and backyards, developing a gardening hobby in the process. Vũ argues
that "In a short space of twenty years, the exiled Vietnamese managed to re-create
an imagined home through taste. In doing so, they inadvertently preserved several
traditional and favourite Vietnamese dishes. At the same time, as with any language
in exile, if it had a voice Vietnamese food in the West would speak with a different
accent and many borrowed words, for it has evolved, branched out or modified to
suit local conditions."[96]

As a demonstration of their resilience, ingenuity, and adaptability, the Vietnamese diaspora has planted their traditional yet vibrant foodways in the United States and around the world. In fact, Vietnamese diasporans in the United States have enhanced the American palates, adding their unique, flavorful cuisine with a strong emphasis on fresh ingredients, herbs, vegetables, and fruits to make or complement traditional and new Vietnamese dishes. Nowadays, Vietnamese dishes such as phở and bánh mì have become almost ubiquitous "American" food staples, commonly found and delightfully devoured across the four corners of the United States. Furthermore, new variations of such popular Vietnamese staples, as well as fusion dishes that combine with other American dishes and flavors, have been created and reinvented, demonstrating the adaptability and durability of Vietnamese food, which aptly reflects the overall resilience of the Vietnamese populace in the United States. One such reflection is shown in the personal home gardens raised and nurtured by Vietnamese Americans, particularly in Texas, the state with the second largest Vietnamese diasporic population.

From colonized and war-torn Việt Nam, to grim refugee camps, and to resettlement in the United States, Vietnamese refugees utilized gardening as a political act to remember, value, and recreate what was lost and left behind. The act of digging and foraging the land to create a fruitful garden was a genuine attempt to remember who they are, where they come from, and where they have been. The remainder of the book focuses significantly on Vietnamese Texans and how they not only saved a part of their culture via their home gardens, but also preserved and expanded their foodways. Furthermore, home gardens remained essential for the working class, supplementing their diets with familiar herbs, vegetables, and fruits; lowering their grocery expenses; and beautifying their modest, crowded urban spaces. Plus, home gardens gave gardeners immediate access to fresh herbs, vegetables, and fruits. Home gardens allowed Vietnamese Americans to preserve and maintain their food heritage and sovereignty, giving them a leisure activity that promotes wellness, healthy living, and sustainable practices. They also granted Vietnamese Americans the opportunity to frequently use their home-grown produce to make specific dishes, enhance flavors of traditional meals, and serve as accoutrements to their home-cooked family dinners. Such home gardens, no matter the size or production, may have additionally serve as cultural, religious, spiritual, familial, and/or healing places for the gardeners; places that no doubt reminded them of their homeland. Thus, these home gardens have a double meaning for Vietnamese Americans: they assist them in planting—literally and figuratively—their own roots in their adopted country while serving as poignant reminders of their former home country of

Việt Nam, more specifically South Việt Nam. Home gardens help free Vietnamese Americans to live a better life, shedding away—albeit never entirely—their hopelessness, statelessness, and rootlessness. They have toiled, farmed, and gardened their way to freedom via emancipatory foodways of food sovereignty, culinary citizenship, and homeland duality; these three concepts will be explored in greater detail in a later chapter.

In addition, for Vietnamese who eventually resettled in Texas and become refugee settlers,[97] they have brought their Global South foodways to the US South, further enhancing Southern foodways, which are always changing, adding, mixing, and creating new cuisines that eventually become traditional culinary staples. While the next chapter will mention Vietnamese diasporic communities across the United States, the concentration of this book will be on Vietnamese Texans, as stated in the introduction. But before the Vietnamese resettlement in the United States is thoroughly explained and analyzed in the next chapter, a discussion on Asian Pacific American foodways, brought forth by eighteenth, nineteenth, and early twentieth century immigrants from Asia and the Pacific, is necessary. Attention will be given to farming and gardening practices and productions by Chinese immigrants during the exclusion era and Japanese Americans in the World War II internment period; two notably horrific experiences in Asian Pacific American history made possible by racist and xenophobic US policies. Nevertheless, like their future Vietnamese counterparts, the Chinese immigrants in the exclusion years and the Japanese American internees during World War II would find ways to cultivate vegetables, herbs, and fruit trees to subsist, earn a modest living, and preserve their food heritage, despite living in times of terrible duress, hostility, statelessness, and uncertainty.

CHAPTER 2

Gardens on the Margins

Asian Immigrants and Vietnamese Refugees Resettle in America

In early autumn the farm recruiters arrived to sign up new workers, and the War Relocation Authority allowed many of the young men and women to go out and help harvest the crops. Some of them went north to Idaho to top sugar beets. Some went to Wyoming to pick potatoes. Some went to Tent City in Provo to pick peaches and pears and at the end of the season they came back wearing brand-new Florsheim shoes. Some came back wearing the same shoes they'd left in and swore they would never go out there again. They said they'd been shot at. Spat on. Refused entrance to the local diner. The movie theater. The dry goods store. They said the signs in the windows were the same wherever they went: NO JAPS ALLOWED. Life was easier, they said, on this side of the fence.

—Julie Otsuka, from *When the Emperor Was Divine*

The hardest part is the beginning.

—Cap Xuân Hồ

The aforementioned passage and quote are juxtaposed in historical references: the passage from award-winning novelist, Julie Otsuka, on the subject of Japanese American internment;[1] and the quote from Cap Xuân Hồ, who worked as a resettlement case manager for the Alliance for Multicultural Community Services in Houston, Texas.[2] The passage from Otsuka's brilliant debut novel and the short yet wise quote from Hồ open a small window into the experiences of Japanese Americans and Vietnamese diasporans, yet they also reflect the difficulties of two racialized and marginalized Asian Pacific American groups throughout the course of US history. One shows the wartime mistreatment of Japanese Americans incarcerated during World War II; the other, a few words about the expected early challenges and difficulties that lie ahead for Vietnamese diasporans, as they attempt to heal and recover, if possible, from the sufferings of war, loss, refuge, displacement, and resettlement. Here, two histories of two Asian Pacific American groups intertwine when they push their hands into the dirt, dig the soil, plant seeds, nurture crops, and raise their gardens on the margins—in search of victory, emancipation, and home— even as they deliberate on whether to fence themselves in or brave a new country. And always in the back of their minds was the question: How could they best reshape their lives now that their former lives had been stripped from them?

Although this chapter spotlights the migration of Vietnamese refugees to Texas, I will begin by briefly discussing the history of Asian immigration to the United States during the nineteenth and early twentieth centuries. I focus on nineteenth century Chinese immigrant gardeners in the US West, and the "victory" gardens of the Japanese American internees during World War II. I also examine the significance of home gardens for Asian Americans today. In the second half of the chapter, I delve into the first wave of Vietnamese refugees and their secondary migration to Texas in the late 1970s. Finally, I hope to expound on the farm-to-freedom concept and how it applies to the racialized and marginalized Asian immigrant gardeners and farmers throughout US history, right up to Vietnamese refugees and political asylees in late twentieth century America. Farm-to-freedom as a concept also pertains to contemporary refugees and immigrants in twenty-first century America, which I will elucidate in the epilogue.

For many Asian immigrants and refugees, farm-to-freedom begins with their gardening traditions. Valerie J. Matsumoto argues that "tradition is a changing and selective process rather than a static body of customs and belief."[3] According to

Virginia D. Nazarea, our attachments to food also exist "in more intimate marginal spaces like home gardens and kitchens where people quietly tend to what they enjoy, and what gives meaning to their lives and their relationships."[4] Nazarea remarks, "Whether rooted or transported, people, plants, and places may have been bent and bruised but, on the whole, have remained remarkably pliant and disarmingly plural."[5] Robert E. Rhoades further argues that "localized responses based on everyday attachment to place, foodways, memory, and identity form powerful countervailing forces to homogenization and genetic erosion."[6] With great certainty, Vietnamese refugees and political asylees seek ways to regain and replicate their familiar foods and produce, protect and preserve their food-producing and cooking traditions, and expand their foodways, all to survive and succeed here in the United States, where they have been displaced and marginalized. Vietnamese were not the first Asian immigrant group (nor the last) to cultivate home gardens as part of their effort to resist against homogenization and racialization while they struggled to adjust to their American life. Throughout nineteenth century America, Chinese immigrants planted and raised food gardens for survival, as an income supplement, to earn a living wage, to create immediate access to fresh produce, and to retain their rich food heritage. Of course, Chinese cuisine and foodways have a strong influence on Vietnamese culinary history—in Việt Nam and in the United States.

CHINESE IMMIGRANTS AND THEIR FOOD GARDENS

Long before Vietnamese refugees and political asylees arrived on the shores of North America, Asian immigrants from China, Japan, Korea, India, and other Asian countries settled in the United States, establishing immigrant and diasporic communities in the eighteenth and nineteenth centuries. Yet today, much work still remains to uncover the rich and complex pasts of Asian immigrants, refugees, and diasporans in America. Matsumoto sums up the Asian American historiography well, echoing the wisdom of a notable historian: "Not only have Asians largely been ignored in US immigration history, but, as Roger Daniels has asserted, there has been more emphasis on those who sought to include them than on the immigrants themselves; few scholarly works have conveyed a sense of their own agency with the parameters of their social and economic situations."[7] I wholeheartedly agree with Matsumoto and Daniels, and in this work, I hope to clearly demonstrate the quotidian activism of Vietnamese American gardeners and farmers in Texas, and how they have searched for and employed numerous strategies to regrow, protect, preserve, and expand their traditional foodways in America.

While facing challenges upon their arrival in the United States due to racial discrimination, xenophobia, marginalization, and limited economic upward mobility, Asian Pacific American immigrants and diasporans sought to establish, maintain, and expand their foodways. Consequently, they made a concerted effort to gain food security while preserving their food heritage. Asian Pacific Americans cultivated vegetable gardens shortly after they arrived here in the United States. In 1848–49, when news of the discovery of gold in Northern California reached around the world, thousands of Chinese immigrants were attracted to the prospect of striking it rich, and so they crossed the Pacific Ocean to resettle in the United States, which Chinese sojourners referred to as "Gold Mountain." They cultivated their own vegetable gardens to satisfy their palates and cook traditional Chinese dishes familiar to them. "Much of this produce [cabbage, beans, peas, celery, potatoes, turnips, carrots, parsnips, apples, pears and small fruits] was grown on the small Chinese garden plots that ringed many communities and on larger farms tilled by Chinese owners or leaseholders," explains food scholar Andrew Coe.[8] He further explains, "Using skills learned on the intensively cultivated plots of the Pearl Delta, the immigrants had begun to grow vegetables soon after arriving—at first, the greens were for their own use, as they craved fresh toppings for their midday rice."[9] Regarding the significance of having such familiar vegetables that are suitable to their palates and diets, Coe writes about the Chinese miners meeting their nutritional needs via food gardens. He describes how the Chinese immigrant laborers from South China subsisted on rice with some vegetables or meat for seasoning. In addition, their daily diet would be supplemented with what they managed to cultivate in little food gardens near their camps.[10] Coe also remarks on the Chinese gardeners' incredible ability to cultivate vegetable gardens, not only to sustain themselves but also to sell produce to generate an income, even in northern Idaho where winters are long and the growing seasons are short.[11]

Historian Liping Zhu describes the Chinese immigrants who eventually dominated the vegetable market in the Rocky Mountain West region where mining towns and miners lacked immediate access to fresh produce: "Because many of the Chinese immigrants had been farmers before leaving for the United States, they entered the gardening business easily."[12] With a much shorter growing season in the Boise Basin than in the Guangdong Province, where many Chinese immigrants were from, "they tried to harvest as many vegetables as they could in just three months," states Zhu.[13] "An individual gardener usually cultivated a small piece of land on the outskirts of town. Using copious irrigation, both by hand-carried bucket and by ditch, as well as effective manures, the Chinese gardeners were able to raise six crops from the same ground in a single season. Chinese cabbage was the main crop in Chinese gardens. Local production immediately reduced the price to a few cents a pound. As early as the 1860s, whites had already realized that the Chinese were 'the most thorough gardeners in the world.'" Chinese immigrants in the nineteenth century Rocky Mountain West region communities were also savvy entrepreneurs. Zhu explains that not only were the Chinese immigrant laborers skillfully proficient at farming, but they were also business savvy and competitive in the commercial produce market. Every morning, they gathered fresh produce from their gardens and partake a door-to-door strategy to peddle their daily supply of fresh vegetables. Consequently, the Chinese immigrants controlled the produce market.[14] He goes on to discuss Chinese horticultural savvy and entrepreneurial prowess, and how they managed a successful produce business and made substantial profits, further demonstrating their production and marketing skills.[15] Zhu also mentions how Chinese miners had greater accessibility to fresh, organic produce by cultivating their own backyard gardens and how their diet was thus more nutritional and balanced in comparison to their Anglo-American miner counterparts.[16]

This book would be remiss if it simply bypassed the Asian Pacific American identity and spoke only of immigrant gardens. Identity formation and exploration are difficult, if not impossible, in the face of constant and persistent marginalization, racialization, perpetual foreign-ness, and seemingly always other-ness. For Asian Pacific Americans to establish or reclaim their identity, holding onto traditional foodways is one opportunity to do so; and farming and gardening offer opportunities to preserve and enlarge their food heritage. Cecilia M. Tsu's astounding work, *Garden of the World*, centers on the agricultural labor of Asian immigrants in Santa Clara Valley, California. She explains:

From 1880 to 1940, the region's peak decades of horticultural production, the participation of Asian immigrants in agriculture challenged, modified, and consolidated the white family farm ideal. Asians who labored in agriculture also redefined this ideal for their respective communities, eschewing the exclusive white American version. For Chinese immigrant men, who espoused a trans-Pacific view of family farming, their labor on California farms became a means to support immediate and extended families in rural villages of southern China. Japanese immigrants, increasingly intent on settling permanently in California as family units, came to see farming as the basis of a secure, thriving immigrant society. In the Japanese incarnation of the American dream, the ability of an immigrant man to succeed as a farmer and thereby support a wife and children in California signified his status among his countrymen and became a means of bolstering his community standing. For Filipino migrants, the majority of whom struggled as poorly paid seasonal agricultural laborers during the Great Depression, the search for work on dignified terms led them to form multiracial coalitions in the farm labor movement.[17]

In the Santa Clara Valley of California, Chinese, Japanese, and Filipino immigrants contributed significantly to the advancement of agricultural labor and produce in the United States. In the late nineteenth and early twentieth century America, Asian immigrants in farming communities of California, Idaho, Washington, Hawai'i, and elsewhere experienced a modicum of economic success as farmers, gardeners, and fruit and vegetable peddlers; a few like George Shima (Ushijima Kinji), a Japanese immigrant who arrived in the United States in 1889, even prospered. Asian immigrant farmers and gardeners protected and extended their food heritage in America, adding to the burgeoning cornucopia of foodways that African slaves and European and Latinx immigrants brought before them. Unfortunately, throughout the course of US history, Asian immigrants were not always welcomed in America, and racist exclusion laws, immigration policies, and presidential executive orders would be enacted to negate the rights and marginalize the labor and livelihoods of Asian immigrants.

A GARDEN GROWS IN THE DESERT: JAPANESE AMERICAN INTERNEES AND THEIR "VICTORY GARDENS"

Throughout the late nineteenth and early twentieth centuries, many Asian immigrants cultivated their own small vegetable gardens on American soil. An influx of Asian immigrants from colonized places such as South Asia and the Philippines also immigrated to the United States, resettling mostly in the western states and laboring for little pay in backbreaking and dangerous occupations that most native-born Anglo-Americans shunned. To provide sustenance, gain immediate access to fresh produce, and consume the food they missed and relished, it was not uncommon for Asian immigrants to plant and raise food gardens in what little green space was available. Some Asian immigrants, such as the Japanese, became distinguished and successful farmers within a couple of generations, particularly in Northern California, demonstrating their ingenuity, perseverance, and incredible work ethic despite anti-Japanese sentiment and racism present even before World War II.

In the immediate aftermath of the Japanese attack on Pearl Harbor, growing public pressure and a rise in anti-Japanese hysteria led to an unconstitutional attempt to punish an Asian minority in the United States because of their race and ethnicity. President Franklin D. Roosevelt issued Executive Order 9066, which led to the US military round-up of Japanese Americans living in the western states and their forceful removal and relocation to internment camps. Approximately 125,000 Japanese Americans were unceremoniously uprooted to internment camps during the American involvement in World War II. Unjustly incarcerated, Japanese Americans challenged this racism, ostracism, and marginalization throughout their internment. Japanese Americans, a majority of whom were US citizens, and none of whom were proven disloyal to the United States, were indeed discriminated and incarcerated against their will and forced to live in prison camps located in desert, mountainous, and isolated areas. They were trapped behind barbed wire and forced to live in military barracks where they were closely monitored by armed US servicemen. Japanese American internees endured the humiliation of being rounded up and placed under heavy scrutiny by armed US military guards, forced to live in subpar conditions, and most of all, were dehumanized by the US government and visible will of the American people. Nevertheless, despite being forced to sell their property at a substantially lower value, give up their livelihood and wealth, and being stripped of their citizenship rights, identity, and humanity, Japanese American internees fought to recover and regain their dignity with tremendous perseverance, hard work, and ingenuity. In fact, they demonstrated not only resilience but also food resistance and justice by cultivating beautiful vegetable gardens despite limited resources, lack of freedom, and less-than-ideal soil and climate conditions. By planting and nurturing camp gardens and producing an abundance of vegetables, Japanese American gardeners transformed negative spaces of internment and imprisonment into positive places by their own accord and will. Many were productive and successful farmers before the war. They regained some food sovereignty by producing, raising, and controlling their vegetable gardens, and thereby established culinary citizenship using their traditional foodways of farming and gardening to retain their food heritage and some sense of normalcy and control, while also demonstrating their right to belong to a country and a land they cultivated before and during their imprisonment.

While American civilians at home supported the US war effort by raising victory gardens and contributing to the defeat of Nazi Germany, fascist Italy, and imperial Japan, Japanese American internees cultivated their own victory gardens in isolated, far-flung prison camps. Not only did they demonstrated their ingenuity, persever-ance, diligence, horticultural savviness, and food justice, but they certainly proved their own self-worth, regained their food sovereignty, improved their physical and mental health, demonstrated resilience and resistance, and made a concerted effort to protest and overcome the inherently racist, flawed, and contradictory US policy that relocated and condemned them to internment camps in the first place. They responded positively to the egregious and blatant violation of their civil liberties and the US Constitution. Indeed, their victory gardens unveiled the farm-to-freedom movement as they worked to gain their freedom from imprisonment.

On the internment of Japanese Americans during World War II, prominent his-torian Gary Y. Okihiro asserts that "more than a violation of civil liberties, the gov-ernment's actions sought to deny Japanese Americans their dignity and essential humanity."[18] Okihiro elaborates further: "Registered and given numbers after wait-ing in long lines, the nameless were herded onto trucks, buses, and trains 'like cattle and swine.' They were dumped in makeshift 'assembly centers,' often county fair-grounds and horse racetracks, and made wards of their government, which arbi-trarily stripped them of their rights and possessions, told them nothing about their destinations, and even denied them their futures. And they knew that their victim-ization was by virtue of their 'race,' deemed inferior and repugnant, and self-hatred and loathing might have been nurtured by that startling recognition. One's face and culture might have required, thus, denial and erasure. That was the heart of the matter for Japanese Americans in Hawai'i and on the US continent."[19] By transform-ing their dreadful internment landscapes into lush gardens of their own cultivated crops, Japanese American gardeners created personal green spaces of redemption and emancipation.

Distinguished historian Roger Daniels analyzes the self-determination and resil-ience of the Japanese Americans who were incarcerated and transported to assembly centers and internment camps during World War II. He remarks on their need to regain some control over what they were given to eat: "There were no individual cooking facilities. Everyone ate in the mess hall. Three times a day, prisoners lined up with trays to receive wholesome, starchy, cheap food, not usually prepared in the most appetizing manner . . . the diet was often supplemented with vegetables grown by the camp inmates."[20] For the thousands of Japanese American internees, the food issued by the US government at the internment camps was unappetizing and unhealthy. The internment experience left them hungry for the vegetables, fruits, and herbs they savored before their incarceration. Consequently, Japanese American internees had a strong desire to raise their own vegetables that they wanted to plant, prepare, and consume. For Japanese American internees, they created their version of victory gardens, cultivating their culinary citizenship despite the "alien citizenship" status bestowed on them before and during incarceration. They preserved and expanded their Japanese foodways amid excruciating and humiliating internment, while experiencing heavily guarded confinement, poor nutrition, inclement weather, and harsh terrain.

Scholar Thy Phu analyzes the complexities behind the cultivation of citizenship. "While internees were banned from starting private enterprise, they were encouraged, as was the case with other Americans who were not incarcerated during World War II, to cultivate victory gardens, as an act of resourceful, not to mention patriotic, self-sufficiency," says Phu.[21] Phu is praiseworthy of publishing photographs taken by Japanese American internees themselves, including Toyo Miyatake. She declares: "After all, in the photo taken by Miyatake, the men are arranged *among* the harvested vegetables, not instead of them, so that while a celebration, a thanksgiving, is to be recognized, so too must the sacrifice that would otherwise be too easily forgotten."[22] Phu aptly summarizes, "Despite the approach that Toyo Miyatake and other photographers offer for tackling the challenge of memorializing labor without reifying cultivation, these lessons were not fully taken up in the post-internment period. Given the ways that cultivation provided, through a laudatory screen focused on industry and self-sufficiency, an effective means of symbolically vindicating the state for the internment, it may seem surprising that this theme persisted beyond the closing of the camps. Nevertheless, far from fading into obscurity, as the camps themselves were inexorably reclaimed by dereliction and desert dust, cultivation survived the ignominy of the internment as a controversial strategy for redressing the injustices of Executive Order 9066."[23] Here, Phu takes a critical view on the cultivation of citizenship, arguing and pointing out the fallacies of the cultivator (US government and society) to determine, facilitate, impose, and showcase the cultivation of citizenship on the cultivator's terms against the will of Japanese American prisoners.

On the flip side, one could assert that the Japanese American internees in the cultivation of citizenship discourse, are the actual cultivators themselves, preserving and protecting their culture and identity, demonstrating resilience and resistance, and advocating for a truer democracy via food gardens to the rest of the United States during the nation's troubling and unjustifiable internment of Japanese Americans. Such Japanese American food gardens in internment camps are victory gardens in their own right, with an emphasis on victory over American racism, state terrorism, and social and economic injustices. By contrast, history textbooks typically mention victory gardens as civilian-led initiatives that were solely focused on defeating enemies abroad, but neglect their effect on defeating the discriminatory behavior at home.

Through the camera lens of history, renowned historians Linda Gordon and Gary Okihiro provide a thorough analysis of the fascinating photos taken by Dorothea Lange in *Impounded: Dorothea Lange and the Censored Images of Japanese American Internment*. Here, Lange—one of the most revered US photographers in history—captures images of Japanese Americans adjusting to their new norm of surviving in internment camps such as Manzanar, California. In these black-and-white photos, she gives back the Japanese American internees something valuable that was stolen from them during World War II: their humanity. For instance, by taking photos of what the US government labeled as "hobby" gardens of vegetables and flowers, Lange furnishes glimpses of the internees' creativity, horticulture savviness, determination, and resilience—all signs of their humanity growing in the middle of Manzanar, in middle of nowhere.

Linda Gordon lauds the legendary work of Dorothea Lange and asserts that Lange managed to photograph, as best as she could, the Japanese American internees and what they accomplished while toiling, creating, and cultivating a civilization of their own in the desert camp of Manzanar.[24] Gordon further examines how Japanese Americans attempted to find a gravity of normalcy and carve out a dignified existence while imprisoned: "They decorated their 'apartments' with curtains, rugs, pictures, flowers, and room dividers. They made themselves partitions, shelves, closets, chairs, benches, and tables out of scrap lumber. They cleared the brush, irrigated, and planted both vegetables and flowers. . . . They created rock gardens and set up art classes in both Western and Japanese styles."[25] Gordon assesses the impact and powerful work of Dorothea Lange's photography collection of Japanese American internees in their unsettled surroundings. Here, she argues that Lange successfully captured the dignified work and creativity of Japanese American prisoners, while acknowledging their resilience and desire to return to normalcy and create and nurture sovereign spaces, cultivated their own citizenship, even while they were victimized. Gardening became a powerful vehicle of remembering their former lives. The act of digging in the dirt to cultivate organic produce of their own turned into an act of food sovereignty, resistance, and justice as well (figures 2.1 and 2.2).

Commenting on Japanese American food gardens raised and crafted at desolate internment camps, Okihiro poignantly asserts, "For many, the act of creating restored a semblance of self-control and self-determination. Inscribing one's tracings

Figure 2.1   Manzanar Relocation Center, Manzanar, California. Evacuee in her "hobby garden," which rates highest of all the garden plots at this War Relocation Authority center. Vegetables for their own use are · grown in plots 10 × 50 feet between rows of barracks. Manzanar concentration camp, California. (Photo by Dorothea Lange. Dorothea Lange Collection. https://ddr.densho.org/ddr-densho-151-372/.)

upon the intractable earth helped to dispel the threatening darkness. Gardens transformed the desert into places of beauty. Even the hostile alkaline soil could not resist this labor of love. Using sticks, stones, and native trees, shrubs, cacti, and wildflowers, Japanese Americans landscaped their blocks and erected hedges and facades around their barracks to shield their dwellings from the dust storms and splash the pitiful tar-paper barracks and bleak surroundings with a mantle of color and life."[26] Okihiro astutely sums up the driving force and significance behind the works of Japanese American prisoners. He argues that in spite of the paralysis that comes with their rejection, confinement, humiliation, and uncertainty, creativity surged

Figure 2.2 Manzanar Relocation Center, Manzanar, California. Evacuees of Japanese ancestry are growing flourishing truck crops for their own use in their "hobby gardens." These crops are grown in plots 10 × 50 feet between blocks of barracks at this War Relocation Authority center. Manzanar concentration camp, California. (Photo by Dorothea Lange. Dorothea Lange Collection. https://ddr.densho.org/ddr-densho-151-467/.)

for Japanese American internees.[27] In this case, they found the will, need, and strength to create food gardens that became their own victory gardens to consume, remember, heal, and resist.

Notable historian David K. Yoo also describes general camp life for Japanese American internees and their varied and strong reactions: "As time wore on, Japanese Americans exhibited a range of responses to their circumstances. In late 1942, riots broke out in the camps at Poston and Manzanar, and protests also took other forms, including draft resistance at Heart Mountain, Wyoming. Some Nikkei channeled their energies into camp-based jobs that paid a mere pittance but filled time."[28] He further states, "Others tended to vegetable and flower gardens or expressed themselves through the fine arts."[29] Here, Yoo remarks on how the "routineness" of cultivating vegetable and flower gardens was an indicative response to their imprisonment. Vegetable and flower gardens granted Japanese American internees the opportunity to express their identity, creativity, and food resistance. "Part of the pain of the war and the camps for many Nisei was the realization that the country of their birth and allegiance had failed them miserably," Yoo poignantly explains. "The concentration camps caused many Nisei to become disillusioned about the core nature of American democracy . . . nearly all carried with them the emotional and psychological freight of having been prisoners of their own country.”[30]

Japanese American internees remember some of the vegetable and traditional Japanese gardens that their parents and neighbors built and raised, while living in their World War II prison barracks. Hikoji Takeuchi recalls: “So in between rows of barracks, we eventually got seeds, and we made lawns, we made gardens out in— let's face it, Manzanar was a barren desert, no grass growing. So eventually, the people got together and put in lawns and gardens.”[31] Takeuchi further elaborates on the gardens and states, “Well lawns went up and gardens were put in. . . . They tried to make it look homey. Rather than seeing nothing but sand, it's so nice to see greenery. And then as for the farmers, you know, they started raising watermelon, cantaloupe. . . . And eventually as time went on, every camp was raising their own agricultural things. So Manzanar was sent to Poston, Poston was sent to Manzanar and so forth, I guess.”[32] Sue Kunitomi Embrey also remembers some of the camp gardens cultivated by Japanese American internees: “And the people also built gardens in front of their unit. They planted flowers, they had vegetable gardens, and it was a real attempt to beautify their surroundings, and I think it really helped the morale of the people.”[33] Willie K. Ito reflects on the Japanese American camp gardens at Topaz and what they managed to produce and consume. “So finally when we started getting rice, we noticed that a lot of the pickles that the Japanese like to accompany their rice, were local grown vegetables, squash, zucchinis and squashes, even watermelons, the rind would be soaked in brine and made into *tsukemono* as we called it, to eat with our rice,” explains Ito. “And, of course, the white radishes, the *daikons*, were great. . . . They were pretty much grown in our so-called victory gardens.”[34]

Despite the discernible fallacies of the American origins behind the cultivation of citizenship discourse (one established, shaped, and narrated by a racist US government and society in wartime), I argue that for Vietnamese American home gardeners, cultivating the herbs, fruit trees, and vegetables that are culturally significant to them demonstrate one way to cultivate their own brand of US citizenship. In other words, by taking ownership over a small plot of land and planting a spatial sovereignty, Vietnamese American food producers are defining their own cultivation of citizenship, pivoting the discourse that was certainly incomplete, irksome, shortsighted, and flawed regarding the World War II internment of Japanese Americans. Of course, there is one major difference: while the Japanese American internees suffered this dehumanizing experience during wartime, Vietnamese Americans suffered the visceral carnage of war, exile, displacement, and racialization, and continue to suffer today. Nonetheless, Vietnamese Americans, akin to their Japanese American predecessors, attempted to cultivate their American citizenship, despite their "alien" citizenship status, as experienced by Japanese American internees. One way to cultivate their own American citizenship—and culinary citizenship—is to raise home/food gardens to preserve and expand their traditional foodways, rooting themselves in the United States, and by this act of food sovereignty and remembrance, rooting themselves in their Việt Nam.

FARM-TO-FREEDOM FOR ASIAN PACIFIC AMERICAN HOME GARDENERS

Not only were food/kitchen gardens essential to the economic survival and success of Chinese immigrants, Japanese American internees, and other Asian immigrant gardeners toiling in nineteenth and twentieth century America, but even today food/kitchen gardens remain important to modern-day Asian immigrants and refugees residing in urban areas. Scholar Robert E. Rhoades astutely observes that "In their adopted countries, reflecting on the old adage that the last thing to change in an immigrant's home is the cupboard, immigrants seek to grow or obtain plants essential to their native cuisine. Aside from fulfilling food memories, gardening also performs another function, namely, to help immigrants set down roots in the new place."[35] Rhoades stresses the significance of maintaining traditional foodways for immigrants to remain connected to their homeland. He alludes that such foodways are integral links to their past, strengthen their ethnic identity, and offer the greatest resistance to cultural loss and erasure.[36] Furthermore, immigrants grow home gardens rife with familiar herbs, vegetables, and fruit trees; utilize their fresh produce to make familiar culinary dishes; and share favorite comfort foods with immediate family members and friends to lessen the burden and anxiety of their resettlement in a new country.[37]

Freelance writer and food journalist, Alana Dao, argues that "cultivating a kitchen garden becomes a significant rite of passage that's almost subversive in nature—it involves digging into the ground to mark not only a physical place to grow what one is familiar with."[38] Dao notes that many Asian immigrants and refugees in the United States and around the world need to plant their own gardens and grow their own food, so that they may have some control over their own diet and preserve their culture.[39]

Such food/kitchen gardens are indeed *home* gardens. Historically, home gardens have helped Asian immigrants in the United States not only to remember their homelands, but they have also used them to reassert and regain their food sovereignty and culture, especially in the face of anti-Asian legislation, vitriol, and violence that occurred in nineteenth century America and onward. In addition, home gardens give Asian immigrant gardeners opportunities to take root in the United States—on their own terms. The same could be said of Vietnamese refugees of the late twentieth century who sought ways to grow, make, and import the Việt foods they missed and enjoyed. For Vietnamese diasporic homes and neighborhoods in Texas, the US South, and throughout the United States, one way to garner produce that is to their taste and liking is to dig the soil and plant their own home gardens, which have become tremendous emancipatory foodways to preserve their cuisine and heritage *and* help liberate them from the horrors of war, refuge, relocation, and racialization.

POLYCULTURAL FOODWAYS IN THE US SOUTH

Polycultural foodways have always existed throughout the US South, particularly in Texas. Such polycultural foodways were brought forth and introduced in the region by Indigenous peoples, followed by Mexicans, African Americans, and Europeans. Their foodways were established long before Vietnamese refugees arrived in Texas and the US South. Like their predecessors, Vietnamese refugees would also bring their own food heritage and enrich and diversify Southern foodways. Despite facing the travails and challenges of marginalization and racism as perpetual foreigners, Vietnamese refugees would seek and find ways to preserve and expand their food traditions, including the cultivation of their own home gardens.

Although Vietnamese refugees and immigrants have their own share of adversities, it is clear that without the culinary trails previously blazed by early immigrants and refugees in Texas, who endured, confronted, and contested social injustices, institutional racism, historical erasure, cultural memory loss, and marginalization, Vietnamese foodways would not have found a more receptive audience in Texas today. For instance, on the origins of Texas Mexican cuisine, renowned chef Adán Medrano briefly traces the history of the Indigenous peoples in Texas: "Between 1492 and 1900, 90 percent of the native peoples of Texas died. European diseases such as cholera, smallpox, measles, and influenza devastated huge populations within weeks and even days. The Indigenous peoples who remained in Texas married into other tribes, with European settlers, and with Mexicans coming up from Southern Mexico. They sometimes lived in Catholic missions and eventually came to be known as the Mexican people of Texas. It was a process of continuous change and adaptation."[40] Chef Medrano further explains, "Food production and cooking were essential to Texas Indian survival and self-identity.... But as native cooks fled from their homelands and took shelter in Catholic missions or in newly established European towns, they encountered new animals such as pigs, cattle, and goats, and new bulbs such as garlic and onion, and could no longer depend on their traditional hunting, fishing, gathering, and gardening. From the sixteenth century to the twentieth century, their cuisine would evolve quite remarkably, even deliciously (!), and begin a new phase that would marry Texas Indigenous cuisine with European dishes. These are the origins of today's Texas Mexican cuisine."[41]

It is not uncommon for immigrants and refugees who have resettled in the United States to partake an assertive role in influencing and transforming American culinary tastes and choices. Donna R. Gabaccia discusses the immigrants' historical influences on Southern and Texan foodways. For instance, she comments on German immigrant foodways: "As early as the 1720s, Germans specialized in providing New Orleans with cabbage, fruit, salads, greens, beans and peas, and fish. In Texas in the 1840s and 1850s, they developed truck gardening around port cities like Galveston and Indianola."[42]

HOUSTON AS A CITY OF CULINARY REFUGE AND CULTURAL CONTINUITY

Historically, particularly in Houston, ethnic cultures and foodways take precedent because Black slaves, Mexicans, and other ethnic and racial groups have partaken in the building of the fourth largest metropolis in the United States. Historian Tyina L. Steptoe writes, "City founders Augustus and John Allen saw the potential of a city located 'in the heart of a very rich country' of pine and swamp. In 1836, they used Black slaves and Mexican prisoners of war from the Battle of San Jacinto to clear the 'marshy, mosquito-infested' bayou land that originally formed Houston, named for the commanding general who led the attack on the Mexican army that year. Human chattel and crops traveled between the city and the farms and plantations of the Sugar Bowl [Ft. Bend, Wharton, Brazoria and Matagorda counties] via the San Felipe Trail, a path that allowed the city to prosper on the productivity of the slave-filled countryside."[43]

In Houston, there exists a long tradition and history of residents growing their own vegetable gardens, and that practice remains today. Ethnic groups have been cultivating their own kitchen gardens throughout the city's history. Steptoe analyzes the migration of Black Southerners from Louisiana and East Texas to Houston in the Jim Crow era of racial segregation and violence toward African

Americans. She describes Houston's development and the Black settlement of its residential wards during the late nineteenth and early twentieth centuries. Steptoe argues, "The wards made Houston feel like a collection of small towns rather than one city. Thelma (Scott) Bryant, who was born in Third Ward in 1905, commenting that her neighborhood felt 'very much like the country' in the early twentieth century."[44] She further asserts, "Likewise, musician Arnett Cobb, who came of age in Fifth Ward, described the community of his youth as a 'country town.' Indeed, many of the people who moved to his neighborhood from the country continued the same customs and agricultural practices they had brought with them from the countryside. Most families raised chickens and grew okra, greens, corn, and other subsistence crops in their backyards." Here, African American migrants brought to Houston their own customs of raising their own vegetables, herbs, and farm animals when they lived in the countryside, and kept these practices when resettling in Houston to preserve their cultural praxis. Historian, author, and colleague Malcolm Frierson refers to the aforementioned practices as a "cultural continuity," which is integral to curtail cultural appropriations and marginalization of food heritages.

The cultural continuity of carrying farming customs from the rural to an urban environment is one of many contributions Black southern migrants have brought to Houston, enriching the city's "polycultural world"[45] despite living under Jim Crowism. They introduced the concept of urban farming in the early twentieth century, long before the term itself became part of the American vernacular and trendy in our twenty-first century dialect. Furthermore, African Americans' cultural continuity via urban farming adds to the unique characteristics of Houston's urban development and growth and the people who make the city. *Houston Chronicle* journalist Leah Binkovitz writes, "Houston has long been a different kind of South, a different kind of city. Throughout Houston's history, culture has given it its topography."[46] She further remarks, "In the same way, decades later, Vietnamese immigrants in Thai Xuan Village near Hobby Airport created 'microfarms,' Black communities made space to meet their needs. Here space is written and rewritten. Boundaries are crossed even as they are reinforced elsewhere. Houston is, it turns out, many things. It includes and has included many cultures."[47]

In Houston's history, early immigrants planted their own vegetable gardens and played an integral role in the constructing the city's polycultural foodways. Local writer David Leftwich talks about the immigrants of the nineteenth and early twentieth century Houston: "Most of Houston's early residents were Anglo immigrants from the United States and the enslaved Africans they forced to move with them. By 1900, German immigration, which had been significant between 1836 and 1860, had slowed but German settlers and their descendants were well established. Many were prominent businessmen. . . . Other Germans were growing vegetables, cultivating rice and raising dairy cattle in northern Harris County and along Brays Bayou, where the Texas Medical Center and Meyerland are today."[48] Leftwich explains the arrival of Italian immigrants from farming communities in southern Italy and Sicily during the 1880s. By the early 1900s, they operated truck farms in what is today the Galleria area of southwest Houston, cultivating vegetables and running grocery stores. Immigrants from Ottoman Syria (modern-day Syria, Lebanon, Jordan, Israel, and northwest Iraq) also started to settle in Houston, in the Near Northside and the Second Ward, with many becoming integral players in wholesale and retail produce and in the grocery business.[49] They were joined by Jewish refugees from Russia and Eastern Europe, fleeing from the pogroms, many of whom also entered the produce and grocery businesses. As for the arrival of Japanese immigrants, they were rice farmers who brought their expertise to cultivate a Japanese variety of rice known as Shinriki (or "power of god" in Japanese), which performed better than other varieties grown on the Gulf Coast. Consequently, the Texas Gulf Coast was momentarily transformed into a major rice cultivation region. Leftwich explains that "Even then a century ago, one needed to look no further than its restaurants to see that Houston was and would remain a city of immigrants . . . a Japanese entrepreneur [Tsunekichi 'Tom Brown' Okasaki] hired a German head waiter and a British chef to serve Houstonians a menu of chop suey (an Americanized take on Chinese food), along with gumbo (a blend of African, Indigenous, and French cuisines), standard 'American' fare of that time . . . and a handful of Chinese and Japanese dishes . . . Okasaki and his fellow immigrants had helped lay the groundwork for the multicultural city Houston would become."

Local writer and author of *Lot*, Bryan Washington, makes a profound proclamation about Houston and the city's gastronomic scene today: "What's really genuine about our culinary culture is the blending and adapting and adopting by its residents."[50] Washington also postulates that "Vietnamese-Cajun, for instance, is hardly innovative here. It's no shock to find Salvadoran folks cooking pounds and pounds of biryani. Italians, Egyptians, and Thai folks simmer hot pot in bunched up strip malls, beside spaces selling dakos and étouffée and char siu. In the Medical District, there's this spot called M&M Grill, which stands for Mexican and Mediterranean, since they serve shawarma and guac, and halal chili con queso, and the place is always packed."[51]

Houston has grown leaps and bounds since Okasaki first settled in the city more than a century ago. In fact, in the twenty-first century, Houston remains the most diverse large city in the United States, according to the 2020 US Census. Brittny Mejia of the *Los Angeles Times* writes, "Houston boomed through the mid-twentieth century, thanks to the oil bonanza, and most of those who came to get rich were white. Large numbers of Vietnamese refugees began arriving in the 1970s, and after an oil collapse in 1982, they were followed by an influx of Latinos driven by cheap housing and employment opportunities. Whites, meanwhile, started drifting out."[52] Demographists claim that the Houston metropolitan is now home to the third-largest population of undocumented immigrants in the country, trailing only New York and Los Angeles, and foretelling the demographic trends of what US cities will look like in the next few decades as whites become minorities in the metropolitan areas.[53] Mejia also reports the changing demographics in Houston, from 1970–2010. In 2010, the Latino population accounted for 43 percent of the city's population, a substantial increase from 10.6 percent in 1970. Whites accounted for 25.6 percent in 2010, noticeably down from 62.8 percent in 1970. Meanwhile, Houston's Black population has decreased slightly, with 23.1 percent of the city's populace in 2010, in comparison to 25.7 percent in 1970. Finally, Asian Houstonians made up 6 percent of Houston's 2010 population, which was a considerable increase from 0.7 percent in 1970.

Along with significant demographic shifts in the past forty-plus years, Houston's food scene has transformed dramatically, too. Change is constant in the culinary world, and cultures—so long as their preservation and continuity remain—also evolve and diversify over time. In addition, Houston was booming with available jobs and affordable homes during the late 1970s, and today it continues to be an affordable place for immigrants and refugees to resettle their families. To add to the aura of Houston as a booming modern-day metropolis with a diverse cityscape and population, food scholar Francine Spiering writes, "It's a city with leading performing arts, a walkable museum district, landmark street art, and myriad restaurants, bars, and microbreweries. And just a stone's throw from downtown are quaint neighborhoods, urban vegetable farms, and community gardens."[54] Spiering also analyzes the local growing seasons. "In winter, trees here are heavy with an abundant variety of citrus, including satsuma, kumquat, grapefruit, and all kinds of oranges. Summer is for eggplant, okra, peaches, and hot peppers."[55] The city's climate and topography, in proximity to the Texas Gulf Coast and nearby rural farms for fresh seafood and crops, made Houston an attractive place for Vietnamese newcomers to resettle.

Today the city, infamous for its urban sprawl and multiple nodes of center, continues to contract, shift, gel, and implode—and the "center" dissipates. And then it begins anew again, with a new wave of immigrants and refugees rebuilding a

commercial district or mixed-use neighborhood in decline, adding another diasporic community to layer and enrich the burgeoning, moving, and restless urban
population that is the most diverse in the United States, yet still racially and ethni-
cally segregated in many neighborhoods. As mentioned by sociologist Dr. Stephen
L. Klineberg, Houston shows the prophecy of America, one that is increasingly
diverse in population, while also featuring its paradox—one that remains significantly segregated by race, ethnicity, and class.[56]

MIỀN NAM MỚI: VIETNAMESE REFUGEES FORGING A NEW(ER) SOUTH

Oftentimes, the US South is viewed from a Black–White racial binary. However, the
region is in constant change and in flux, demographically and culturally, as has been
for centuries. The Creolization of the South is nothing new, and neither is the Creolization of Southern cuisine. Southern foodways have been consistently transformed by Indigenous peoples and communities of color, as they contribute mightily
to the prominent stature that Southern foods have earned; this is not just because of
the talented and creative chefs in the region, but also because of the thousands
of home cooks, farmers, gardeners, food purveyors, restaurateurs, small grocers, fish-
ermen and women, fishmongers, shrimpers, ranchers, beekeepers, brewers, viticultur-
alists, rice and grain millers, and so forth. The South continues to attract a unique and
diverse population with an equally impressive, unique, and diverse gastronomy. Much
of that Southern uniqueness and diversity has been pushed aside, minimalized, marginalized, and erased by White terrorism that has haunted and continues to haunt the
region and its communities of color, starting with the colonization of Indigenous
peoples and cultures, and trampling on through slavery, Jim Crowism, racial segregation, and anti-Black violence and voter suppression today. Perla M. Guerrero astutely
declares: "The South can no longer be defined, if indeed it ever could, through a racial
binary. As scholars, we need to pay attention to how migrants, immigrants, and
refugees—and reactions to them—are altering regional racial mores, meanings, and
understandings."[57] I could not agree with her more. The incredibly diverse Southern
foodways that have been built by immigrants, refugees, and diasporans, surface and
resurface throughout the region's history and thus reorient the South, not just for
native-born Southerners, but also for non-Southern visitors.

Guerrero also asserts that the New South is "a regime built on white supremacy,
the exploitation of racial difference, and increasingly, legal statuses such as citizen,

refugee, or undocumented immigrant that define the experiences of new Southern-ers."[58] The 1975 arrival of thousands of Vietnamese refugees in Fort Chaffee, Arkansas, created quite a stir and mixed feelings among Arkansans. For certain, there was strong opposition to both what was perceived from locals as an intrusive federal government operation and anti-Asian racism and xenophobia.[59] However, numerous Arkansans were also well aware and cognizant that "people fleeing from Vietnam and other Southeast Asian countries were doing so as a direct result of the United States' failed understanding."[60] Second, in a predominantly Protestant region, many Arkansans held "the Christian belief in helping those less fortunate than themselves," which "spurred some Arkansans to mobilize in support of relocation efforts at Fort Chaffee and in Arkansas communities." Within the first three weeks after the fall of Sài Gòn, approximately 26,500 refugees from Việt Nam were relocated to Fort Chaffee, many of whom were from the professional class of doctors, lawyers, and teachers.[61]

Although more will be discussed about the intersection of Vietnamese gastronomy and Southern cuisine in a later chapter, it is essential to ground this work and discuss the impact Vietnamese Americans and their home gardens would have on Southern foodways and history. How and where do Vietnamese refugees, particularly those who resettled in Texas, fit in the cultural and culinary landscapes of the New South? Regarding the study of the US South as a region, Guerrero articulates that "space is a construction that is produced through an inherently political process because it is the outcome of social relations. Place is a particular form of space, and likewise, also the outcome of social relations."[62] Viewing the New South as a regional place with a distinct geography, dialect, gastronomy, history, culture, and population, Vietnamese refugees in the US South and Texas did not automatically fit into the New South persona and narrative, nor would they automatically gain acceptance from native-born Southerners. Instead, what made Vietnamese refugees unique of their own accord, as with their Black, Indigenous, immigrant, and migrant predecessors of the past and present, was the ability to preserve, maintain, and expand their "outsider" culture, despite their outsider status as "alien" citizens in the New South.[63] Therefore, Vietnamese Americans sought and found ways to dig and plant their own cultural spaces, such as home gardens, to establish their food sovereignty, culinary citizenship, and homeland duality. Vietnamese Texan home gardeners raised and cultivated gardens replete with traditional and familiar herbs, vegetables, and fruit trees to survive and live a new life in a new homeland. They planted and rooted themselves in the New(er) South and the Lone Star state.

"Gone to Texas": South Vietnamese Nationals in the Lone Star State

Even before the fall of Sài Gòn in 1975, a handful of South Vietnamese nationals were working, training and living in Texas. Although they would eventually make up a small minority of the refugee population, Vietnamese emigration to the United States occurred during the middle of the Việt Nam War. Before the war's end, quite a few South Vietnamese nationalists lived in Texas as college students, RVN military personnel in training, and war brides. For instance, Yen Ngọc Huỳnh came to America in 1971 to pursue and complete her college education.[64] Yen transferred to the University of Texas at Austin where she earned a bachelor of business administration degree, majoring in management.[65] However, when the South Vietnamese government was overthrown, she remained in Texas under the care of her college roommate's family, and they helped Yen cope with the emotional loss and concerns for her fallen country and for the safety of her brothers and sisters. Eventually, Yen moved to Houston to work for the YMCA of the Greater Houston Area as a Business Operations Manager for Indochinese Refugee and Urban Services, assisting thousands of refugees for whom she helped to resettle in Houston.

Some of the first Vietnamese to set foot in America were sent to this country for military training and preparation, and then return to Việt Nam to fight the war, as part of President Richard Nixon's Vietnamization policy. Many RVN military personnel were sent to US military bases in Texas. In 1969, the US Air Force was scheduled to train 1,200 Vietnamese, and the Navy would train another one thousand Vietnamese, according to Pentagon figures.[66] An unspecified number of Vietnamese in this Air Force unit were those who studied English at Lackland Air Force Base in San Antonio and then moved on into US Army programs. One of the most successful experiments in training RVN forces on a large scale occurred at Ft. Wolters, the home of the Army's Primary Helicopter Center in Mineral Wells, Texas.[67]

A handful of Vietnamese scholars and intellectuals were also sent to American universities and colleges for academic training. They were sent by the RVN government to not only create a burgeoning group of well-trained scholars and academics, but to represent the RVN in positive public relations and garner greater support and sympathy from the American public. They consisted mostly of students, professionals, war brides of men formerly stationed in Southeast Asia, and officials on temporary assignment in the United States.[68] By early 1975, no more than thirty thousand had lived in the United States, with fewer than one hundred in Houston. The pre-

1975 group of Vietnamese Houstonians included twenty to forty wives of former servicemen, thirty to fifty students, and a small number of instructors. At the time, the Vietnamese were but a small fraction of the Asian immigrants of the post–World War II period, particularly before the passage of the monumental Hart-Cellar Immigration Act of 1965.[69] Such numbers were too small to be considered as the first major wave of Vietnamese refugees and immigrants; the Vietnamese population in the United States would grow exponentially immediately after the Việt Nam War.

The main legislative catalyst behind the dramatic increase of the Vietnamese population in Texas and throughout the United States would be the historic Refugee Act of 1980.[70] Vietnamese refugees, particularly those who fled as part of the subsequent waves in the 1980s and 1990s, benefited from the Refugee Act of 1980 and the Hart-Cellar Immigration Act of 1965, which granted them legal entrance into the United States. Unlike other immigrants, Vietnamese expatriates who were part of the 1975 exodus received refugee status; they were "exempt from numerical quotas and may enter the US without regard to population figures."[71] Refugees are technically not considered immigrants, and thus at the time they were not counted in the data used to regulate the number of immigrants accepted into the United States.[72] A clear distinction was made in order to identify and classify a political refugee versus an economic migrant as the US government shifted its admission policy to consider people whose freedom and well-being had been seriously jeopardized.[73]

As mentioned in the previous chapter, under US government's Operation New Life, tens of thousands of first wave Vietnamese refugees were temporarily housed at four makeshift refugee camps. The Vietnamese exiles received great assistance and coordination from the Interagency Task Force and Army personnel in setting up their own temporary self-governing infrastructure.[74] The initial refugee resettlement patterns were in marked contrast to where Vietnamese refugees actually wanted to settle to keep the nucleus of their families intact. Instead, the US government's initial attempts to resettle the refugees reflected US efforts to find what was suitable for government organizations and voluntary agencies: "First, refugees in the first wave tended to be resettled close to refugee holding centers. . . . Second, much of the placement also reflected the contacts of the voluntary agencies. The Lutheran Immigration and Refugee Service, for example, found individual sponsors among Lutheran communities in the Midwest."[75]

After the cessation of Operation New Life, not all Vietnamese refugees remained in their initial places of resettlement. Instead, a majority of them relocated once more, making a secondary migration because of social, economic, and familial reasons.

A majority of Vietnamese newcomers made a secondary migration to resettle in states with a warmer climate, healthier economy, lower cost of living, and greater government assistance programs. Other reasons included family reunification, desire to be in proximity of a sizable Vietnamese community, better workplace training and schooling opportunities, and more job prospects.[76] As a result, the Sunbelt states such as California, Texas, and Louisiana became attractive places for Vietnamese refugees to resettle their families. Linda Gordon asserts, "In California, Texas, Louisiana, Oregon, and Colorado, these states saw increases between 53 and 88 percent, indicating that they have all been targets of significant secondary migration or have received a disproportionate share of the late entries."[77]

Scholar Bill Ong Hing is perceptive in his analysis of the socioeconomic interests of Vietnamese expatriates, or *Viet Kieu*, in the decision to make a secondary migration within the United States and resettle in states such as California and Texas. Hing criticizes the government's failed attempt to disperse the Vietnamese refugees throughout the forty-eight contiguous states and concludes that most of them resettled in California and Texas because relative isolation quickly proved unacceptable to the Vietnamese diasporans.[78] These two states became popular for a secondary migration; California for its warm climate, large Asian Pacific American population, and reasonable welfare programs; and Texas for its job opportunities from the state's economic boom in the mid-1970s, mild winters, and robust fishing, crabbing, and shrimping industries.

Many of the first wave of Vietnamese refugees decided to make a secondary migration to Texas and relocate to cities like Houston. Scholar John Kong Leba declares that "Houston, during the booming years (1976–80), was typical of the hottest job market for blue collars, because the oil-drilling equipment factories such as Hughes Tools, Cameron Works, [*sic*] Dresser Industries, [and] FMC Corp . . . were working at full capacity. Responding to such high demand for factory hands, thousands of out-of-state workers were immigrating to Houston to fill those openings; among them were a great number of Vietnamese factory hands, who were then relatively experienced and had sufficient knowledge of English to get along with their employers as well as their fellow American workers."[79] By 1976, hundreds of Vietnamese refugees had made a secondary migration to Houston and begun to resettle their lives in earnest by working in low-paying, less desirous occupations or holding down multiple jobs. Vietnamese newcomers also started building up their ethnic enclave economy as an essential part of their community formation strategy.

Vietnamese Diasporans Grow New Roots in Texas

We should not be surprised or find it exceptional for Vietnamese Texans to have had a tremendous impact on Southern foodways. Equipped with long growing seasons and warm weather, Vietnamese refugees and immigrants would come to find the Houston metropolitan area and nearby Texas Gulf Coast communities to their liking with the lower cost of living, and the climate hospitable to planting a large quantity of various herbs, fruit trees, and vegetables. Here, I will share a few stories of Vietnamese refugees and how they arrived in Texas. These short vignettes serve as an introduction and insight to the early struggles and challenges for new Vietnamese arrivals. They also elucidate the circumstances that rationalized their relocation to the Lone Star state. Their stories also provide a window into their early resettlement years and how they unfolded, as they replanted their diasporic lives.

Professor Nguyễn Văn Nam patiently waited for us and smiled when my wife and I finally arrived at Lee's Sandwiches on Bellaire Boulevard—our agreed meeting place to conduct his interview. Apologetic, we explained that we were stuck in heavy traffic, as Bellaire Boulevard is notoriously known among Houstonians who frequent this urban retail mecca of predominantly Chinese and Vietnamese restaurants, cafés, and shops. After the conclusion of his interview, Professor Nguyễn, ever cognizant of his surroundings, warned us to be extra cautious when exiting the sandwich shop and returning to our vehicle parked in a car-friendly lot, as if we were to make one of those infamous pedestrian street crossings in congested Sài Gòn. He was always looking out for us, as well as his students and Vietnamese brethren. Professor Nguyễn, or Thầy Nam, as his colleagues, students, community leaders, and friends affectionately and respectfully called him, had taught Vietnamese language courses at the University of Houston for more than a decade.

Thầy Nam recounts his arrival in America: "In 1975, I came to the United States. I was sponsored by an American family in Covington, Kentucky. Here, I got a job teaching French at a high school."[80] Six years later, Nam got in contact with old friends whom he worked with in the Catholic Confederation in Việt Nam. "My wife and I moved to Houston in 1981 to join the Lạc Việt group," recalls Thầy Nam. He and his wife, Thị, and their children eventually moved to Cypress, a suburb in northwest Houston, where they started their own home garden.[81] Nam recollects, "When we moved to Houston, we met a few old friends who own several nurseries around town. They helped me to plant a few vegetables in the backyard both for fun and for food."

The terrifying moments of the war's end, the chaos that ensued, and the separation of loved ones, reunited a decade later, provides a compelling and heart-
wrenching story that is all too common for Vietnamese refugees. At the tail end of
a second wave of the Vietnamese exodus, Hoàng Quang and Nguyễn Lan resettled in the United States in 1985.[82] Mr. Hoàng learned to garden as a four-year-old
child growing up in Việt Nam.[83] His wife, Lan, started gardening soon after they
relocated to Pearland, Texas. At their former Pearland home, they maintained a
lush, immaculate home garden that featured an abundance of vegetables, fruit trees,
and herbs that would rival the produce section of a neighborhood grocery store.
The couple grew fruits and vegetables such as mustard greens (dưa cải), chili
peppers (cay ớt), papaya (đu đủ), satsuma oranges (cam satsuma), kumquats (cây
quất cảnh), bitter melon (trái khổ qua or mướp đắng), fuyu persimmons (trái
hồng), and various herbs.

Their son, Son Hoàng, recounts a more detailed and heart-wrenching story of
his parents that is all too familiar for Vietnamese refugees and immigrants. Son
recalls his parents' remarkable journey, from courage and desperation to separation
and deep sorrow to finally a reunion and absolute joy. Here is Son's retelling of his
parents' miraculous reunion and their family's relocation to Pearland, Texas:

My parents were a young couple with an eighteen-month-old child (me), at
the end of the Việt Nam War.[84] In the midst of the chaos leading up to April 30,
1975, my dad and relatives made the decision to escape through Tân Sơn Nhứt
Airport. He and his family were all military personnel, and he himself was a
pilot. . . . The next day, they came to the airport with my uncle's family because
he had secured a military lift out of the country. . . . My mom and I got in but
my dad was stuck because he left his badges at home. (Military personnel all
changed into civilian clothes to avoid being targeted.) After a long while, my
mom became frantic because she could not see my dad coming in. At the same
time, I was having a high fever. She then decided to come back out to find my
dad so that we all could stay together no matter what.

What she did not know was my dad had bribed the guards with his motor-
cycle to enter the gate.[85] That is where the two of them were separated and lost
from one another, leading to a decade-long separation with limited contact
and knowledge of the whereabouts of each other. Both of them suffered from
severe depression, and mom was on the verge of suicide to have lost her young
husband and most of her own family. What kept her going was me and the
comfort of having my maternal grandmother in Biên Hòa.

When my dad and relatives finally arrived at Camp Pendleton, California (Vietnamese refugee camp), they were separated when the family split everyone up based on the availability of host families . . . my dad found a Hispanic host family in Houston, Texas. My parents did not know how to contact each other for years. . . . In Houston, my dad became a machinist and gradually rose to the rank of management. He finally managed to contact my mom after almost eight years and then quickly sponsored me and my mom to reunite in Houston.

My mom, on the other hand, had a sister in Paris who left Việt Nam in the 1950s and was working on the documentation to sponsor me, my mom, and my grandma to France. We already received the paperwork to leave the country when my maternal grandmother died and my parents finally reconnected via mail. The reunification process to the US was expedited thanks to the existing paperwork to leave Việt Nam to France. My mom and I finally met my dad in July 1984. It was the first time (except when I was a baby) I met my father.

As for my own parents and siblings, they fled from Việt Nam when Communist forces entered Sài Gòn in late April 1975. They escaped from Việt Nam by my maternal grandfather's fishing boat, sailing for three days until they were rescued by a US naval ship. From there, they were relocated to Subic Bay Naval Base in the Philippines. After a month-long stay, they were flown to Andersen Air Force Base in Guam, where they stayed for three days. Then, they boarded another military plane to Hawaii for an overnight stay, before making land in the continental United States, where they arrived at Fort Chaffee, Arkansas. After their three-month stay in the Vietnamese refugee resettlement camp at Fort Chaffee, my parents made the decision to move the family to Texas, where they found family sponsors in a small town called Winnie. Upon hearing stories of economic growth and great job opportunities in Houston, they decided to make a secondary migration to nearby Pasadena, where they were sponsored by the Martin family, and later by the Jacoby family via Associated Catholic Charities, one of nine voluntary agencies approved by the US government to help resettle the thousands of Vietnamese refugees who survived the terrifying exodus and made it to the United States. Our family moved a couple of more times before we settled in our current home in the working-class, South Belt neighborhood of southeast Houston. When we moved into our home in South Belt with our own large front and backyards, my father, Vũ Kiến An Quân, and my mother, Trần Thị Diem Dũng, rekindled their passion for gardening. They could finally start to build a home garden and plant their favorite herbs, vegetables, and fruit trees. They were also replanting their Vietnamese food heritage to root themselves here in the United States.

As we consumed some refreshing and flavorful chè (iced sweet pudding dessert) at Phở Danh inside Hong Kong Food Market on Bellaire Boulevard, during a hot and balmy August afternoon in Houston, Tammy Đình retells her story of growing up in Việt Nam, leaving her home country, adjusting to a new life in Boston, and how and why they moved to Texas. Subtly yet meaningfully, she would reflect on her late husband, Nicholas Đình, quilting thoughtful details of his military career; their civilian menial and office jobs in America; their long, memorable drive to migrate once more, this time from Boston to Houston; and the early socioeconomic challenges that they successfully overcame together. Nestled in between these stories of labor, loss, refuge, and love, she discussed her herb garden and flower bed, as well as the traditional Vietnamese dishes she still makes. To trace her family lineage to traditional Vietnamese foodways, we returned to Việt Nam in dreams and stories—like so many Vietnamese refugees and immigrants here do.

On April 29, 1975, one day before the fall of Sài Gòn, the Đình made their exilic departure from their beloved home country, not knowing whether they would ever return; nor did they know what their future would hold for them or where they would live.[86] Tammy Đình's parents and siblings chose to remain in Việt Nam. It was a heartbreaking family separation for her. On April 29, she and her husband, along with his mother and thirteen siblings (sixteen altogether), made the emotional decision to leave the land of their birthplace, saying tearful goodbyes to loved ones, including Nicholas's father, who chose to remain in Việt Nam. As for those who were leaving, the Đình were thankfully fortunate to be granted permission to board a US naval ship and leave Việt Nam, just one day before the Vietnamese Communist forces captured Sài Gòn. Their US naval ship made its way to Subic Bay Naval Base, Philippines, where they stayed for a day. The following day, they were flown and transported to Andersen Air Force Base in Guam, where they remained for approximately a month. Finally, they took a military flight to Fort Indiantown Gap, Pennsylvania, one of four makeshift Vietnamese refugee camps in the United States, created under US Operation New Life and designed to proportionately disperse and resettle Vietnamese refugees throughout the country.

The Đình remained at Fort Indiantown Gap for a couple of months, where Nicholas assisted as an interpreter, since he studied English in Việt Nam and was fluent.[87] Eventually, they ran into an acquaintance who sponsored them to move to Boston and offered Nicholas a job to work for his insurance company. The Đình lived in Boston for two years, and during this time they welcomed their newborn son, Tino (Vietnamese name Thanh), on January 6, 1976, the Day of Epiphany. However, the brutally cold New England winters, their rat-infested apartment, and a job offer from Tino's godfather to work at his convenience store all persuaded them to make a secondary migration to Texas where they discovered warmer weather and an extensive summer season more to their liking. So, in 1978, they packed up their belongings in a used car that they had purchased for two hundred dollars and made a long yet memorable two-day journey to Pasadena, Texas, where the Đình family would live in an apartment in a working-class neighborhood for the next three years.

The Dallas–Fort Worth (DFW) metroplex is also home to thousands of Vietnamese refugees and immigrants, as well as Laotians and Cambodians. Although the Vietnamese population in the DFW metropolitan area is less populous than Houston's, the Vietnamese diasporic community here remains quite significant and visible. According to the 2021 American Community Survey by the US Census Bureau, the estimated Vietnamese population in the Dallas–Fort Worth–Arlington metropolitan area is numbered at 91,866.[88] Trần Thị Lừng and Phạm Minh Thứ are two of thousands of Vietnamese refugees and immigrants who decided to resettle in the DFW metroplex. After a long separation due to the extreme chaos and confusion in the final days of the Việt Nam War they were fortunately reunited in 1991 and resettled their family in a home, first in Duncanville, and then later in Grand Prairie, two suburban cities that make up part of the DFW metropolitan area.

Like my parents and thousands of other Vietnamese refugees, Trần Thị Lừng left Việt Nam after the Communist takeover of Sài Gòn. In the tumultuous last days of the war, Lừng and her husband, Phạm Minh Thứ, were separated when Thứ decided to return home to find and retrieve his mother.[89] As their situation became even more dire and exasperating, she and her two young daughters finally departed with three younger friends and countless strangers who boarded the Đông Hải, a South Vietnamese cargo ship, desperately trying to escape from the Vietnamese Communists.[90] Lừng and her children were refugees, and she did not know when she would ever see her husband again. She and her two young daughters, the oldest just a toddler of eighteen months, and the other a four-month-old infant, were traumatized and anguished as they embarked on their journey, yet they were also relieved and determined to travel to America in search of a new homeland, even as they mourned what was lost from the war.[91]

Their voyage at sea was treacherous and filled with angst, sorrow, and uncertainty, as their vessel sailed from Sài Gòn to Singapore. They were lost at sea for

several days, finally reaching Singapore after nine days of sailing. Here, about a quar-
ter of the refugees on board were able to leave their ship and eventually resettled in
refugee camps in Singapore. The remaining Vietnamese refugees onboard were
given some food and water. Then they made their way to the Philippines, but their
nine-day voyage was rocky and treacherous. They survived a heavy nighttime storm
and strong waves. When they finally reached the Philippines, the oceanic refugees
were given plenty of food and water. After a brief stay in the Philippines, the Đông
Hải vessel lurched onward to Guam, where Vietnamese refugees were at sea again
for a couple of more weeks—33 days combined at sea for this group of forlorn oceanic refugees.

    In Guam, Lừng and her two young daughters stayed at a temporary, makeshift
refugee camp at Andersen Air Force Base for approximately two months. Here, they
received some new clothes and a pair of new shoes. Lừng vividly remembered
receiving two new outfits, one of them a lavender double-knit suit. While waiting
for their paperwork to be processed, she and her daughters slept on cots under a
military tent shared with other Vietnamese refugees. Finally, they, along with their
three younger friends and many others, boarded a US plane and headed to mainland
United States. Their long flight included a three-hour stopover in Alaska for refuel-
ing, before Lừng and her daughters finally arrived in Ft. Chaffee, Arkansas. It was
late summer when they arrived in Ft. Chaffee, and they resided at the refugee camp
for another couple of months before being sponsored by a Methodist church group
in Leavenworth, Kansas. Unfortunately, the winter months in Leavenworth were
bitterly cold. In hopes of finding better job opportunities and warmer weather, Lừng
decided to take her daughters and her three younger friends—who were living with
her as roommates in a small apartment in Leavenworth—to Dallas, Texas. Another
friend from the Guam refugee camp was living in Leavenworth at the time. He happened to have an old car and agreed to drive them all to Dallas, where they arrived
sometime in February or March of 1976.

    For a year, they lived in an Oak Cliff apartment complex in south Dallas, where
Lừng found a job and worked at a sewing factory. In 1977, Lừng and her daughters
moved into a subsidized apartment unit in Duncanville, Texas. Here, Lừng learned
to garden from a Vietnamese friend.[92] At first, she planted herbs and chili peppers in
a little plot next to the apartment building that was typically used for landscaping.
Despite severely limited spaces, Lừng managed to plant some herbs and greens on a
small plot of land next to their apartment building for a while, demonstrating her
ingenuity, resourcefulness, and determination to garner some food security and sovereignty on her own. However, she was later forced by apartment building managers

to remove her garden.[93] Unfortunately, the apartment building managers did not foresee the importance of gaining food security and sovereignty for Lừng and other residents living sparsely in a public housing neighborhood. For Lừng, this was another bump on a long road to recovery and redemption; one that would ultimately lead to her emancipatory foodways of cultivating herbs, fruit trees, and vegetables in her own home yard. Once more, she would replant and raise homegrown produce to cook Vietnamese dishes that she loves to eat and share with others.

For Vietnamese American home gardeners, the act of gardening and cultivating fruits, herbs, and vegetables remind them of their homes and lives back in Việt Nam. Gardening serves as a leisure activity to maintain their health and wellness; a way to remember their Việt Nam days; forge a newfound freedom from the nightmares and lifelong pains of war, loss, and refuge; and dig their roots under the Texas soil, which in turn would become their small but monumental plots of a homeland they miss. These food gardens are places of sanctuary and refuge, where Vietnamese refugees root themselves and become Vietnamese Americans, anchored to a new citizenry and homeland.

Historian Kyle Shelton coined the phrase "infrastructural citizenship," arguing that "by transforming elements of the built environment from inert materials into arenas in which they could claim and assert political power, residents crafted a set of rhetorical and political actions that constituted what I term infrastructural citizenship. In this case, citizenship is not defined by nationality or legal standing, but instead by the quotidian acts residents used to construct themselves as political participants. . . . They argued that their homes and local streets should be held in the same esteem as regional highways and downtown redevelopments."[94] Here, I am in agreement with Shelton, defining citizenship beyond nationality and legal standing. While Shelton emphasizes urban history, zeroing in on the built environment of highways and structures, as well as processes of urban planning, development, and redevelopment to define infrastructural citizenship, I focus on his analysis of "quotidian acts residents used to construct themselves as political participants." For Vietnamese American home gardeners, their quotidian acts of caring for their gardens—digging into the earth, planting the seeds, watering the plants, replenishing the soil with biodegradable compost, clearing the weeds, and nurturing the produce—are significant political acts that define their culinary citizenship. Such political acts demonstrate their assertiveness to gain food security and sovereignty. In addition, the gardeners' actions are evidence of their attempts to preserve and enlarge their food heritage, and also to remember their Vietnamese roots while planting their new roots on American soil. Gardening allows Vietnamese American home gardeners to cultivate a homeland duality, and in the process, they gain a sense of belonging and earn their culinary citizenship in the United States. The end result for Vietnamese American home gardeners is a liberation from the tragedies of war, displacement, and marginalization, and a new sense of freedom found in cultivating a homeland of their own.

CHAPTER 3

Sowing the Seeds of Freedom

Gardening an Emancipated Life

Why did I come here to be so lonely?
I have clothes, I have food, but I think about my country.
I remember my farm in the valley.
Though here I have three meals a day, still I remember my country.
I live here with plenty of clothes, but still I recall
My country, the trees, the grasses, my own farm, the town.

—a translated excerpt from a traditional Hmong song

When I put Vietnamese veggies, herbs, and fruits in my mouth that
is very special to me. When I eat them . . . I feel like I have
Vietnamese spirit in my mouth . . . they all taste so good to me . . .
especially the food from my garden.

—Trần Thi Lừng

These two passages capture and epitomize a dichotomy of homesickness and rediscovering home, of longing and belonging. A state of paralysis or in-betweenness resides in the hearts and spirits of Vietnamese and Southeast Asian refugees as they traverse between losing one homeland and finding another. Along their journey they have grown home gardens and cultivated a more sustainable life where they have sown the seeds of their own freedom—a life finally free of stateless-ness, rootlessness, and anonymity, somewhere between homesickness and finding a home. These home gardens may be in-between or liminal spaces for Vietnamese and other Southeast Asian Americans, but such positive, green spaces provide them the fruits, herbs, and vegetables, as well as a taste of their homelands that they miss dearly. Whether they are backyard gardens, makeshift hanging or potted gardens on small patios, or communal microfarms, these green liminal spaces nourish their bodies and spirits. Once again, when gardening and farming, they become who they are and more than perpetual sojourners.

This chapter showcases Vietnamese Americans, particularly in Texas, who culti-vate home gardens that yield a wide array of food to nurture the body, sooth the mind, mend the heart, and heal the soul. Here, Vietnamese Americans demon-strate their farming and gardening skills to help reconstruct an emancipated life and transform their own yards and neighborhood lots into beautiful, colorful, and lush vegetation. Preparing and cultivating food gardens results in stronger bonds between loved ones, families, relatives, friends, and neighbors. They share a com-mon praxis of laboring on the land with their hands, tools, and ingenuity, toiling for hours each day in the sun and rain. Consequently, the more they spend time in their home gardens, the deeper their roots are bound to this adopted homeland of America.

Immediate access to fresh vegetables, herbs, and fruits is vital for the Vietnam-ese, and cultivating their own home gardens fulfills the needs of raising, picking, and consuming produce that is fresh, convenient, affordable, and healthy. In turn, having fresh herbs, fruits, and vegetables is an indispensable option for cooking and prepar-ing Vietnamese dishes and meals. Celebrated chef, restaurateur, cookbook author, and a Vietnamese refugee herself, Mai Phạm aptly writes, "The Vietnamese have a high regard for vegetables, in large part because meat is too expensive to be con-sumed on a regular basis. But beyond that, we were raised with the notion that veg-etables are just as important as meat proteins and starches."[1] Notable chef and cook-book coauthor, Chef Helene An, declares, "Using our natural resources wasn't a trend back then, it was a part of our culture. Fresh food that you grew yourself in good soil made you feel healthy. Today, modern food can make you feel bloated or weighted down. This is very against my philosophy: food should never make you feel bad, it should always make you feel good. The key is to use the freshest ingredients possible. Fresh food makes you feel light and gives you energy."[2]

Resettled in California, Chef An discusses the significance of kitchen gardens at home: "I grow everything I can in my own kitchen garden now. The thyme I grow at home is so much better than the thyme in the supermarket. You don't need a lot of room, especially for herbs. You can plant them in a container outside or inside on a windowsill. Plant what you know you will use frequently. I have a small kaffir lime tree since I use the leaves and the fruit in a lot of my cooking; the dwarf citrus trees will grow extremely well in containers and indoors. To grow the best food you must respect the cycle; you must feed the soil with compost, and it will produce more beautiful food for you. When I polish and rinse rice, I always save the soaking water and pour it over my plants."[3] Here, Chef An alludes to the importance of not only cultivating a kitchen garden at home as a return to "normalcy" from the terrible and deadly disruptions of war, refuge, resettlement, and marginalization, but she also expresses the need to practice sustainable gardening by growing produce seasonally and not wasting water.

Her daughter and coauthor, Jaqueline An, hints at some of the resettlement challenges for refugees and immigrants if one did not have a home garden. "Since almost every cook has a kitchen garden in Vietnam, plucking a fresh spring of mint to muddle into a sparkling limeade or picking an orange right off the tree for a freshly squeezed flavored iced tea is common practice. My grandmother Diana continued this tradition when she moved to San Francisco," explains Jaqueline. "Since my family lived with my grandparents until I was nine, I was lucky enough to be able to help my grandmother with her garden. She had an amazing rose garden with roses that would bloom to the size of a large rice bowl, kumquat trees, and a variety of Vietnamese herbs and vegetables that were otherwise hard to find in San Francisco at that time."[4]

Robert E. Rhoades examines the significance of home gardens to the Vietnamese diaspora in the United States: "Vietnamese cuisine requires particular spices, herbs, fruits, and fresh vegetables, which are often prepared with meat. Faced with a new environment devoid of these key plant ingredients, however, Vietnamese families in America seek mechanisms and connections to acquire seeds or planting materials necessary to recreate their traditional cuisines. . . . The primary mechanism, therefore, of acquiring appropriate cooking ingredients in the United States is gardening, which in turn requires space, knowledge, and the essential planting material . . . the home garden provides readily available, fresh, and often organic produce to the family and their friends."[5] Rhoades emphasizes the importance of home garden produce for Vietnamese Americans, in particular how gardening helps them recreate place and memory. Gardens are small, personal refuges where Vietnamese refugees may temper the stresses of uprootedness and living in a foreign land.[6] He also remarks on how Vietnamese American home gardeners deftly gather necessary seeds to cultivate a garden: "Planting material is obtained through five sources: saving one's own seed, exchanging with family and friends, obtaining directly from Vietnam, purchasing seed packets, and extracting from fresh fruits and vegetables bought in local Asian stores."[7] Such seed-gathering techniques display the resourcefulness and persistence of Vietnamese Americans to grow a successful home garden.

Shampa and Sanjoy Mazumdar conducted an insightful study on Vietnamese American home gardens in Southern California. In their valuable research, the authors assert that home gardens could assist immigrants uprooted from war, sociopolitical upheavals, and religious persecution to "remember and embrace landscapes lost."[8] They further describe a Vietnamese refugee's sentiment on home gardens: "Having a garden in America . . . brings her back to the landscape she left behind. [Because] of war, my mom had to leave Vietnam [for] fear of political persecution, therefore, she misses Vietnam a lot. America can sometimes be overwhelming and the environment is completely different. . . . The garden makes her feel more comfortable, secure and in familiar territory."[9] In addition, the Mazumdars state that kitchen gardens can be a source of pride and joy, particularly for first generation immigrants. Such gardens and their produce provide immigrant gardeners an opportunity to remember, redeem, and rebuild their homeland on their new home soil, allowing "for cultural continuity with the past and yet anchors them in the present." Furthermore, the first generation's offspring, the second generation of immigrant families, would learn and absorb more of their own food culture, and thus a significant part of their ethnic heritage.

Shampa and Sanjoy Mazumdar elaborate on the home gardens cultivated by Vietnamese Americans. In one example, they detailed a home garden belonging to another Vietnamese American family: "Our front yard is Americanized but our backyard tells a different story. In the side of our house is a patch filled with various Asian herbs. It reminds [us] of [Vietnam] where growing your own food is a very common thing. My family actually uses these herbs in our meals . . . when you look out of the patio door you can see *bi dao* (winter melons) hanging down waiting to be harvested. There [are] okra and lemongrass growing along the back exterior wall of the house." The Mazumdars also explain how gardens provide Vietnamese refugees and immigrants an opportunity to rebuild the natural living environs they missed and yearned for when they fled from Việt Nam. Therefore, the gardens they raise and the vegetables, herbs, and fruit trees they cultivate provide an essential comfort—a healthy coping mechanism.

The researchers share another story and explain that "When Mrs. Tran (an elderly Vietnamese American) first came to America in 1990 she lived in an apartment. Depressed and lonely, she longed for a garden, to work the soil, to cultivate, to feel the earth, to connect to her rural roots and natural vegetation of Vietnam. When she moved to her house and could have a garden, she began to feel more secure and content. When everything around her was changed or changing, she finally could control a small segment of her life, her own garden where she could connect once again with the familiar. As a young Vietnamese American poignantly stated, the garden 'is a space that allows [my dad] to bring a little piece of Vietnam to our house.'"

The authors further examine the lives of Mrs. Trần and Mr. Trương to reflect and reiterate their previous assessments about Vietnamese refugees and immigrants and their home gardens. They observe that Mrs. Trần and her elder friends often shared and exchanged the fruits and herbs they successfully raised in their garden. Such exchanges also serve as their reason to meet and socialize with one another. Furthermore, Mrs. Trần packages some fruits, vegetables, and herbs to give to each of her children. For Mr. Trương, his pride and joy are his bí đao (winter melons), which he successfully grows in large abundance and gives them to his friends and coworkers. The Mazumdars also articulate that Vietnamese refugees and immigrants strategically utilize their yard space to build unique cultural spaces, which play an integral role in preserving, protecting, and expanding their traditional foodways. Consequently, the kitchen garden is a home garden in more ways than one. Not only does the garden provide the necessary raw ingredients to advance Vietnamese gastronomy, but it also demonstrates the strong desire among Vietnamese American home gardeners to preserve their food heritage, cultural and familial ties, and even ethnomedicine, as they use familiar produce and cooking techniques to connect with their family members, neighbors, and friends.

It is not uncommon for Vietnamese refugees and immigrants to create a sacred ancestral space within their home gardens to connect with their ancestors. The Mazumdars elaborate on the sacred spaces that are home gardens. "Several of the plantings in Mrs. Trần's garden tell the story of past relationships—the dragon fruit reminds her of her mother, the mint of her father and the pomelos of her grandmother who rewarded her with this fruit whenever she was good," they explain. The Mazumdars conclude that home gardens not only function as a family memorial space but a sacred one as well, offering home gardeners some peace and solace. They assert that home gardens are also sacred landscapes, especially for first generation immigrant families. To support their domestic religious life, such gardens would include trees and flowers instilled with significant symbolic and religious meaning. Here, the Mazumdars offer a plethora of valuable reasons why home gardens are vital and sacred to Vietnamese American home gardeners.

I will attempt to expand on the Mazumdars' pertinent and relevant analyses and confirm their conclusions regarding the tangible and meaningful uses of home gardens for Vietnamese newcomers in the United States. For instance, I will expound on the farm-to-freedom manifestation experienced by Vietnamese refugees and immigrants via individual home gardens and microfarms in "village" communities in Texas.[10] Here, Vietnamese Texans utilize the limited spaces of their yards and sidewalks to cultivate home gardens, transforming spaces into greener places that remind them of home. Their transformations of such spaces are an attempted reclamation of their own Việt Nam; a South Việt Nam they could never duplicate nor truly return to ever again. Nevertheless, the home gardens still heal and nurture, provide sustenance and strength, and preserve and expand Vietnamese foodways. Unbeknownst or not, they have created these in-between or interstitial spaces of Vietnamese America where they can claim home in the land here, too. They are sowing the seeds of emancipatory foodways for themselves and for future generations.

VIETNAMESE AMERICANS AND THEIR HOME GARDENS: WHAT THEY PRODUCE AND PRESERVE

In this section, I examine the specific types of vegetables, herbs, and fruit trees planted and nurtured by Vietnamese American home gardeners, as well what their gardens represent. The home garden has layers of meanings; it evokes powerful memories, connections, and foodways for Vietnamese diasporans who cultivate familiar produce and then wash and prepare them to make their comfort food of traditional culinary dishes. What they produce and preserve from their home gardens is essential to keep and extend their Vietnamese foodways. Here, I will impart a few stories of Vietnamese Texans, some of whom I first introduced in chapter 2, and share what exactly they cultivate from their own home gardens.

Professor Nguyễn Văn Nam enjoys cultivating his home garden not only for the food it produces, but also to see the plants grow each day—plants such as water spinach (rau muống), spearmint (hung lủi), okra (đậu bắp), and winter melon (bí đao). But more importantly, Thầy Nam believes that gardening helps the Vietnamese in the United States maintain a part of their tradition. Thầy Nam explains that "This is an effort to preserve and extend the traditions of our ancestors. The Vietnamese, when leaving their homeland, promise to themselves to preserve and to develop their traditions and culture. To preserve and develop the traditions and culture doesn't [just] include books, songs . . . but also [a] way to live such as planting and eating [traditionally grown vegetables]."[11]

Son Hoàng provides a detailed account of what his parents, Nguyễn Lan and Hoàng Quang, grew from the spacious backyard of their Pearland home. Son remembers how his father was such an avid gardener, while his mother would partake gardening after her husband:

> My dad grew all sorts of trees: pears, peaches, persimmons, etc.[12] On the other hand, my mom did not take up planting until we moved off the land and into a Pearland subdivision. I guess to her, planting and managing a seven thousand square feet lot was much easier than two acres. Since retirement, they have been planting and growing both decorative and practical gardens, each year improving on their techniques and craft. They were able to crossbreed the fruits and vegetables to achieve the sweetest kumquats and graft plants to produce seedless oranges. . . . Life in Pearland became home for both of my parents because they never imagined living elsewhere.[13]

As for Son's mother, Lan, she enjoys thinking of these beautiful plants as the product of her hard work and appreciates that the fresh produce strengthens and improves their health (figure 3.1).[14] His father, Quang, strongly believes that gardening helps him remember the past, connecting them with their previous life in Việt Nam. They both find gardening a nurturing daily activity that not only reduces stress but provides a connection to nature. Quang explains, "Gardening makes you live close to nature and makes life more beautiful!" Lan adds, "It's also good for our relationship because it gives us things to do together."[15] In 2019, Quang and Lan sold their Pearland home with a large yard space and moved into a much smaller home in southwest Houston. In 2020, they relocated once more, this time moving to a home closer to the de facto Little Sài Gòn along Bellaire Boulevard and west of Beltway 8.

After moving a couple of times in Pasadena, Texas, my parents, Trần Thị Diem Dũng and Vũ Kiến An Quân, took their four children and finally settled into what

Figure 3.1   Lan T. Nguyễn sitting by a papaya tree. Quang V. Hoàng and Lan T. Nguyễn's home garden in Pearland, Texas. (Photo by Son Hoàng.)

would be our family home for the next forty years. My parents still reside in this very house that we still jokingly yet fondly nicknamed the "Vũ Chateau" for its humble appearance and location in a working-class neighborhood of southeast Houston. But surrounding this modest abode is where they would grow okra, persimmon trees (quả hồng), peppermint (húng cay), chili peppers (ớt), and many other vegetables, herbs, and fruit trees they fondly remembered back in Việt Nam.[16] Interestingly, they did not plant home gardens when our family first lived in Pasadena, during the first few years of resettlement. It was not until we moved into our unassuming three-bedroom house and settled in the South Belt neighborhood that my parents started to raise a home garden. This is where they began to feel at home, and their garden, year after year, would produce refreshing and delicious greens, fruits, and herbs (figures 3.2 and 3.3). My parents would also pick and prepare their home-grown, fresh, and organic crops to make a variety of Vietnamese dishes that were familiar and comforting to them.

Growing up in our humble dwelling in southeast Houston, I had a cursory interest in what my parents grew. I neither understood nor gave much thought as to why they would grow opo squash (trái bầu) and peach trees (cây đào). At the time,

Figure 3.2 An old photo of my father, An Quân Kiến Vũ, showing his granddaughter, Aislinn Ennis, how to use the garden hose to water the produce grown at my parents' backyard. (Photo by Ngọc Vũ.)

Figure 3.3 White eggplants at An Quân K. Vũ and Đung T. Trần's home garden. Houston, Texas. (Photo by Roy Vũ.)

I could not exactly comprehend what they were practicing was considered "garden-to-table" since planting fruit trees and vegetables was a daily ritual for them. I did not truly appreciate their recreational gardening to be organic and healthy in more ways than one. As a young adult, what began to pique my curiosity was that while our family printing business, Houston Vàng, was struggling and we had to live rather frugally, my parents continued to raise fruit trees, chili peppers, and opo squash, and in spite of our situation they gave away most of what they cultivated to relatives, friends, and fellow churchgoers. I was completely unaware of the communal act that they shared with other Vietnamese Houstonians. Like so many of their kinsmen and kinswomen, in spite of their working-class struggles, my parents were always willing to literally share the fruits of their labor with others.

So, what was their reward? For certain, my parents take great pleasure and a little pride watching their herbs, vegetables, and fruit trees grow. For them, gardening is not a business venture, but a leisure activity to enjoy. Like Thầy Nam, Hoàng Quang, Nguyễn Lan, and many other Vietnamese American home gardeners, they give their fresh produce to their own children, relatives, and friends. Perhaps equally important, my father believes that gardening gives them "a greater sense of our mother country."[17]

In addition, much like other Vietnamese American home gardeners, my parents compost with food scraps and spoiled leftovers, using them as a natural fertilizer to enrich the garden soil.[18] For my mother, having an organic and sustainable home garden brings her joy.[19] She believes that the physical exertion of gardening and spending some time outdoors will make a person stronger and healthier, too. Today, they continue to grow and raise an assortment of greens, such as mint leaves (rau thơm), water spinach, malabar (rau mồng tơi), and jute leaves (rau đay), along with okra, white eggplants (cà pháo), and short, plump, sweet bananas (trái chuối).

For the Đinh family, after living a couple of years in Boston, they decided to make a secondary migration to Texas. Their early years in Texas were arduous and labor-intensive, but they were together, their family intact. Tammy Huyen Đinh and her late husband, Nicholas Đinh, worked eighteen hours a day at the Pasadena convenience store while raising their son.[20] She describes her daily routine for those first few years in Texas: "We only had one car [the used vehicle they purchased for a couple of hundred dollars], so we woke up early each morning and my husband would take the car to drive to the convenience store and open the business. I would take care of household chores and get my son ready for daycare. Luckily, the daycare facility was nearby the convenience store. So, I took Tino on a stroller, and since the sidewalks and streets were in poor condition, I would push the stroller and cut across the South Houston High School parking lot since the pavement there was a lot smoother. Fortunately, the daycare facility was right next to the high school, and I would drop him off at daycare. Then, I would walk to the convenience store, which was nearby, and join my husband to work."[21] After three years of toiling eighteen-hour days and living frugally to save their meager earnings, the Đìnhs managed to save enough money to mortgage a home in the Sagemont neighborhood of southeast Houston. Through their hard work, perseverance, resourcefulness, and resolute determination, they had moved into a middle-class neighborhood. They also welcomed a second son, Maurice. Yet, they continued to be diligent workers. Nicholas would work for an insurance firm in Houston, while starting his own life insurance company with an office of what used to be old Chinatown, but is now better known as East Downtown (EaDo) since gentrification has taken over much of this former Asian ethnic commercial district. Tammy worked a variety of part-time jobs, while devoting most of her time and energy to raising her two sons and managing the household responsibilities. Nevertheless, their lives were less stressful than in previous years as they settled comfortably into their middle-class residence.

They had also earned some leisure time on weekends, and gardening was one of Tammy's favorite hobbies. She loved growing aromatic flowers and adored roses. Like other Vietnamese American home gardeners, Tammy shared the herbs she used to grow and raise in the backyard of their Sagemont home: lemongrass (sả), chili peppers, chives (hẹ), perilla (tía tô), and mint leaves. She cultivated and maintained an herb garden in the backyard of their abode for nearly forty years until Hurricane Harvey flooded and severely damaged their home in late August 2017. After one of the most devastating storms in Houston's history, they returned home, removed all the debris, gutted the interior, and made extensive repairs and additions before selling their house in 2018. Looking back, their old house reminds her of countless fond memories, particularly those nostalgic times with her late husband who passed away in 2007. What she also missed were the bright, beautiful, and radiant flowers that once surrounded their dwelling. She loved planting flowers, particularly roses. Moving in with her son, Maurice, daughter-in-law, and (at the time) toddler grandson, she resumed planting and cultivating roses and other fragrant flowers in front of their new home in Katy. However, the common Vietnamese herbs and vegetables she had grown at her old Sagemont home always reminded her of Việt Nam. She hopes to teach her grandson (now she is living with two of her grandsons) to learn the Vietnamese language so that he will not forget about his Vietnamese heritage.

The DFW metropolitan area also has a notable, albeit dispersed, Vietnamese American population throughout the region, especially in suburb cities such as

Arlington, Haltom City, Garland, and Grand Prairie. Anthropologists Caroline B. Brettell and Deborah Reed-Danahay have written and studied the growing yet out-spread Vietnamese American community residing in the DFW area. "There is a Little Saigon in Houston, but no place in DFW has that label," write Brettell and Reed-Danahay. "Because of this residential dispersion—more of a suburban than an urban pattern—activities and spaces for the building of ethnic networks or for engagement with the wider civic sphere take place across a broad geographic space."[22] Additionally, as Brettell and Reed-Danahay point out, "The spatial presence of Vietnamese Americans in Tarrant County is most evident in Asian commercial centers and restaurants in such places as Arlington and Haltom City."[23]

Trần Thị Lừng and her two daughters were still living in Duncanville, a suburb city south of Dallas, when she finally got to see her husband again. In 1991, after more than fifteen years of separation, Trần Thị Lừng reunited with her husband, Phạm Minh Thứ, and her mother-in-law.[24] Thư had been detained by Vietnamese Communists and forced to live in re-education camps because of his political affiliation with the RVN government. A year after their reunion, the family relocated to a Duncanville home with a sizable backyard. The spacious yard made Lừng happy because she could expand her garden and plant persimmon trees and more vegetables. In 2003, the family moved once more, resettling in a new subdivision in Grand Prairie, where Lừng and her husband grow mint leaves, perilla, lemongrass, chives, cilantro (ngò), water spinach, luffa (mướp), bitter melon (trái khổ qua/ mướp đắng), and summer squash (bí mùa hè) (see figures 3.4 and 3.5).

Despite some challenges to gardening under the blazing Texas sun and stifling heat, Lừng believes it is definitely a worthwhile endeavor. She loves all the vegetables, herbs, and fruits that she cultivates. "When I put Vietnamese veggies, herbs, and fruits in my mouth that is very special to me," said Lừng. As cited at the beginning of the chapter, she reasons: "When I eat them . . . I feel like I have Vietnamese spirit in my mouth . . . they all taste so good to me . . . especially the food from my garden." She believes that "Gardening is for relaxation after a long day working or to see the new day with new things growing in the backyard. But the best is [to] share . . . with our friends and relatives."[25]

One of Lừng's gardening friends is Phạm Tuyết Bạch, who currently resides in Fort Worth. Bạch recalls how she raised a home garden of her own. She reflects on her early days of resettlement and why she started gardening: "I never thought that I would grow vegetables myself, but when I came to America, I saw many [Vietnamese] families growing their own vegetables from their backyard garden. It was fun and most convenient to have herbs available for cooking. So, I started

Figure 3.4   In Trần Thị Lừng and Phạm Minh Thứ's home garden they cultivate an array of rau thơm (mints and herbs), as well as trái khổ qua (bitter melons), diếp cá (fish mint), bạc hà (elephant ears), and tía tô (perilla). Grand Prairie, Texas. (Photo by Ngọc Vũ.)

gardening from my early days in America."[26] She considers chili peppers and a variety of mints as indispensable in Vietnamese American home gardens. Bạch also believes that most Vietnamese Americans, at a minimum, grow a few herbs and some chili peppers, and perhaps greens and produce that do not require preparation and could be consumed raw.[27] In the summer, she cultivates an assortment of vegetables and herbs, including basil (húng quế), perilla, lemongrass, endives

Figure 3.5   Trần Thị Lừng and Phạm Minh Thứ also grow cây sống đời (kalanchoe pinnata or life plant) and mù tạt xanh (mustard greens) in their home garden. Grand Prairie, Texas. (Photo by Ngọc Vũ.)

(rau đắng), spinach, squash (bí đao), and a variety of gourds (bầu). She also raises an array of fruit trees like mandarin oranges (cây cam quýt) and passion fruit (cây chanh dây). In wintertime, her gardening options are limited, so she grows scallions or green onions (hành lá).

Bạch understands that although home gardening has no financial reward and requires a lot of time, it does bring numerous health and mental benefits. She declares, "Gardening is healthy for your body and spirit. Shoveling and tending plants keeps you healthy just like physical exercise. Every day, I have a job to do on the garden, but I enjoy working on the garden since it makes me feel comfortable and happy." Bạch also mentions that she raises vegetables and herbs from her home garden "with one serving for the family to use and consume, and two or three servings to give to relatives and friends." Bạch Tuyết Phạm is an avid gardener and is delighted with her home garden and what she has planted and raised. No doubt, she is proud (and should be) of the amazing, elongated gourds she has cultivated in her lush home garden.

Another friend of Trần Thị Lừng and Phạm Minh Thứ is an elderly woman named Lê Đinh Qưới, who currently resides in Arlington, Texas. Although in her eighties, Lê remains fond of cultivating her home garden, which consists of winter melons (bí đao), bitter melons (trái khổ qua), white eggplants (cà pháo), and luffas

Figure 3.6   Lê Đinh Quới's home garden includes cà pháo (white eggplants), mướp (luffas), ớt (Thai chili peppers), and more. Their home garden encompasses almost the entirety of their backyard. Arlington, Texas. (Photo by Ngọc Vũ.)

(mướp) (see figure 3.6). Her backyard includes several homemade trellises with numerous giant mướp hanging down from the vine-wrapped trellises and diapered with a cloth to ensure the mướp will not fall to the ground (figure 3.7). Needless to say, she is proud of her garden and what has been produced by her hands, persistence, and agricultural knowledge. She should be extremely proud of her beautiful and lush home garden; the wide variety of greens, fruits, and vegetables provide aesthetic wonder and appreciation for the quantity of food Lê Đinh Quới has been able to grow from her home garden. Nearly every square inch of her backyard is utilized for food cultivation. Lê's home garden is an amazing sight to behold.

Aside from the elderly still cultivating home gardens, the very young immigrants (i.e., the 1.5 generation), and the second and third generations of Vietnamese Texans have taken up gardening as well. For instance, my younger cousin, Tina Mary Đoàn, definitely has more of a green thumb than I do. As a recent homeowner living in Houston, she is modest about her gardening prowess. Ever since Tina moved into a permanent home, she has raised a garden in her yard. Tina explains what made her decide to garden and plant some herbs and vegetables: "I want to say I always wanted to garden and I never had a green thumb but I think it's because now I have a permanent home to call my own that I can build my own raised garden."[28] In

Figure 3.7 In Lê Đinh Qưới's home garden, mướp (luffas) are cultivated and suspended precariously in midair from a homemade pergola. These luffas are carefully diapered to ensure that they do not prematurely fall to the ground. Arlington, Texas. (Photo by Ngọc Vũ.)

our talks, Tina mentioned the deadly and devastating Winter Storm Uri that swept through Texas in the second week of February of 2021, and how that negatively affected her family. The destructive winter storm also brought a small (but not insignificant) and serendipitous opportunity to expand her home garden. "The second set back is funding," says Tina. "My parents' house got ruined during [the] ice storm and [they] are staying with me now. They have seen how successful my garden has gone and decided to provide plants from my uncle add [to] on to the beds. My uncle is really a big-time gardener." As for the other reasons why she decided to start a home garden, Tina states, "I would say biggest reason is due to pandemic. Lack of going anywhere and lack of fresh food." Tina represents the second generation of Vietnamese Texan home gardeners who cultivate a variety of herbs, fruits, and vegetables. As a result, they gain access to fresh food, have some control over the production and consumption of fresh greens and vegetables, and establish food sovereignty by their own volition.

Home gardens give Vietnamese Texan growers an opportunity to give and share their produce, and in the process, build community with their neighbors when they exchange not only fruits, herbs, vegetables, and seeds, but also gardening strategies, cooking tips, and fond memories. For Vietnamese diasporans, home gardens have become an integral connection to their lost homeland of South Việt Nam. Such gardens not only serve as reminders of the ashes of a terrible war and violent past, but they give Vietnamese American planters the positive spaces to plant their roots in their new homeland *and* recover a piece of their former country. While these small, surviving reminders may fade and possibly escape from memory, these gardens help nurture, liberate, and heal the mind, body, and spirit of Vietnamese American home gardeners.

To maintain their homeland connection via traditional foodways, Vietnamese diasporans find even the smallest of spaces to cultivate a home garden. Showcasing their ingenuity, resourcefulness, and horticultural prowess, Vietnamese American home gardeners living in condominiums or "villages" located in working-class neighborhoods face challenges of scarcity—scarcity of land, scarcity of resources, and scarcity of disposable income. In response, they utilize an assortment of discarded materials and reuse them to raise small home gardens in tight quarters. Abandoned items such as old bathtubs, political campaign signs, cardboard boxes, ice coolers, fish aquariums, newspapers, glass jars, and blankets are repurposed and strategically arranged to grow small gardens and protect their vegetables and greens. To maximize garden space, stairway railings, gutters, fences, balconies, porches, sidewalks, and spaces underneath the stairs are exploited for maximum gardening. Thus, for Vietnamese Texan home gardeners who do not have the luxury of front or backyard spaces to garden can make the most of severely limited green spaces to increase their food production of vegetables, herbs, and fruit trees, showcasing their strong desire and need for food security and sovereignty. None of this is demonstrably more evident than the Vietnamese làngs or villages in the working-class neighborhoods within historic African American wards and Latinx residential areas of southeast and south-central Houston.

THE GARDENS OF ALLEN PARKWAY VILLAGE

I vaguely remember my bà nội's (paternal grandmother) vegetable garden at Allen Parkway Village. I was perhaps six or seven years old when I first saw a lush field of greens in front of her well-worn two-story apartment unit. Little did I know until later that she grew an array of herbs that Vietnamese refugees and immigrants are accustomed and familiar to consuming and using as essential ingredients in traditional Vietnamese meals. I also did not know that whenever my bà nội donned her conical straw hat to tend her vegetable garden on bended knees, that she had rekindled a part of her Vietnamese lifestyle, re-enacting her own Việt Nam in America. Here was a wise, elderly woman living alone and laboring in an impoverished, historic Fourth Ward neighborhood, but she was not lacking the riches of her homeland.

Home gardens also blossom in the smallest spaces and most unexpected places. They exist and thrive in working-class neighborhoods, and are especially prevalent in every Vietnamese "village" or *làng* in southeast Houston. These home gardens are ubiquitous in the villages of Thái Xuân, St. Joseph, Sài Gòn, Thanh Tâm, Đà Lạt, and Huế, blooming in tight corners, nooks, and crannies, or stretching along handrails and beneath stairwells. A seventh village, known as St. Mary's Village in south central Houston, once existed as a sanctuary for working-class Vietnamese Houstonians to reside, but the village was later set for demolition, and its Vietnamese residents were forced to evacuate and find residency elsewhere. For working-class Vietnamese village residents, produce from their home gardens supplemented their diet and lessened the costs of purchasing herbs, vegetables, and fruits from grocery stores. These gardens also provide Vietnamese Texan gardeners with immediate access to bitter melons, water spinach, citrus fruits (trái cây), and more, allowing them an opportunity to control what they cook and consume, and hence regain some food sovereignty. Home gardens help spruce up working-class neighborhoods and improve living conditions by beautifying the dilapidated buildings and crowded living quarters. Consequently, home gardens provide a pleasing aesthetic to the time-worn villages, improving people's immediate surroundings and transforming negative spaces into positive places to relax, enjoy, and socialize with their neighbors.

Before there was a formalized and organized Vietnamese village, there was Allen Parkway Village, a much-maligned and eventually gentrified public housing residency located in the historic and predominantly black neighborhood of Fourth Ward. After the Việt Nam War ended in 1975, with a large influx of Vietnamese refugees resettling in the United States and being widely dispersed throughout the country, many decided to make a secondary migration and relocate to major cities such as Houston, Texas. Consequently, Houston city officials searched for public housing options for Vietnamese newcomers to resettle. Working with Vietnamese refugee leaders, they sought to relocate Vietnamese refugees to Allen Parkway Village, where living conditions had deteriorated and declined by the 1970s.

Allen Parkway Village was constructed during the Jim Crow era of racial segregation, when in 1941, "the HACH [Housing Authority of the City of Houston, now Houston Housing Authority] constructed Kelly Village to house blacks and Allen

Parkway Village for whites only."[29] The father of environmental justice history, Robert D. Bullard, explains the population changes in Houston's public housing: "The most dramatic change that occurred in the city's public housing between 1976 and 1984 was the rapid increase in Oriental public housing tenants, mostly Indochinese refugees, in two family developments: Allen Parkway Village and Clayton Homes."[30] In Allen Parkway Village, where 1,000 units existed in 1984, Asians represented 58.1 percent of the village's population.[31] Bullard further analyzes the effects of urban gentrification of the historic Fourth Ward and continued displacement of Black Houstonians in Allen Parkway Village. He argues that, starting in 1976, which coincides with the influx of Vietnamese refugees in Houston, the HACH intentionally carried out a replacement policy that favored the selection of Vietnamese refugees over African Americans to move into Allen Parkway Village. Bullard explains that, at the time, "physical conditions at Allen Parkway Village have been allowed to deteriorate severely, so that most of the units are not suitable for habitation, the project has become the subject of much speculation, and its cloudy future may put the future of the entire Fourth Ward at risk. . . . As the project's condition worsens and few units are habitable (only 528 of the 1,000 units were occupied in August 1984) it becomes an easier target for redevelopment. And with the gradual replacement of black tenants with Indochinese refugees, especially from 1976 to 1980, in Allen Parkway Village, that community focus of the Fourth Ward was no longer black. Thus, both situations may serve to erase the historic Fourth Ward."[32]

According to Wayne King of the *New York Times*, "Houston's public housing authority has systematically funneled Vietnamese refugees into an inner-city housing project [Allen Parkway Village] to lessen opposition to a plan to clear and develop the property, a prime piece of downtown real estate."[33] King further reports that "the lawyers for the Vietnamese charge that the housing authority is purposely letting the 1,000-unit Allen Parkway Village public housing project deteriorate to the point that the Federal Department of Housing and Urban Development will have no choice but to allow the city to tear it down."[34] According to an internal technical report, Allen Parkway Village housing project "was originally built exclusively for whites, the largest of its kind in the South at the time, but that as racial barriers were gradually lifted the project by 1976 was 66 percent black, 3 percent Hispanic, 26 percent white, and 5 percent Indochinese." That same report states, "the period between 1976 and 1983 has seen the project go from two-thirds black to more than one-half Indochinese. It is unlikely that this demographic change in tenant population was due to random assignment from the waiting list." According to King, the report later concludes that "a decision to demolish a project that house Vietnamese refugees would cause less political 'fallout' than the same decision to tear down a project housing mostly [of] black families." Earl Phillips, the executive director of the Housing Authority of the City of Houston denied the "purported 'steering' of Vietnamese to pave the way for demolition," claiming it was untrue.

Intentional or not, HACH policy over the development of Allen Parkway Village did little to alleviate the social, economic, and environmental problems for Vietnamese and African American residents. As the Allen Parkway Village buildings further deteriorated and living environs worsened for residents, the Village appeared headed for redevelopment, one that would not benefit residents, but instead, would gradually force them to leave and relocate elsewhere. Nevertheless, Vietnamese residents, such as my paternal grandmother (my bà nội) continued to reside in Allen Parkway Village and cultivate the herbs and greens that covered entire front yards of their dilapidated apartments. Bà nội raised and grew an assortment of mints (rau thơm) and water spinach (rau muống) to eat, to share with relatives and neighbors, and to sell. She and other Vietnamese village residents and gardeners lived in Allen Parkway to the best of their abilities despite the uncertainty of how long they could remain there.

By the mid-1980s, Vietnamese residents at Allen Parkway Village were not faring any better than their African American neighbors; both marginalized populations faced greater pressure to leave and vacate their Allen Parkway Village home units, with the latter possibly losing their historic Fourth Ward neighborhood entirely. To reiterate, even before the development of Vietnamese villages in southeast and southwest areas of Houston, a significant number of the Vietnamese refugees who made a secondary migration to Texas were settled in government housing projects, most notably Allen Parkway Village, one of Houston's poorest communities in the 1970s and 1980s.[35]

One source summarizes the socioeconomic struggles and cultural challenges for Vietnamese residents in Allen Parkway Village: "Many would be caught-up in a twenty-year struggle between wealthy developers, government agencies and poor tenants, and their supporters, over the fate of one of the highest valued real estate properties in the nation. The Vietnamese residents, along with fellow Chinese and Cambodian immigrants, soon made up two-thirds of the population in Allen Parkway Village. They raised herb gardens in the peace and quite [sic] Fourth Ward offered, relative to war. Even with many cultural barriers, and faced with high rates of crime in the crowded tenement, they achieved mutual acceptance with many of their African American neighbors."[36] The source also mentions the eventual removal of Vietnamese and African American residents from Allen Parkway Village, as previously contended by Bullard, asserting that the Village was part of the redevelopment plans of the Houston Housing Authority (HHA), formerly HACH, that would lead to further gentrification of the historic and predominantly African American neighborhood of Fourth Ward. Despite claims made by others that the HHA attempted to displace minorities (i.e., Vietnamese refugee and African American residents of Allen Parkway Village) to clear the way for the real estate auction and development of prime square footage near downtown and the redevelopment of Memorial Park, neither Village residents nor wealthy developers prevailed: in fact, "the dispute dragged on in court and energy profits declined, though the residents were ordered to leave in 1996."

Since 1996, Allen Parkway Village has been redeveloped into a low-to-mixed income residential neighborhood, with multiple housing plans for single and family units. Renamed as the Historic Oaks of Allen Parkway Village, the housing is a "blended occupancy community" under the Public Housing Program administered by the HHA.[37] Some of the original apartment building structures remain standing for historical preservation, but the dwellings have been drastically refurbished inside. The grounds have been manicured and landscaped as well. New buildings for housing, facilities, and office space have also been built. And no longer are the residents predominantly poor or working-class Vietnamese refugees and African Americans. Allen Parkway Village buildings and its demographic have changed considerably. For Vietnamese refugees who once resided in Allen Parkway Village, they evacuated once more, moving in with family members, relatives, or friends, and relocating to other low-income housing residences. Many found another village to live in where Vietnamese residents would make up the majority, and the main language spoken would be their native tongue.

THE GARDENS OF THÁI XUÂN VILLAGE

Thái Xuân Village appears to be the largest of the six remaining Vietnamese villages that sprawl across southeast Houston.[38] Approximately 1,400 Vietnamese Texans reside at Thái Xuân today. This Vietnamese village, located at 8200 Broadway and not far from Hobby Airport, consists of well-worn condominium buildings that are predominantly occupied by Vietnamese refugees and immigrants.[39] For Vietnamese diasporic residents living here, the social makeup and environment of Thái Xuân reminds them of their home country. One way to make the place feel like home is the heavy presence of makeshift home gardens cultivated and tended by Thái Xuân Vietnamese Texan residents themselves (figure 3.8).

Figure 3.8   A home garden in makeshift containers. Thái Xuân Village Condominium, Houston, Texas. (Photo by Ngọc Vũ.)

On a warm mid-morning in May, my wife and I leisurely walked through the narrow walkways and open courtyards of Thái Xuân Village, taking photographs of the villagers' makeshift home gardens and microfarms. A couple of Vietnamese residents greeted us, and became curious about our photo documentation of their gardens and their neighbors'. One middle-aged woman and her mother, Trần Thị Mỹ Huệ, stepped outside of her modest condo and greeted us. We exchanged hellos and pleasantries. I then explained why we were photographing her small yet immaculate, makeshift garden. She was pleased and happy that we were taking pictures of the produce from her potted garden and pointed out the elephant stalk ears (bạc hà) that she cultivated underneath the stairway in front of her condo. After we took a few more photos, Trần Thị Mỹ Huệ invited us for tea, but we politely declined, as we had just started documenting the gardens of Thái Xuân Village. We said our goodbyes and thanked her for the permission to photograph her home garden and her offering of tea.

For the next hour, we continued strolling the walkways of the village, taking photos of the countless unique home gardens and microfarms that decorated and beautified the outdoor living spaces of residents. As we made our way to the other end of Thái Xuân Village, we were greeted with a warm hello and smile from Bác Phước, who tended a small home garden that lined up against the wall of her condo.

We returned her greeting and politely introduced ourselves. She, too, was curious about our photographic endeavor. Once more, I explained our objective to photo-document as many small home gardens and microfarms at Thái Xuân Village as possible. Bác Phước smiled once more and was pleased to hear of our mission. I asked her if we could take a photo of her as she started to tend her modest garden. She nodded yes and began to smile and pose for the camera. We took a few photos of Bác Phước sitting beside her small beautiful garden. We thanked her for permission to photograph her next to her garden and exchanged our goodbyes. Nearing the second hour of photographing the greens and fruit trees cultivated by residents, we completed our round of walking through Thái Xuân Village, and circled back to our car. Needless to say, it was a joyous and eye-opening experience to explore the numerous small gardens of herbs, vegetables, and fruit trees being grown by Vietnamese villagers of Làng Thái Xuân.

Of course, we were not the first ones to take notice of the plethora of makeshift home gardens and microfarms in Thái Xuân Village. Claudia Kolker, author of *The Immigrant Advantage*, has written about the Vietnamese diasporic residents at Làng Thái Xuân and their home gardens. She references a connection of the residents' gardens here in the United States to the gardeners' home country of Việt Nam, which would be another good reason for them to embrace their village life. According to Kolker, Vietnamese diasporic residents "cherish it for the sense of community created by their shared origins, customs, and the tiny gardens of Vietnamese vegetables they grow."[40] Kolker also provided an excellent, detailed account of Trần Thị Đô, from Mỹ Tho, Việt Nam, her husband, and their family, who resettled in Làng Thái Xuân. She also shares a comprehensive explanation of the Trầns' home garden. Her interviewee, Trần Thị Đô, comments, "Every morning, at the same time, the first thing I do is check my plants. The lettuce is for the old man and me, the old lady, to eat. When it's windy, I pick up the plants that are tipped over, prop them up with a stick and tie them. Next I check for bugs. I kneel down to get a good look at each leaf and if I see one I'll get a [pair of] scissors and snip the whole leaf off." Trần remarks, "My garden makes me feel at home. It's a little different here: the weather is different than in Vietnam, where you can plant anything anytime. And we don't have much space. But I plant what I can. For winter, I grow lettuce [rau diếp], cilantro, onions, and elephant ears [bạc hà]—a kind of green that you use with pho and soups. That's a papaya tree [cây đu đủ] out front, left over from the previous resident. For the summer I put in basil, lettuce, and water chestnuts [hạt dẻ nước]. And I go around to talk about the garden with other people in the village. We ask, 'How do you get this (to) grow?' or, 'How did you do that?'"

Vietnamese villagers at Thái Xuân have fostered a thriving community; thriving in terms of building a neighborly and close-knit community living that is comfortable, safe, and akin to their lifestyle of the Việt Nam they remember. Consequently, despite the working class and tired facade of the Thái Xuân Village buildings, Vietnamese residents have established a small, but not insignificant homeland of their own, one equipped with a large, open, decorative courtyard and shrine dedicated to a Buddhist deity, and another manicured courtyard and floral shrine surrounding the Virgin Mary for Catholics. In between, from unexpected spaces, they have raised microfarms and small gardens next to their apartment building walls, underneath staircases, and along stairway handrails. Some residents have even dug out circles from the concrete pavement to plant their favorite herbs and fruit trees. Journalist Josh Harkinson describes the plethora of microfarms and their rich bounties in Thái Xuân Village: "Thái Xuân unfurls like a lotus flower. Any sidewalk between any two buildings leads into a valley of microfarms crammed with herbs and vegetables that would confound most American botanists."[41] Harkinson provides a colorful and apt description of their produce: "Entire front yards are given over to choy greens [rau cải ngọt]. Mature papaya trees dangle green fruit overhead, and vines sagging with wrinkled or spiky melons [bitter melons] climb trellises up second-story balconies. Perfumed night jasmine stretches for light alongside trees heavy with satsumas [cam satsuma], limes [chanh], and calamondins [cam calamondin]. Where the soil ends, Vietnamese mints and peppers sprout out of anything that will contain roots: an old US mail bin, an ice chest, two clawfoot bathtubs."[42] Harkinson shows that despite severely limited spaces, small-scale farming and urban gardening in the villages are leisure activities, sources of food security, and even supplemental income for some villagers. Journalist Susan Rogers confirms the visible presence of Thái Xuân Village home gardens and concludes that village residents make the most of constraint spaces by cultivating produce and greens on their balconies or in small yards that are fenced off.[43]

Vietnamese diasporic residents of Thái Xuân use whatever little space they have to maximize the size and productivity of their home gardens. They act creatively, wisely, resourcefully, and sustainably to build their gardens in tight, limited spaces and corners. Vietnamese Texan home gardeners also employ sustainable practices in their gardening by reusing and repurposing old containers and wooden materials for homemade trellises and cobbling together a makeshift home garden of their own. As a result, home gardens here are quite varied, and their contents range from container gardens to hanging ones covering staircase railings, balconies, and trellises. By maximizing their resources and available space, Vietnamese residents have engaged and labored in sustainable practices to develop and maintain their home gardens at Thái Xuân Village, demonstrating their working-class ethos.

Overall, Vietnamese diasporans are content and comfortable, for the most part, living in Thái Xuân Village. For them, the village is a re-imagined and recreated version of their home of Việt Nam. Trần Thị Đô remarks about Thái Xuân Village itself. She states, "Living here feels like Vietnam. You can visit and play and yak with the neighbors. You can leave your house for a whole month, and people will watch it for you. I can't leave the village because I can't drive or go out very easily. Outside, I'm scared. But here I can walk around anytime."[44] Ms. Trần reaffirms the beliefs of her Vietnamese Texan neighbors. For instance, Harkinson reports the story of Phòng and Nước, who attempted to leave Thái Xuân Village and relocate to a house in Bellaire. However, they discovered that they dearly missed the close-knit atmosphere of the village community and decided to return to Thái Xuân a few months later. According to Nước "It's warmhearted here. . . . The people here come in and out. It's the same as my old village. It reminds me of when I was little."[45] Other residents echo similar sentiments. "I like the villages because they have the same culture as in Vietnam," said Hoa Nguyễn, a mother of three.[46] "If we lived in a house, we wouldn't see our neighbors." For most Vietnamese villagers of Thái Xuân, they feel comfortable, secure, and content living in this place (deteriorating condominiums in a working-class neighborhood notwithstanding).

One crucial element that contributes to this feeling is that Thái Xuân Village allows Vietnamese diasporans to live as if they were transplanted to village life in Việt Nam. Yes, the living conditions may appear substandard and even impoverished from the perspective of outsiders. Nonresidents may perceive Thái Xuân Village to be well past its prime, with housing structures deteriorating and the neighborhood under great decline. Strangers may notice the significant number of feral cats roaming and discarded trash strewn on uneven sidewalks and pavement. Outsiders may see the buildings and stairways in dire need of new paint, or the lines in the parking lots that need to be repainted. However, to the approximately 1,400 Vietnamese Texans,[47] Thái Xuân Village is a genuine attempt to recreate and re-imagine their Việt Nam in miniature; it is a return to their homeland that they have lost and can never truly return to. The passing years have changed much of modern-day Việt Nam, almost as much as the Vietnamese diasporans here have changed themselves. But their village is not an impoverished homeland. With their working-class ethos evident in their living environs, the village life of Thái Xuân is safe, secure, stable, and meaningful for the Vietnamese villagers. How the village appears from the outside and to outsiders is merely a facade or shell of what is truly inside the village: a

Vietnamese life where the sidewalks are flanked by an abundance of small home gardens and microfarms and residents form a tight-knit community. This is where they feel at home.

THE GARDENS OF SÀI GÒN CONDOMINIUM

Vietnamese villagers of Sài Gòn Condominium are no different from their Thái Xuân counterparts; they also reside in a working-class neighborhood. The village is just a short drive from Thái Xuân Village, on the opposite side of Interstate 45 (I-45), just past the tent homes of the less fortunate who are living beneath the highway overpasses. Upon entering through Sài Gòn Condo's main entrance where the flags of the United States and the RVN stand sentinel, one sees an open oval-shaped lawn bordered by concrete pavement surrounded by microgardens that contain countless container trees, potted plants, and herb beds. The Vietnamese Texans here fully utilize the green and concrete spaces available in their limited individual residential and communal areas, planting vegetables, herbs, and fruit trees next to the exterior walls of their units, underneath worn stairways, and along rusted iron fences.

Although not as large or prominent as Thái Xuân Village in terms of land size, number of units, and population, the residents here nevertheless grow a plethora of home gardens, just like their Thái Xuân counterparts. At Sài Gòn Condo, the Vietnamese diasporans cultivate home gardens that are certainly noticeable, beautifying the entire well-worn condominium complex. They grow white eggplants, an assortment of mints and greens, citrus trees, dragon fruit (thanh long), elephant ear stalks (bạc hà), and more. Herbs, vegetables, and fruits are plentiful and abundant here. The home gardens serve a dual immediate purpose: they provide direct access to fresh nutritional produce, and the produce and accompanying flowers serve as decorative, organic adornments that enliven and enlighten what otherwise could be described as an uninteresting, dull residential complex that has seen better days.

In one particular home garden, a homemade ancestral shrine stands upright, visibly anchored as a wooden marker, with a small platform large enough to hold a vase with incense sticks, two larger vases, and teacups, all as offerings to their ancestors. These spots within the home gardens serve as significant religious or spiritual spaces for the Sài Gòn Condo Vietnamese. Much like Thái Xuân Vietnamese villagers, a few Vietnamese diasporans here utilize their home gardens to worship, pray, and pay respect to their ancestors. Michael W. Twitty, 2018 James Beard Award-winning author and food scholar, writes that "food is often a necessary vehicle between one's ancestors or the spiritual forces that guide their destiny."[48] Twitty's declaration on the sacrosanct nature of food, especially homegrown produce, is supported by Shampa and Sanjoy Mazumdar's research on immigrant kitchen gardens in the United States and how such gardens are also sacred spaces for Vietnamese American home gardeners, where it is not uncommon for them to have a dedicated, ancestral shrine watching over their greens.

Additionally, Vietnamese Texan home gardeners at Sài Gòn Condo are savvy and ingenious in discovering ways to cover and protect their vegetables, herbs, and fruit trees from the intense sunlight and overwhelming heat during the sizzling summer days, which oftentimes reach triple digit temperatures. From bedsheets to blankets to cardboard boxes, Vietnamese villagers here go beyond the traditional usage of homemade trellises and pergolas, favoring the much less expensive and utilitarian materials to shield and safeguard their produce from the searing heat and stifling humidity.

Much as they have done for Vietnamese villagers at Thái Xuân, these home gardens of Sài Gòn Condo give the residents an opportunity to re-imagine and recreate their own little Việt Nam, all while healing, soothing, and nurturing their war-torn, terror-filled refugee lives. Such home gardens offer hope, respectability, and dignity as well as a regaining of the humanity that was diminished during war, exile, displacement, and racialization. No longer are Vietnamese refugees merely victims; in spite of their victimization, they become agents of change in their own lives. They are here to plant, raise, harvest, cook, eat, and live like Vietnamese citizens they once were, only this time their culinary citizenship and food heritage belong here in the United States.

The Gardens of St. Joseph Condominium

Home gardens are also ubiquitous at St. Joseph Condominium, situated between I-45 and Sài Gòn Condo on Park Place Boulevard. Residents here are also able to create the allure of an abundance of green spaces even though such spaces are severely limited. Herbs, fruit trees, and vegetables are carefully planted and cultivated in home gardens by Vietnamese diasporans to construct positive spaces that momentarily transplant them back to Việt Nam. Papaya and lime trees, an array of mints, white eggplants, and chili pepper plants contribute to the sights, colors, and smells of St. Joseph's home gardens. These gardens also line up along building walls, stairways, and balconies of the old, pink structures, with some plants individually placed in well-manicured brick borders. A few other plants are placed in cut out circles in the middle of the concrete pavement.

Danny Phạm, an exuberant and precocious young boy who resides at St. Joseph with his parents and grandmother, greeted me near the village chapel. "Are you lost?" he asked innocently. "Do you need help?" I kindly replied no, although I probably did look a little lost just wandering from one narrow alley to another, taking photos of the abundant produce cultivated by local residents. Danny offered to help and encouraged me to check out the decorative flowers inside the village's Catholic chapel. After a brief introduction, I followed him inside the chapel, which was small but spotless. I stayed for a few minutes, took several photos of the religious icons and decorative flowers, and then walked outside with Danny. My cheerful, de facto tour guide offered to lead me throughout the village and give a tour of the residents' gardens. As we walked past one home garden after another, Danny happily explained what produce was growing all around us. We walked through the narrow alleys of St. Joseph, passing by towering papaya trees and stumbling upon one of his neighbor's lush home garden, replete with a variety of mints, greens, and fruit trees. Afterward, he led me to his grandmother's house where the garden covered much of the front of her condo unit's facade. Danny's grandmother cultivates bitter melons whose vines stretch across a white trellis and halfway up the stairway railing. She also grows lime and papaya trees, white eggplants, aloe vera plants (cây lô hội), and plenty of mints and other herbs. Needless to say, Danny's grandmother has planted a spectacular and impressive home garden despite such a limited spatial enclosure.

In addition, much like Thái Xuân village, the home gardens at St. Joseph Condo are quite diverse. Container gardens abound, where Vietnamese villagers utilize mismatched containers of different sizes, shapes, and colors. A few hanging gardens also drape the village, blanketing staircase handrails and improvised trellises. Vietnamese Texan home gardeners use their creativity, ingenuity, and horticultural skills to make most of their spatial limitations.

St. Joseph Condominium, no doubt, is a working-class village. Neighbors live in close proximity to one another, residing in small, well-worn condo units. Regardless of their working-class status and subpar living standards, residents have transformed their limited spaces into beautiful home gardens. Vietnamese diasporic residents make much of their crowded quarters by raising and nurturing home gardens next to exterior building walls, beneath stairways, along the rails of balconies and stairs, as well as on paved concrete. These microfarms and gardens are essential to their living and dietary needs. Furthermore, these home gardens help beautify their living places. Finally, they are gentle reminders of what they love to grow and consume, providing small, but not insignificant, reminders of their Việt Nam.

Vietnamese diasporic home gardeners of St. Joseph continue to plant, develop their abundant green gardens, and harvest the produce they proudly raise and grow. Home gardens remain plentiful and essential at St. Joseph. The produce supplies the Vietnamese villagers with valuable nutrition, and offers beautiful sights, tastes, and smells. The gardens are also small yet important reminders of their home country of Việt Nam. Living in a working-class neighborhood and surrounded by incredible home gardens and crops would indeed empower, motivate, and nurture Vietnamese village residents living here, giving them a sense of camaraderie and kinship, as well as a place that they could call home.

The Gardens of Thanh Tâm Village

Another Vietnamese village located in close proximity to I-45 is Thanh Tâm Village, which is nestled in the quiet residential area of the Park Place neighborhood of southeast Houston. Smaller than its counterparts, Thái Xuân Village and St. Joseph Condominium, but larger than Sài Gòn, Đà Lạt, and Huế Condominiums in size and scope, Thanh Tâm appears quaint and calm, encircled by single family unit homes of a nearby subdivision. Like the aforementioned villages, many Vietnamese Houstonians here also plant and nurture their own small home gardens. In addition to their attractive home gardens, Vietnamese villagers have established a grotto of the Virgin Mary with a small, open courtyard and seating area, surrounded with decorative flowers and plants. Further behind and to the left of the grotto lies a gated red and yellow pavilion and an open courtyard shaded by a covered pagoda that houses a female Buddhist deity. Analogous to Thái Xuân Village, religious spaces are crucial to the social and physical environs of Thanh Tâm Village. One condo unit even has a statue of the Virgin Mary atop of a red gateway entrance of their home.

At Thanh Tâm Village home gardens are numerous. Vietnamese diasporic residents grow chili peppers, lime trees, winter melons, luffa, a variety of squash and gourds, papaya trees, an assortment of mints, water spinach, and much more. Such herbs, vegetables, and fruit trees are grown alongside exterior building walls and makeshift trellises. Reusable jars, sitting on a table next to one home garden, are used to pickle some of the homegrown fruits and vegetables. In other words, Thanh Tâm residents maximize their constrained spaces and scarce resources. Despite such constraints, these home gardens are evidence of their willingness, diligence, determination, and creativity to overcome limited space, scarce resources, and little capital. Vietnamese Houstonians here have also embraced their working-class ethos, creating opportunities for themselves to plant gardens and raise fruit trees, herbs, and vegetables that remind them of Việt Nam.

Some gardens are fenced and manicured. Others are container gardens where once again Vietnamese diasporans demonstrate their gardening ingenuity and savviness, using whatever materials available to them. Such container gardens are evident at làng Thanh Tâm, as well as other villages. A few Thanh Tâm home gardens are spread out with makeshift trellises and PVC water pipes, in what essentially amounts to hanging gardens. These hanging gardens demonstrate their foresight and resourcefulness in building, organizing, and sustaining their home gardens. In addition, a number of gardens are multilayered, with lengthy vines and stems from melons and squash covering most of the roof of a trellis and providing much-needed shade for other plants to flourish underneath. Such two-tiered home gardens add another layer of uniqueness and creativity that augments their gardens and makes it possible for them to raise additional herbs, fruits, and vegetables.

A diverse style of home gardens can be seen at Thanh Tâm, further validating the resourcefulness and ingenuity of Vietnamese Texan home gardeners. Using a variety of materials, Vietnamese village residents at Thanh Tâm have made the most of the limited outdoor spaces to cultivate home gardens that supplement their diets, allow them to make traditional Vietnamese dishes, reminisce about Việt Nam, offer a daily regimen of physical labor and exercise, create religious and spiritual spaces, and give much-needed peace and tranquility to their bodies and souls. These home gardens provide sanctuary for Vietnamese refugees while their physical bodies reside here in the United States, even as their inner souls softly ache and long for their old homeland of Việt Nam.

THE GARDENS OF ĐÀ LẠT AND HUẾ CONDOMINIUMS

Also in the Park Place neighborhood of southeast Houston, and just down the street from St. Joseph Condo and Sài Gòn Condo, lie two more Vietnamese villages: Đà Lạt and Huế Condominiums. Làng Đà Lạt is the larger of the two, having more condo units and residents. However, the quantity of home gardens between the two villages is about equal. Although not as plentiful and prolific as their other làng counterparts, Vietnamese Houstonians living in Đà Lạt and Huế Condos also plant and raise a significant amount of produce.

At Đà Lạt Condo, plants, herbs, and flowers decorate the faded white brick walls and red trimmings of several units. In front of barred windows and front doors, cultivated tall plants and trees speckle the subpar condo units, beautifying their homes. Plant vines also crawl up red staircase railings, and container gardens are decked out beneath them. With the Đà Lạt buildings are more sprawling and the concrete parking spaces are more plentiful than làng Huế, the home gardens do not ostensibly appear as visible or evident in comparison to other Vietnamese villages. However, there are plenty of chili pepper plants, an array of mints, potted flowers, elephant ear stalks, and mixed greens that are cultivated here by Vietnamese residents.

Diagonally across the street lies the reddish-brown and pink brick complex of Huế Condo. The village is enhanced by a number of colorful container gardens, numerous herbs, and pomelo trees (trái bưởi) that border the open courtyard (figure 3.8). Old grocery carts are utilized to contain and protect herbs and plants, while antiquated political campaign signs are reused and repurposed to provide some shade for the vegetables growing underneath stairways. Some container gardens are more well-kept and organized than others, yet they are all unique additions to what would have been just a drab looking building, awash in a tired, uninspiring color scheme. Instead, bright yellow, red, and pink flowers punctuate the outdoor living spaces, providing a more pleasant, charming, and dignified front entrance for residents. As for the produce, chili peppers, a variety of mints and greens, lime trees, aloe vera, pomelos, and lemongrass are cultivated here. The flowers, vegetables, fruit trees, and herb gardens provide a nice, stark contrast to the burglar bars that mask the front doors and windows of the substandard living units of a working-class neighborhood. These home gardens are organic indicators for strangers to take notice of the Vietnamese Texans living here, and their efforts to do so in accordance with their traditional foodways via sustainable practices to the best of their ability.

Planting their roots in Texas, literally and figuratively, Vietnamese Texans nurture home gardens of different shapes, sizes, and styles, that allow them to survive, live, and in many cases, thrive. They have come a long way to secure a place they could call home. In these home gardens, no matter how minuscule or insignificant they may initially appear, Vietnamese diasporans have discovered refuge by digging in the soil and transforming plots of earth into an amazing cultivation of herbs, vegetables, flowers, and fruit trees (figures 3.9–3.14). They have planted the seeds of home here in Texas and throughout the United States. Raising such produce also gives Vietnamese Texan home gardeners a sense of pride, achievement, and belonging. They utilize the produce they have planted and raised so that they may prepare

Figure 3.9   Pomelos. Thái Xuân Village Condominium, Houston, Texas. (Photo by Ngọc Vũ.)

Figure 3.10   Home garden in limited space. Sài Gòn Village Condominium, Houston, Texas. (Photo by Ngọc Vũ.)

Figure 3.11 A home garden. St. Joseph Village Condominium, Houston, Texas. (Photo by Roy Vũ.)

and cook familiar and comforting Vietnamese dishes that give them a taste of home. Whether they realize it or not, with their hands toiling the land, they have cultivated a farm-to-freedom movement, freeing a part of themselves and others to live a more peaceful, healthy, and fruitful life—a life taken away from them by the Việt Nam War and the consequent terrors of refuge, displacement, and marginalization.

In Texas, Vietnamese diasporic home gardeners have sown the seeds of food sovereignty, culinary citizenship, and homeland duality. They have attempted to gain the food security inherent in planting and raising produce familiar and comforting to them. With such actions, they resist food alternatives that are less healthy, less familiar, less organic, less nurturing, and less natural to their bodies, minds, and spirits. Instead, they seek food security and sovereignty by rejecting negative food alternatives, opting to cultivate bitter melons, luffas, water spinach, kumquats, jackfruits (quả mít), white eggplants, okra, and many others, using the raw, homegrown ingredients that are readily accessible to make traditional dishes and comfort meals for their families and friends to share together. Consequently, Vietnamese Texan home gardeners not only attempt to regain and preserve their food heritage, but they also magnify and extend their foodways for the next generation, as well as for the non-Vietnamese populace in Texas. The next chapter spotlights the Vietnamese

Figure 3.12   Home garden along a wall. Thanh Tâm Village Condominium, Houston, Texas. (Photo by Roy Vũ.)

American gardeners, home cooks, and chefs who incorporate and cook with their homegrown herbs, vegetables, and fruit trees to prepare and concoct traditional and popular dishes typically consumed by Vietnamese diasporans. They are expanding their borders of culinary citizenship and gaining a greater sense of belonging here in the United States—one ingredient, one dish, and one meal at a time—while establishing a homeland duality of rooting themselves as Americans. They are reclaiming their Vietnamese identity through cooking and consuming their homegrown and home-connected foods. As a result of their farm-to-freedom practices, Vietnamese diasporans are able to live a more emancipated life.

Figure 3.13 Home gardens in a central courtyard. Thanh Tâm Village Condominium, Houston, Texas. (Photo by Roy Vũ.)

Figure 3.14 A home garden under a stairwell. Huế Village Condominium, Houston, Texas. (Photo by Roy Vũ.)

Lan T. Nguyễn standing next to bitter melons in the home garden she shares with Quang V. Hoàng. Pearland, Texas. (Photo by Son Hoàng.)

Bunches of sweet bananas at An Quân K. Vũ and Đung T. Trần's home garden. Houston, Texas. (Photo by Roy Vũ.)

Lung T. Trần with her prized fuzzy winter melon. Grand Prairie, Texas. (Photo by Điệp Besaw.)

Bác Phước tending her home garden. Thái Xuân Village Condominium, Houston, Texas. (Photo by Ngọc Vũ.)

Home gardens at Sài Gòn Condo Village Condominium. Houston, Texas. (Photo by Roy Vũ.)

Nua Nguyễn picking Thai chili peppers from her backyard. Grand Prairie, Texas. (Photo by Ngọc Vũ.)

A papaya tree at St. Joseph Village Condominium. Houston, Texas. (Photo by Roy Vũ.)

Home gardens at Thanh Tâm Village Condominium. Houston, Texas. (Photo by Roy Vũ.)

A pomelo tree at Huế Village Condominium. Houston, Texas. (Photo by Roy Vũ.)

A home garden along a stairwell at Đà Lạt Village Condominium. Houston, Texas. (Photo by Roy Vũ.)

Luffa squashes hanging from a trellis at Thanh Tâm Village Condominium, Houston, Texas. (Photo by Roy Vũ.)

Lê Đinh Qưới and her husband standing in their home garden, surrounded by white egg plants, Thai chili peppers, gourds, bitter melons, and more. Their home garden encompasses almost every square inch of their home backyard. Arlington, Texas. (Photo by Ngọc Vũ.)

Nua Nguyễn picking Thai chili peppers from her backyard. Grand Prairie, Texas. (Photo by Ngọc Vũ.)

Satsuma oranges grown in Nguyễn Lan and Hoàng Quang's backyard in their old home in Pearland, Texas. (Photo by Son Hoàng.)

CHAPTER 4

Global South Meets the New South

Perseverance and Expansion of Vietnamese Foodways

Food, like love, is a basic human need. Everyone needs sustenance to survive. Food can unite people regardless of culture, ethnicity, religion, political ideals, or socioeconomic backgrounds. Two people who may not speak the same language can sit down to a meal together and thereby instantly have something in common: the desire to partake.

—Christine Ha, from *Recipes from My Home Kitchen: Asian and American Comfort Food*

But now that Mother was suddenly taken away from us, this house never would be the same. On this day, only three days after her death, my siblings and I and our father gathered in her favorite room to cook a meal in her honor. In truth, it probably was the only thing we wanted to do. . . . As comforting and satisfying as these foods were, in the end it was the rhythms of peeling, chopping and being in the kitchen together that most eased our pain. We realize—more than ever—that food is simply love.

—Mai Phạm, from "Cooking Together Threads Past with Present, Grief with Joy"

To this day, my family has a propensity to snack late at night, well after dinner. Reflecting on my childhood years, I remember my mother would occasionally make bánh chuối chiên (pan-fried banana cakes) as a post-dinner snack for us, even after she had a long day at work at my parents' print shop, or after coming home from her shift at Burger King. The bánh chuối chiên was delicious and sweet. Because I was a finnicky eater as a kid, she would even make bánh danh (pan-fried sweet cakes without the bananas) just for me. Strangely, I loved the bánh danh even more than the bánh chuối chiên! It was fried, sweet, doughy, and delicious. I am absolutely sure that it had zero nutritional value, but I was six or seven years old, so nutrition was not my biggest concern. What I did learn, even more so today, was that my mother showed her greatest love for us through her own cooking. Cooking was then, and still is, my mother's utmost labor of love; and her food is her love for us.

This chapter connects the garden-raised produce with the home-cooked meals prepared by Vietnamese Texans. Here, I delve into Vietnamese American home cooks and the fresh herbs, fruits, and vegetables they gather from their gardens to make traditional Vietnamese dishes in the kitchen. *Where* they cook familiar dishes is also discussed, as Vietnamese American home cooks sometimes equip themselves with nontraditional kitchen spaces, in comparison to American mainstream standards. I also examine the importance of dining together as a family unit. Home-cooked meals with some use of homegrown ingredients from the garden would lend to dining together as a family as an essential quotidian ritual. Thanks to Vietnamese American home gardeners, cooks, restaurateurs, and chefs, Vietnamese cuisine in America remains alive and well. In fact, Vietnamese food has become more ubiquitous and ever-present, adding another integral cuisine to the already varied gastronomy of America, particularly Southern cuisine. Furthermore, by embracing their own unique gastronomy, Vietnamese diasporans have gained culinary citizenship—a greater sense of belonging here, thanks to the expansion of Vietnamese foodways by gardeners, home cooks, chefs, and restaurateurs.

Farm-to-table, from start to finish, is typically practiced among Vietnamese diasporic home cooks; to grow, pick, and use their own fruits, herbs, and vegetables and create their own recipes and meals in their own unique kitchens allows them to preserve their food heritage (see figures 4.1 and 4.2). In Texas, Vietnamese diasporic home cooks frequently cultivate an expansive home garden, or even a

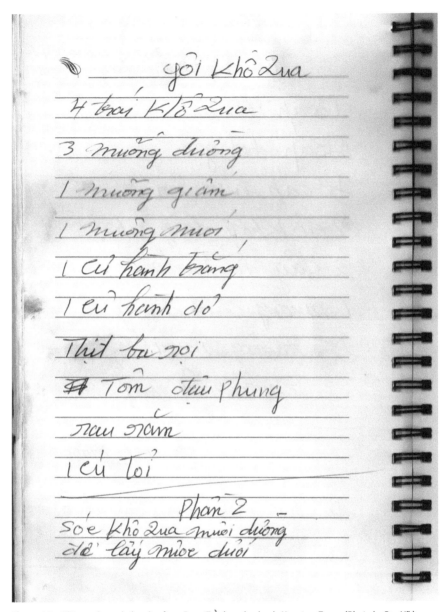

Figure 4.1 Bitter melon salad recipe from Đung Trần's recipe book. Houston, Texas. (Photo by Roy Vũ.)

microfarm, exhibiting their traditional farm-to-table practices. In this chapter, I hope to reveal an in-depth look into Vietnamese Texan home cooks and chefs and their performance of farm- and garden-to-table practices when they use what they produce to create recipes and cook meals in their outdoor and makeshift kitchens for family dinners and gatherings. Dining together as a family exemplifies significant

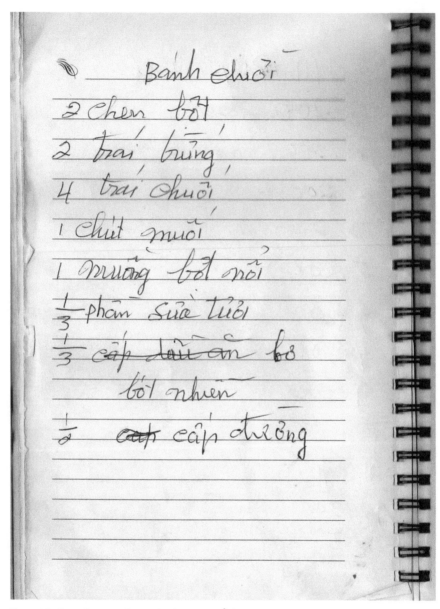

Figure 4.2 Sweet banana crêpes recipe from Đung Trần's recipe book. Houston, Texas. (Photo by Roy Vũ.)

traits that are central to the Vietnamese household: family unity, stability, and quality time. Furthermore, dining together as a family is an important ritual for Vietnamese refugees and immigrants. Dinner is the most important meal of the day for a Vietnamese diasporic family. A family that dines together, stays together. Consequently, Vietnamese refugee parents do their utmost to ensure that the entire family—which often includes grandparents and extended family members—eats together for dinner.

Using food items from their own gardens to create Vietnamese dishes in their own kitchens also shows the significance of retaining their identity and culture. The construction of makeshift indoor and outdoor kitchens echoes their traditional food preparations, harking back to their days of Việt Nam. For Vietnamese Texan home cooks, it is not uncommon for the kitchen to be a separate shed, outdoor patio, or car garage that exists outside the house they live in. As mentioned in the Introduction, in Vietnamese, a kitchen is called nhà bếp, which literally translates into "kitchen house." The kitchen is typically separate from the living quarters, so it is not always considered part of the house—in fact, the kitchen is traditionally not considered as a room inside the house or as part of the living quarters. One reason is that Vietnamese Texan home cooks prefer not to have the lingering smell of cooked food inside the house. To them, the smell of cooked food inside their homes would often be considered as adulterating the air. In other words, the aroma from the cooking would actually be considered an unsavory smell if lingering inside the house.[1]

Making meals and dining together brings a lot to the table, literally and figuratively. The family/communal meal metamorphosizes into a bountiful harvest of conversations and quality time to bond, while patiently sharing the home-cooked dishes. It collectivizes and highlights the strength of every individual, demonstrating how each person helps, and what she or he brings to the table. The dining table showcases a beautiful repast—no matter the amount or type of dishes—of familial community. Food is the focal point that remarkably, momentarily, and sometimes unintentionally, brings people together. Robert E. Rhoades asserts that "While immigrants have few options in coping with the strangeness of a new language, confusing laws, discrimination, and racism, one area of their lives they can control is what they cook in their own kitchens and eat in the company of compatriots."[2] Rhoades further states that Vietnamese diasporans share with their American Southern counterparts a cultural upbringing that includes the desire to cultivate plants in order to preserve and remember a cuisine that reminds them of their homeland.[3] For the parents who cook daily from home, they believe that cooking familiar meals and sharing the foods together are significant actions that help them to preserve and extend their Vietnamese culture foodways to their children.

A Vietnamese Home Meal: The Importance of Consuming Fresh Produce and Ingredients

Both of my parents, Vũ Kiến An Quân and Trần Thị Diem Dũng, have a passion for gardening. They have nurtured a home garden in their front and backyards for decades. As mentioned in the previous chapter, An Quân and Dũng plant a variety of crops each year. In recent years, they have focused on growing đậu bắp (okra), cà pháo (white eggplants), and chuối (bananas). For each harvest, they cut the okra and chop them into bite-size pieces so that my mother can make canh chua cá (sour soup with fish, typically catfish). They pickle the white eggplants in jars and then eat the fermented white eggplants as a condiment, which is also sometimes mixed with fish sauce to enhance the flavors for dipping other foods. As for bananas, Vietnamese love the short, plump, and well-ripened ones, and my parents are no exception. They eat them as a snack. When overripe, the bananas are sometimes be used to make bánh chuối chiên. Renowned home cook and James Beard Award-winning cookbook author, Andrea Nguyễn, remarks, "The Vietnamese adore bananas, arguably the country's national fruit. Many kinds—small, large, scrubby, sweet, starchy—are available, and people know the seasonal and regional differences. A giant herb related to lilies and orchids, the entire banana plant (leaves, fruits, blossoms, trunk, and roots) is used in cooking."[4]

In addition, my parents continue to plant tía tô (perilla), rau thơm (mint leaves), cây lô hội (aloe vera), rau muống (water spinach), ớt (Thai chili peppers), and cây đào (peach trees). They consume perilla, mint leaves, and water spinach as garnishes for phở, bún, and other hot soups. Thai chili peppers are incorporated into the cooking, added to a bowl of fish sauce, or eaten separately as a condiment. In years past, their home garden included produce such as bí đao (winter melons), mướp (luffas), and cây quất (kumquat trees). The winter melons would be cut into small pieces to make canh bí (winter melon soup), while the luffas are sliced into thin, bite-sized pieces to make another soup.

It is no surprise that both of my parents love to garden. They take tremendous care and pride working in their home garden, cultivating herbs, vegetables, and fruit trees. Using their bare hands, my parents pluck tía tô, rau thơm, rau muống, and other herbs, and use scissors to snip off đậu bắp from the stalks and cà pháo from the stems. My mother frequently uses some of the handpicked herbs, plants, and vegetables as essential ingredients for the next family meal. For instance, she or my father will cut and wash their homegrown đậu bắp. Mom then uses the fresh đậu bắp to make canh chua or xào (stir fry vegetables).[5] My mother also handpicks her favorite greens, organic rau đay (jute leaves), to cook a refreshing and healthy pot of canh rau đay (jute leaf soup).[6] Sometimes, my parents plant and pluck mướp from their backyard, so that mom can make canh mướp (luffa soup) for us. In addition, she incorporates homegrown herbs as garnishes and condiments for traditional Vietnamese dishes such as cây me chua (or sorrel, which is what my mother calls it in her Vietnamese accent) and rau muống for phở (beef noodle soup) and rau thơm for bún riêu (crab-based egg soup with noodles). For condiments, she pickles cà pháo and dưa muối or dưa cải chua (pickled mustard greens) as accoutrements to accompany a meal. These herbs, vegetables, and fruit trees grown in their front and backyard are critical for preparing traditional Vietnamese dishes and sauces, preserving the flavors, tastes, textures, and smells of the food they ate when they lived in Việt Nam. Today, my parents' home garden remains a transnational foodway linkage to their Vietnamese past. Their garden is a small plot of home that reminds them of their homeland.

Trần Thi Lừng cooks traditional Vietnamese dishes with some herbs, vegetables, and fruits cultivated from her home garden as well. With her homegrown herbs, she makes stir fry dishes and soups such as canh chua.[7] As stated in the previous chapter, Lừng grows a variety of rau thơm, húng quế (Thai basil), hành lá (green onions), and ngò or rau mùi (cilantro or coriander) to make dishes such as bánh xèo (savory crispy pancakes).[8] Lừng uses her bí đao to make canh bí (winter melon soup) or a stir fry dish. She eats bạc hà (elephant ear stalks) raw like a salad or uses it as an ingredient for canh chua. Lừng explains, "The herb we use the most is rau thơm. . . . That's what we like the most. For we eat with soup—we eat many different kinds of soup." She also notes that her family enjoys raising mướp (luffa) and trái khổ qua or mướp đắng (bitter melon) and using them as the primary ingredients in traditional Vietnamese soups, salads, and stir fry dishes. In addition, she pickles ớt to make a dipping sauce that complements Vietnamese dishes and enhances their flavors.

Of interesting note, Ms. Trần, who has lived in the DFW metropolitan area for almost her entire American life, makes a horticultural comparison between DFW and Houston, commenting on the differences in climate and geography that affect home gardening cultivation. She says, "We like cà tím (purple eggplants), too. But over here in Dallas, we don't plant that much cà tím. But in Houston, I see some people, they plant that a lot." Home gardens appear in greater abundance and tend to be more prolific in the Houston metropolitan area versus the DFW metroplex due to Houston's warmer and more humid climate. Plus, the Vietnamese American population in the Houston metropolitan area remains larger than in North Texas.

As for Houston transplant Tammy Đinh, she did not learn how to cook until she got married. That was when she learned Vietnamese cooking from her friends. After the war and relocation to Texas, she remembers growing and picking organic rau thơm in the backyard of her house in the Sagemont neighborhood of southeast Houston. She would use the rau thơm to make gỏi cuốn (spring rolls) and stir-fried dishes. In addition, Ms. Đinh would make traditional staples such as phở and chả giò (Vietnamese egg rolls, sometimes referred to as fried spring rolls). However, her favorite dish to cook is canh chua cá.

Bạch Tuyết Phạm also cooks a variety of dishes using her home garden produce as vital ingredients and raw garnishes. Bạch explains in great detail: "For vegetables and greens in my garden, I use them for boiling. I boil gourds, water spinach, cabbage, etc. to make squash soup, gourd soup, cabbage soup, melon soup, bitter melon soup, etc. I also use a variety of produce to make stir fry dishes. Soups or stir fry dishes are cooked with shrimp and flavored with cilantro. A variety of mints are used the most on weekends. Herbs are eaten together with egg rolls, vermicelli dishes, beef noodle soup . . . [and] wrapped inside spring rolls . . . each food must use different herbs for the right taste."[9] In addition, Bạch thinks that every vegetable, herb, and fruit has its own characteristics, and she prefers to consume fresh spinach, endives, squash, luffa, and bitter melon.[10] She grows her favorites every year, and so do her friends. Bạch cultivates fresh herbs, vegetables, and fruits to seek flavors commonly found in many Vietnamese dishes. Such home-produced ingredients enhance the richness of dishes consumed by her family. Bạch adds that she neither wants to nor likes to eat flavorless foods that are not Vietnamese dishes. It is safe to assume that she finds Vietnamese dishes to be well-flavored and balanced in taste.

For Vietnamese Texan home cooks, having readily available crops are crucial to preserving traditional recipes, meal-preparation techniques, and dishes. Picking and gathering fresh herbs, ripe fruits, and edible vegetables from the home garden personifies *and* amplifies the working-class ethos, which was the most common descriptor of the Vietnamese refugee and immigrant population when first resettling in the United States. For the Vietnamese diaspora, having a home garden, no matter how small, provides them with not only nourishment, but also allows them to preserve their cooking and meal-preparation traditions. Such farm-to-table praxis grants Vietnamese diasporans an opportunity to retain a huge part of their cultural identity while adjusting and struggling to earn a decent living in America. Ultimately, Vietnamese Texan home cooks demonstrate their refugee resilience by gardening; and some of them truly thrive, becoming successful restaurateurs, chefs, food purveyors, and cookbook authors. Their success creates a niche for Vietnamese cuisine in the American multicultural palate and introduces the world of flavors, textures, and freshness present in Vietnamese gastronomy. Such remarkable resilience and success often start with the produce from home gardens, flow into traditional recipes that are cooked in the nhà bếp, and end in home meals shared by family members dining together.

Cookbooks continue to play an important role in recording, cataloging, and preserving recipes, particularly from food cultures that are marginalized by mainstream society or traditionally passed on via oral history. Scholar Delores B. Phillips writes that "the Vietnamese cookbook performs work other than the mere cataloging of recipes. Most cookbooks do, but the Vietnamese cookbook has a special relationship with its English-speaking diaspora—particularly those cookbooks that blend the functions of cataloging recipes with those of cultural recovery."[11] Phillips continues, arguing that cooking goes well beyond the table: "The pervasiveness of eating in Vietnamese culture means that food gestures toward every aspect of Vietnamese identity: as a daily offering to the ancestors, as the centerpiece of every celebration, and as a way of sharing love and binding the family. Cooking articulates Vietnamese culture as fluently as its language."[12]

According to James Beard Award-winning cookbook author, Andrea Nguyễn, "Displacement often leads people to seek solace and comfort in simple pleasures that give them a sense of stability. My parents, in their forties when they fled their homeland, placed great importance on maintaining Vietnamese culture in our family. . . . Mom and Dad believed that food was a practical and easy way for us to experience and express our ethnic identity."[13] Nguyễn also shares how when her father prepared and consumed Vietnamese food, it would remind him of home and ease the burden of starting life over in the United States.[14] She stresses the importance of having raw, fresh herbs to accompany Vietnamese dishes as a heaping plate of garnishes. Such raw ingredients heighten the flavors of a traditional Vietnamese dish, particularly when herbs are added toward the end of cooking. Having a full plate of herbs and greens on the dining table is a uniquely Vietnamese custom that differentiates Vietnamese gastronomy from other Asian cuisines.[15] "Vegetables are woven throughout the Vietnamese table," Nguyễn claims. "A plate of vegetables and herbs arrives with a bow of noodle soup; cucumbers, jicama, and greens join meats and seafood in rice-paper rolls; and everyday soups (canh) usually include a vegetable for flavor, texture, and color."[16] Nguyễn states how conspicuous vegetables are in Vietnamese cuisine; they are notable as one of the four integral components of the traditional Vietnamese four-dish meal, which consists of a soup, a meat or seafood dish, a vegetable dish, and rice. She adds that, similar to many other Asian cuisines, pickled and preserved vegetables are essential to Vietnamese gastronomy by providing contrasting texture and flavor to other dishes on the table.[17]

Esteemed California chef, cookbook author, and owner of Star Ginger and Lemon Grass restaurants, Mai Phạm, notes the prominent role of herbs in Vietnamese cuisine: "The Vietnamese eat an enormous amount of herbs. . . . A family meal often consists of a table salad, which includes lettuce and different varieties of mint and basil. To eat, diners just snip off the sprigs and add to their bowls or plates, creating little salads as they go. Fresh herbs are also used as garnishes and accompaniments to soups, salads, and noodle dishes."[18] She believes that Vietnamese people highly valuable fresh vegetables for consumption. For an average Vietnamese, meat was not always an affordable option for daily consumption in Việt Nam. And Phạm was also raised to believe that vegetables are as important, if not more so, than meat and starches in a balanced and healthy diet.[19]

Chef Mai Phạm writes extensively about vegetables, herbs, and fruit trees commonly grown by Vietnamese. She discusses the variety of gourds consumed by Vietnamese and how they are cherished in Việt Nam: "Homes are framed with front trellises, all wrapped in thick vines of *trai bau*, a variety of bottle gourd, and clusters of brilliant white flowers. A beloved plant and a popular architectural feature of sorts, the gourd is prized not only for its lush green starlike leaves, which provide ample shade, but for its sweet flesh."[20] Phạm further observes that "In Vietnam, *trai bau* often appears in soups, but my favorite way of eating it is a simple stir fry with shrimp. For me, even without remembering those homes with the flowering gourds, I know that a meal with *trai bau* is as delicious as it is comforting."[21]

For distinguished author Monique Trường, a cookbook is also a memoir: "For an immigrant, a refugee, or a racial or ethnic other, there's often a difference between the food that you eat in public and the food that you eat at home. . . . That goes hand in hand with the language that you speak in public versus the language that you speak at home. There's a clear linguistic divide, and you need both languages to survive. The language spoken at home is the language of love and family. Similarly, the food eaten at home is the food of comfort and belonging. We learn to pivot back and forth, to create a 'double' of ourselves who can go into the public realm to attend school or to work. That's how we survive the trauma and loneliness of displacement, immigration, or racism."[22] She focuses on the state of in-betweenness that is often evoked and experienced by refugees and immigrants, a feeling of not belonging here in the United States, as well as not belonging over there, back in their homelands. This in-between sentiment also applies to what we eat in public and in the privacy of our home. For Trường, comfort food eaten at home is synonymous with belonging.

For Vietnamese American home gardeners, cooks, and chefs, having raw ingredients from their gardens to prepare and make Vietnamese comfort food gives them a greater sense of satisfaction and belonging—here and there.

HOME COOKING IN THE VIETNAMESE KITCHEN(S)

Vietnamese refugees and immigrants carry on cooking traditions unbroken by war, exile, displacement, and xenophobia; these culinary traditions are a large part of their survival, resilience, and ability to establish a sense of place. Historian Kurt E. Kinbacher writes, "Food preparation in the home was vital to the maintenance of Vietnamese identity. . . . In diaspora culture, Vietnamese food functioned as a focal point for maintaining long-standing social and historical continuity."[23] Because most people cook from rote memory and experience, not many Vietnamese American home cooks record and collect recipes. The few fortunate ones kept or inherited recipe books from their parents. Andrea Nguyễn recalls that her mother carried a little orange notebook with her when her family was forced to evacuate from Việt Nam in 1975: "My mother squeezed her best jewelry, a couple of important photos . . . and a small orange notebook filled with her handwritten recipes into her handbag. . . . Surely, she thought, all the Vietnamese refugees heading for the states would want a bit of home to chew and savor. She guarded her handbag at all times, and the notebook traveled with us from Saigon to Guam to Hawaii and finally to California."[24] Regarding the significance of her mother's small, orange recipe book, Nguyễn reflects how she wanted to preserve the recipe book because it was a family heirloom and therefore a part of her heritage. When Nguyễn began writing her first cookbook, *Into the Vietnamese Kitchen: Traditional Foodways, Modern Flavors*, her mother no longer needed the recipe book because she had replaced it with a large recipe-card box. So she gifted her small yet remarkable recipe book to her daughter Andrea.[25] Using that diminutive orange notebook as her cooking foundation, Andrea Nguyễn forged ahead to write what would be her first of many stellar Vietnamese cookbooks.

My mother Dũng also has a recipe book that she safeguards inside a cluttered and dusty office desk inside our two-car garage, which has been transformed into a makeshift nhà bếp. Her recipe book is fairly thin, and her recipes are not an exact science. Recipes are not typically written down but remembered and improvised through memory and oral history. However, what is atypical is the fact that my mother has a recipe book of her own. Penning recipes inside a small notebook is an uncommon practice among Vietnamese home cooks. My mother's slender recipe book contains approximately forty (and counting) of her recipes. These recipes for traditional Vietnamese meals are mostly simplistic, not quixotic, and require only a handful of ingredients. The instructions are rather straightforward, but some are incomplete, indicating that she prefers to prepare some dishes from rote memory. For baking, my mother uses her recipe book. However, for cooking traditional Vietnamese dishes, she relies on her memory and instincts. When preparing a new dish, she resorts to trial and error and cooking intuition. Sometimes, she watches cooking shows aired on Houston's PBS station to observe and learn from other chefs and cooks. [26]

My mother's recipe instructions are written in her own language of cooking. For instance, instead of specifically marking the exact measurements for each ingredient in a meal recipe, she adequately lists the numerical equivalence measured in preparation to other ingredients: one part this, two parts that, and four parts other, to get an idea. Such an inexactness does not betray her taste for cooking. Rather, her recipe instructions are suitable and comfortable to her as a home cook, a working mother of more than thirty-five years, and now a retiree. The recipes are her own language for cooking delicious, healthy Vietnamese meals daily. It is a language that she understands and is familiar with, a jarring contrast to her experience of being forcibly uprooted to live in the United States, speaking little English and not knowing much about American mainstream culture. My mother's recipe book is a foodway artifact that allows her to retain a part of her Vietnamese culture, identity, and own way of cooking.

My mother is not alone on how she portions her ingredients. Andrea Nguyễn argues, "Traditional Vietnamese cooking measurements are impressionistic. People measure by the rice bowl, handful, and odd-sized spoon. While that approach has its charm and pushes you to cook intuitively, it provides little practical guidance for anyone unfamiliar with the cuisine and culture."[27] Helene An, executive chef of the famed Crustacean Restaurant in Beverly Hills, California, and her daughter, Jacqueline An, share Andrea's sentiments on recording recipes, or the lack of, by Vietnamese home cooks. Jacqueline An claims, "Traditionally in Vietnam, recipes are not written down. Instead, they are passed along orally. You learn from your mother and your aunt and your sister who learned from theirs."[28] The Ans elaborate further, noting, "Vietnamese cooking is also unscientific and decidedly forgiving, a blessing to both the inexperienced and the perpetually busy cook. Unlike in baking, the measurements don't have to be precise. Everyday meal preparation is about throwing together whatever you have on hand in the kitchen, mixing and matching flavor profiles to make almost anything work. The heart of Vietnamese cooking isn't all

rolling and steaming, it's a light stir fry in a good, homemade stock that pairs different proteins with fresh vegetables in whatever ratio you prefer."[29] Cookbook author
and food writer, Ann Lê, reaffirms the Ans' comment on the lack of written recipes, and she adds the importance of having them written in a cookbook to preserve
Vietnamese foodways. Lê states that Vietnamese cuisine "is a cuisine with recipes
that are never written down, but ingrained in memory."[30] Houstonian Christine Ha,
executive chef of The Blind Goat Restaurant, cookbook author, and winner of
Gordon Ramsey's *Master Chef*, season 3, poignantly recollects her mother's cooking: "My mama never used recipes, so when she passed away, I had only my memory
and senses to re-create her delicious food. . . . In the years following her death, I
made many attempts to reproduce the dishes she seemed to pull together without
thinking, and I botched most of them. But I refused to give in and ultimately found
my way to some of my childhood favorites."[31]

FINDING HOME IN THE VIETNAMESE KITCHEN

Even before the kitchen became a centerpiece of the twenty-first century modern
home, the nhà bếp has always been integral to the Vietnamese household. One key
difference is that, for many Vietnamese home cooks, they like to utilize two kitchens
whenever feasible to save time, with the second nhà bếp sometimes used more frequently than the main kitchen in the home. The second nhà bếp could be constructed in the backyard, right outside of the actual house; it could be a makeshift
kitchen in the garage or patio; or there could be a backyard toolshed that doubles up
as a kitchen. Why have more than one kitchen or cooking station? One reason is that
having an alternative nhà bếp grants the Vietnamese home cook the flexibility and
utility to make several Vietnamese dishes for a four-course, balanced meal for the
family, or create a more extravagant dinner for a large gathering or special occasion.

My mother Dũng still cooks Vietnamese food utilizing two kitchens, with the
second nhà bếp stationed in their transformed and repurposed two-car garage. My
parents retrofitted their garage to expand their living and cooking quarters. Even
before, the garage was where they once operated their own machinery to run their
print business. My mother manages the garage as her second kitchen, mainly to boil,
steam, and stir fry an array of Vietnamese dishes. The meal preparations range from
frying Texas Gulf Coast shrimp to sautéing crab to making a variety of soup dishes
and so forth. In fact, she cooks in her garage kitchen more frequently than in the
built-in kitchen of their 1,400-square foot home that was constructed from the late
1960s. She also prefers to prep meals and cook in her garage kitchen so that the rest

of the house will not be overwhelmed by the smell of cooked food. "Để nó sẽ không hôi nhà (so it won't smell up the house)," she says.[32] My mother also likes the ability to choose a kitchen, or even operate from both kitchens when she is cooking for a large party or making more intricate and time-consuming Vietnamese dishes. Her garage kitchen is furnished with a stove with four burners, a toaster oven, a deep fryer, and a chopping table. In addition to having two kitchens, my mother also has an extra freezer in the garage to store a variety of seafood and meats. For many Vietnamese American home cooks, it is not unusual to see more than one kitchen and/or freezer inside their house.

Trần Thị Lừng concurs with my mother on frying food outside the house instead of inside the home: "Yeah, when [you have] a new house like we have [in Việt Nam], they don't want the house [to] smell. That smell is bad for the house. And they make a little, like a shed, a small one. And they cook outside."[33] As for her house in Grand Prairie, Texas, she explains, "I have a gas stove outside [on the patio]. When I fry fish . . . then I put it over there [outdoor gas stove], I feel better. . . . But lately, I feel old. I don't get out. But I love to cook outside because all the smell stay outside."[34]

Cooking Vietnamese comfort food and preparing familiar dishes at home are not to be taken lightly. For my mom, cooking traditional Vietnamese meals help her remember Việt Nam.[35] Vietnamese American home cooks also find great joy and satisfaction in cooking, where they may express their creativity in making Vietnamese cuisine and share their love and exultation with family and friends through their food. Also, cooking together may be comforting, particularly if a family is grieving over a lost loved one, providing members with some solace, introspect, and peace. Chef Mai Phạm affectionately reflects on the passing of her mother: "Now that Mother was suddenly taken away from us, this house never would be the same. . . . On this day, only three days after her death, my siblings and I and our father gathered in her favorite room to cook a meal in her honor. In truth, it probably was the only thing we wanted to do. . . . When the meal was ready, we followed the Vietnamese custom of placing food on an altar we had made for my mother to remember her and share our lives and meals with her."[36] She ends her stirring tribute with a heart-aching but tender reflection: "As comforting and satisfying as these foods were, in the end it was the rhythms of peeling, chopping and being in the kitchen together that most eased our pain. We realize—more than ever—that food is simply love."[37] For award-winning chefs Christine Ha and Mai Phạm, cooking good Vietnamese food is a daily tribute to the mothers who shaped their lives, in addition to being an outlet for their culinary interests and creativity. Their mothers displayed love and care in their cooking. In return, Chefs Ha and Phạm prepare traditional Vietnamese dishes and create new ones that become foodways to share their memories of and love for their own mothers. Food is love, as my own mom demonstrated when she made bánh chuối chiên and bánh danh for us, even after a long day of work, child-rearing, and household chores.

A VIETNAMESE REPAST: THE IMPORTANCE OF CONSUMING A BALANCED MEAL

As stated before, for a traditional Vietnamese dinner, a four-course meal is customary for a family. Such a four-course meal typically includes rice, a soup, a vegetable entrée, and a meat dish for the entire family to share together. Sometimes dessert, often a fruit serving, is offered and eaten at the dining table. Tracing Vietnamese food history, Vũ Hồng Liên describes a typical, multicourse, balanced Vietnamese dinner from the mid-twentieth century: "The ordinary Vietnamese meal started with appetizers and then soup, meat or fish, vegetables and/or salad, and rice—all served at the same time—followed by fruit, sweets, and tea."[38] Thus, a Vietnamese dinner commonly resembles a balanced meal with several dishes for the entire family to share.

On the topic of dining habits of Vietnamese diasporans, author Claudia Kolker writes, "The Vietnamese template for dinner is also considerably more involved than the American one. Always, for instance, the meal must include a clear soup and steamed rice. There should be crisp vegetables, savory protein, tart pickles, or salad. And rather than one hunk of protein per diner, meat or fish must be hand-chopped to bite-size chunks."[39] For Vietnamese American families, such a four-course meal represents a balanced and healthy diet that is crucial to their health and wellness. Also, the traditional four-course dinner allows the Vietnamese American family to maintain and continue their own foodways. In addition, regaining their own foodways give Vietnamese Americans the opportunity to garner and extend their own food sovereignty, offering a control over what foods they secure, prepare, and consume.

Kolker sat down with Đại Huỳnh, Houston food writer, journalist, and gourmand, for a Vietnamese meal at a cơm tháng (monthly rice) home-cooked food delivery business. Huỳnh says, "Vietnamese food is all about texture and contrast. . . . Every meal, including *com thang*, has to include dishes that are salty, sour, crunchy, and soupy. So . . . the sour part of the meal is this mix of fresh sprouts and pickled spinach. . . . My mom used to make it and preserve it in a big jar on our counter."[40] Helene and Jacqueline An reiterate the need to balance the flavors in Vietnamese food. They explain that Vietnamese cuisine is all about balance. It is not too salty, too sweet, too spicy, too oily, or too filling. It is not 'too' anything. It is balanced for flavor with a subtle blend of sweet, salty, and umami, the fifth, secret savory taste. It is balanced for the seasons, highlighting what's fresh and locally available alongside preserved foods from previous harvests. And it is balanced for the body, employing ingredients that work together for optimum digestion and wellness."[41] Chef Mai Phạm also stresses the importance of balanced, layered flavors in Vietnamese cooking: "Flavors are built on several levels—by layering meat or seafood with starch and fresh herbs, by contrasting the hot with the cool, the soft with the crunchy, and by using dipping sauces and condiments to blend them all together on a plate or in a bowl."[42] As a result, quality Vietnamese cuisine not only contains a plethora of varied and tasty dishes, but also typically requires a balance of flavors and textures that, when combined for a household meal, adds up to an irresistible, delicious, and healthy gastronomic experience. The simplicity of mixing a symphony of ingredients, leads to a rich complexity of balanced flavors. This is the enchanting sensory experience that good, home-cooked, traditional Vietnamese food combined with fresh herbs, garnish, and ingredients delivers.

No doubt, vegetables, fruits, and herbs occupy a sizable portion of each meal, and the visual spectrum displayed on the dining table signifies their importance to the Vietnamese daily diet and consumption. Chef Phạm states, "Unlike the European approach of blending and harmonizing ingredients as one sees in slow braises or sauce reductions, the Vietnamese prefer to cook by layering flavors, textures and temperatures so that the ingredients remain separate and distinct. Take *pho bo*, for example. The noodles and broth provide substance and by themselves the flavors are rather delicate. However, when eaten with fresh herbs, chilies and limes, the flavors are immediately transformed, becoming spicy, aromatic and tangy all at the same time."[43] She illustrates her point with another great example: "Picture another scenario at a typical multiple-course family meal: simmered ginger chicken, which is fairly well seasoned, is served with a delicately flavored soup, a steamed vegetable dish, a stir fry and some steamed unsalted rice. But the meal isn't quite complete without a platter of fresh herbs and a bowl of spicy salty fish dipping sauce to tie together all the flavors. For the cook, the ultimate aim is to present the diner with a feast of contrasts across the entire meal, as well as with each bite."[44]

Chef Mai Phạm also reflects on her early days of owning and managing Lemon Grass, her first restaurant in Sacramento, California, looking for fresh herbs such as tía tô (perilla) and Vietnamese rau mùi (coriander): "Looking back, it was really the availability of these herbs that most influenced the cooking that I do. When I opened the restaurant in 1988, I'd wanted to feature fresh herbs and Asian greens, but supply was limited. . . . And sometimes when I get the chance to talk to a customer about the herbs, how you should eat them, and, of course how we got them, they invariably ask where they can buy them. But even better is when they ask if they can take some sprigs home and root them in water."[45]

Andrea Nguyễn also mentions the noticeable presence of greens and vegetables on the dining table that adorn a family meal: "One of the distinctive aspects of eating Vietnamese food is the large plate of lettuce and herbs that accompanies many grilled and fried dishes. . . . For example, sizzling crepes would be incomplete without the texture, flavor, and color of the lettuce, herbs, and cucumber that arrive with them. It is the final layering of cooked and raw ingredients that contributes to the uniqueness of Vietnamese food."[46] On what is typically consumed for dinner, Helene and Jacqueline An concur that "Vietnamese meals always include a vegetable side dish—whether raw or steamed, stir-fried or pickled."[47] Cookbook author Ann Lê echoes their sentiment. She writes,

> The Vietnamese pride themselves in cuisine that uses only the freshest ingredients—a principle applicable to everything from produce to seafood. Fresh herbs and vegetables play a pivotal role in the dining experience. From the citrusy, cumin-flavored rice paddy herb to the licorice and cinnamon tastes of the perilla leaf, herbs wrap a second layer of flavor around the food they adorn. Fresh produce is also important to help achieve the contrast of textures that Vietnamese cuisine is known for. Crunchy, crispy, al dente textures derived from vegetables and fruits make all the difference to otherwise simple dishes. The ubiquitous salad platter consists of sliced or julienned cucumbers, green or red leaf lettuce, bean sprouts, sprigs of mint, coriander, Thai basil, and whatever else the local garden yields.[48]

Lê further explains that "Garnishes are important for taste as well as presentation. It is common to garnish a dish with some fresh herbs like mint, cilantro, or parsley, or to top off a dish with crushed peanuts, chopped scallion rings, or fried shallots or garlic. These final touches add a layer of fragrance, flavor, or texture. Whole Thai bird chiles are also added as a garnish for the sake of appearance; most people, however, can manage only a few bites of one chile at a meal."[49]

Of course, vegetables and fruits are essential and healthy to anyone's daily nutritional intake. Vegetable soups as part of the main course and plated fruits as desserts represent a quintessential balanced meal for Vietnamese Americans. Fresh, raw ingredients of herbs, vegetables, and fruits are desired for a healthy, delicious, and balanced meal of Vietnamese comfort food. For Houstonian Trung Đoàn, his wife and children consume traditional Vietnamese food on a daily basis.[50] Trung describes how they "make vegetable soup almost every day, some kind of vegetable made into a soup . . . and then we eat a lot of rice at home. And when we do eat meat, it's normally a small serving of salty meat of some sort."[51] Houstonian Lê Phú Nhuận considers himself half Vietnamese and half American. "I am half and half. You know I grew up in Vietnam. Forty-three years. Then I came here about less than forty years. Not equal. Even the,—my way of life now is kind of American way. But the other side, I still have some way of uh, Vietnamese culture. The food I eat, vegetable I eat, you cannot eat . . . [referring to his native-born American interviewer] so strong."[52] Michelle Trần, another native Houstonian, asserts, "We Vietnamese so we eat rice we don't eat bread every day. We eat rice. We don't eat hamburger. So we eat . . . fried rice, regular rice and fruit, vegetable, and soup you know for dinner."[53]

Not surprisingly, fruits, herbs, and vegetables are essential in the Vietnamese diet and family meal setting. For người Việt (Vietnamese people), greens, vegetables, and fruits are indeed vital to their daily food consumption, offering a balanced diet consisting fresh ingredients and garnishes with great nutritional value, as well as an opportunity to display diverse Vietnamese dishes with unique flavors and textures. In addition, fresh produce help bring a family together over a delicious, home-cooked meal, helping them bond when they consume traditional Vietnamese comfort food and taste the herbs, vegetables, and fruits plucked from their own home garden. Andrea Nguyễn feels her heritage is rooted in food, saying "Ultimately my parents were successful in educating us about our heritage through food. Most of what I know about Vietnamese culture and history evolved from exploring the country's culinary traditions."[54] These in-between or liminal spaces that have become home gardens are where Vietnamese food culture is sustained. Home gardens are "movable" gardens, from Việt Nam to refugee camps to Vietnamese diasporic communities throughout the United States. The soil, climate, and temperature may change, but because the garden exists the culture persists and lives on in the stories and memories that are cultivated and guided by the hands of Vietnamese American home gardeners.

A VIETNAMESE FOOD RITUAL: THE IMPORTANCE OF FARM- AND GARDEN-TO-TABLE PRAXIS

Microfarms remain ubiquitous at Thái Xuân Village, Thanh Tâm Village, St. Joseph Village, and other Vietnamese village communities that dot the urban landscapes of southeast Houston. A significant number of Vietnamese Texans in the Greater

Houston and DFW metropolitan areas continue to cultivate their own home gardens of herbs, vegetables, flowers, and fruit trees. The produce and the product of their labor extends to their kitchen table (or two), where the magic arises from a Vietnamese home cook's nhà bếp. When the cooking is finished, the multidish, multidimensional flavored meal is served on the dining table set for family members. Before loved ones devour the multicourse dinner, children pay respect and deference to their elders or guests (grandparents, aunts, and uncles) and then to their parents, by politely inviting them and saying "mời [parent, relative, or guest] ăn cơm"; this figure of speech can be interpreted as "please eat first." The parents, relative, or guest then acknowledges the presence of younger ones and responds, "Con ăn đi," or "you may now eat." It is a minor ritual, yet nevertheless, it displays the importance of a family meal eaten together while establishing a family hierarchy where children demonstrate their respect to their parents, elders, relatives, and guests. Such a meal is consumed and celebrated together, representing time and effort well spent. Plus, such a ritual gives homage and thanks to the home cook and provider of the family meal.

Dining protocol is commonly practiced and followed in Vietnamese households that dine together as a family. Dinner is crucial family time, and remains so for many Vietnamese American families today. Andrea Nguyễn observes, "Traditional eating practices were always followed at the table. . . . A meal wasn't only about filling our bellies, but also about weaving elegance, refinement, and tradition into what was otherwise a modest situation."[55] Ann Lê asserts that "food is an important part of the Vietnamese culture. It represents the time for families to be together after a busy day, and it is the principle component of celebrations and festivals."[56] She also believes that dinner is the most important meal of the day because it is when a family comes together and dine on a healthy, balanced four-course meal.[57] For the Vietnamese American family, sitting down for dinner together is cherished not only as a crucial daily routine, but the ritual also helps the family retain their Vietnamese foodways through sharing food, conversation, and quality time together. Trần Thị Lừng elaborates on why Vietnamese people find it important for their family to sit together and feast over a home-cooked meal: "They're (Vietnamese) so proud they say to tell to friends, 'My family always sit down together to eat.' That means they have a happy family."[58]

Home gardens provide Vietnamese Americans another physical and tangible safe haven in the United States. They also help build a social community of like-minded individuals with similar shared experiences. Home gardens help raise, nurture, and feed Vietnamese American families. These foodways give Vietnamese diasporans an opportunity and time to remember, rebuild, maintain, strengthen, cherish, celebrate, and share their heritage in spite of the past and current anti-Asian racism, anti-refugee nativism, anti-immigrant xenophobia, and the lingering negative sentiments tied to an unpopular war. Food identity and culture are not superfluous but rather unique, dynamic, and essential. Food scholar, freelance writer, and magazine editor David Leftwich remarks on the significance of the countless intersections of food and culture in Houston's expansive food scene. He offers a great question, "You may go and eat the food and that's good, that's the first step, but are you understanding more about why a particular culture came here?"[59] He quickly zeros in on the answer: "Food is one of the first and last things a culture hangs on to, if that makes sense."[60] In other words, our Vietnamese food represents người Việt, and người Việt are represented in our food. Familiar produce, cooking techniques, dining rituals, and home-cooked meals allow displaced Vietnamese refugees and immigrants to stay alive, literally and figuratively. Food gives us hope, warmth, comfort, community, nourishment, and a sense of security and achievement. Food emancipates us.[61] Food also democratizes us, giving us a chance to have a seat at the table, figuratively and literally, and commune for a meal together.

Some Vietnamese American chefs and home cooks praise Vietnamese food as the "original" farm-to-table cuisine. For instance, Helene and Jacqueline An believe that "true Vietnamese food is based on simply mixing good meat, especially lean seafood, with lots of fresh vegetables. Typically, food is cooked in water or broth instead of oil. Flavor comes from aromatic herbs rather than heavy sauces. Vietnamese cooking is organic, paleo, and naturally gluten-free—the original farm-to-table cuisine."[62] Whether original or not (since many other notable, delectable, and multifaceted cuisines from around the globe could also stake such a claim), in Vietnamese food preparation has always been farm-to-table, well before the term was introduced in the English language or became a fashionable practice in the twenty-first century. The farm- and garden-to-table praxis in Vietnamese culinary culture extends beyond the microfarms of a specific village or any person's home garden. Such culinary practices are also preserved through the ingredients, recipes, cookbooks, kitchens, makeshift cooking stations, and dining etiquette that families practice when they gather together for a meal full of their own unique rituals. It is a way of living healthily together. The fresh produce, essential ingredients, mixing of diverse tastes and complex flavors, and meal preparation strategies of Vietnamese cuisine necessitate a farm- and garden-to-table praxis. Whether deliberately or not, Vietnamese gastronomy—from cultivating home gardens to preserving cooking techniques to embracing familial dining—lend itself to farm- and garden-to-table customs that aid Vietnamese diasporans in preserving their food heritage. It is also a celebration of their survival—a feast that speaks, "I have made it, and I am alive."

Sociologist Michéle Companion asserts that "consumption patterns are a form of cultural capital. Cultural capital refers to sets of knowledge, skills, and behaviors that enable individuals to embed themselves in specific subcultures and be recognized as members of that group. Cultural capital is also expressed through the explicit rejection of assimilative forces and reaffirmation of Indigenous identity through food."[63] While studying the impact of urban gardening upon Native American cultural continuity, Companion observes that gardens create positive spaces for Native American gardeners by imbuing them with greater purpose and direction, providing them a sense of accomplishment, and empowering them personally and socially.[64] She concludes that Native American home cooks and gardeners transmit personal and cultural knowledge with their own cooking of traditional meals in much the same way that Vietnamese gardeners do. For Native American home cooks and gardeners, food serves as a catalyst for a family to discuss and share their memories of food preparation techniques, unique recipes, or cultural traditions.[65]

Vietnamese diasporans cultivating microfarms and home gardens may seem insignificant, but to the growers, procurers, makers, purveyors, and servers of these unique cultural dishes the aforementioned activities revolving around food are no small feat. They go beyond filling bellies and are acts filled with pleasure and joy. Scholar Erica Peters writes, "In these endeavors to determine when people ate particular foods and why, the field of food studies is deeply indebted to the work of French sociologist Pierre Bourdieu on taste in daily life. In his seminal work, *Distinction*, Bourdieu showed how people do not choose their diet and other daily practices in a vacuum; they learn from their families and social environments the appropriate foods and other essentials for their station in life."[66]

Growing, gathering, and prepping food is strenuous and tedious labor. Choosing to remember, preserve, and act upon traditional ways of making Vietnamese food is uniquely political. Food politics go beyond the home gardens, makeshift kitchens, and daily gathering; the struggles to retain and extend such culinary traditions are critical to constructing the memory and post-memory of what constitutes Vietnamese cuisine. The planting, growth, and procurement of vegetables, herbs, and fruits, along with reviving, practicing, and maintaining traditional cooking techniques, recipes, dishes, and dining customs are all crucial to the Vietnamese diasporic community and their emancipatory foodways. Especially in Texas, where the third and fourth largest Vietnamese American communities reside, such food preservation politics demonstrate an integral part of preserving culture and heritage.

The preservation of Vietnamese heritage in Texas endures via foodways, not just as an ode to Việt Nam, but also as a way to connect different cultures. Food politics recognizes the growing influences of America on Vietnamese food *and* the influence of Vietnamese food on of Texan, Tex-Mex, Cajun, and Southern cuisines. Such new and exciting foodways are expanding boundaries and elevating palates, thanks to the creativity and inventiveness of Vietnamese Texan chefs, home cooks, gardeners, and restaurateurs. For a refugee or an immigrant, America is their wilderness, not to adopt or master, but to grow and live with, to accept and nurture, to preserve their culinary landscape and heritage. For the first peoples, America is their home, and we, the colonial settlers, must too cherish, protect, and enhance their culinary landscape and heritage if our very own foodways are to survive.

VIETNAMESE FOOD ON THE SOUTHERN TABLE: PRESERVATION AND EXPANSION OF VIETNAMESE CUISINE IN THE SOUTH

> *To abandon immigrant food traditions for the foods of Americans was to abandon community, family, and religion, at least in the minds of many immigrants.*
>
> —Donna R. Gabaccia, from *We Are What We Eat*

My Vietnamese refugee parents and siblings and I still celebrate an original—but historically inaccurate in its reenactment and retelling—American holiday known as Thanksgiving. Growing up, every fourth Thursday of November, my parents would create their humble version of a Thanksgiving meal. With limited means and knowledge of how to prepare an American Thanksgiving feast, my mother would cook traditional Thanksgiving sides such as yellow corn (whole or frozen kernels) and mashed potatoes from a box. In lieu of a five-pound Thanksgiving turkey as the main course, my parents prepared a dish that they would call gà hộp lo,[67] or roast peppered chicken, with miến (clear glass noodles), chopped mushrooms, and cilantro as the "stuffing." At first glance, gà hộp lo is a bizarre-looking dish, and it definitely does not rekindle one's nostalgia for a traditional American Thanksgiving feast. Yet, my siblings and I fell in love with this impostor substitute for a golden brown, succulent, and juice-dripping turkey. My parents took turns cutting the chicken and made sure that their four children would have enough faux "turkey" on their plates. To make the meal last, we added a starch to our Thanksgiving repast:

Sunbeam white bread. And if we were fortuitous, my parents would cook *two* gà hộp lo for Thanksgiving dinner, which was a rare treat. Such an occasion was a glorious and sumptuous meal for our working-class, refugee family. I did not realize it at the time, but my parents were making their own Vietnamese version of a Thanksgiving meal to celebrate a traditional American holiday. They resorted to Vietnamese food-ways to make their own American feast for us to enjoy.

As stated before, food effectively democratizes us. Consider a potluck dinner: food serves as an equalizer wherein everyone brings her or his own dish to contribute to a colorful, mosaic repast. Each person can come to the table and be seated next to one another, facing others, to consume a home-cooked meal together and converse with one another: hosts with guests, cooks with diners, and friends with strangers. Food draws us to the dining table and gifts us the precious moments to share our food, our thoughts, our stories, and our lives. These are some of life's comforting moments we cherish, live for, and remember, no matter how foreign or familiar the meal may appear.

For the remainder of the chapter, I analyze how Vietnamese Texans manage to preserve and expand their food culture by not only using their homegrown herbs, vegetables, and fruit trees to cook Vietnamese dishes, but also how they utilize their home gardens to cultivate crops that are commonly grown in Texas and the US South, thanks to the warm weather and long, sweltering summer days similar to Việt Nam's climate. Taking advantage of the warm climate and extended growing season, Vietnamese Texans plant not just the produce cherished and commonly grown in Việt Nam, but they also grow cây đào (peach trees), đậu bắp, rau đắng, and ớt; produce that is typically cultivated and consumed in Texas and the US South. Such produce may have been familiar to Vietnamese refugees and immigrants before they resettled in Texas, but they grow them here in abundance and use them as essential ingredients to make or complement Vietnamese dishes. In addition, Vietnamese Texan home cooks and chefs apply their artistry and creativity to come up with new twists on Vietnamese food, while still retaining the tastes, textures, and smells that Vietnamese consumers come to expect. Consequently, new hybrid cuisines and gastronomic delights are made by and served to younger generations of Vietnamese Texans, while still catering to the palates of the first generation of refugees and immigrants.

Oftentimes, it starts with the home garden and a wide range of crops. As previously stated, Vietnamese Texans who live in villages and homes located in working-class neighborhoods of southeast Houston demonstrate an ethos to match their socioeconomic status: resourceful, resilient, savvy, creative, and diligent. The hard-working Vietnamese diasporans who reside here demonstrate how their home gardens bloom, produce, and thrive under the hot, sweltering, and long Texas summers. Preserving their home gardens, and in turn, their culture and tight-knit community, are necessary ingredients to their working-class ethos and livelihood.

Even though it seems a thing of the past, the Việt Nam War still looms large in the minds and hearts of the Vietnamese diaspora. No doubt, they could never completely extricate themselves from that deadly conflict nor the brutality, depravity, destruction, and uprootedness it caused. One path to unpackage the memories of conflict, refuge, and resettlement is to construct, maintain, and control foodways to ease their post-war trauma and pain, preserve Vietnamese culinary heritage, and build a supportive community. These foodways include a connection to the Texas soil, and highlight their working-class ethos, their ingenuity, and their "make do" attitude in the face of uncertainty and capital scarcity. A symbiotic culinary connection emerges in the places where refugees settle, and such gastronomical marriages and offspring of divergent cuisines are not unusual in history. In fact, they occur rather frequently, even in Vietnamese refugee history. As noted historian Donna R. Gabaccia points out, "Culinary Americanization work now more often emphasizes immigrant gifts and cross-cultural communication than the benefits of American food."[68] As an example, Gabaccia describes how:

> In a YMCA program for refugees at Eglin Air Force Base in Florida in spring and summer 1975, newcomers from Southeast Asia received instead a quick introduction to ethnic pride, American style. YMCA workers encouraged the refugees to produce a cookbook (*Happy in My Stomach: Toi Vui Trong Long*) as "one way of building a bridge of understanding" between the two cultures. Social workers with low-income clients planned a cooking school for Vietnamese and attempted to show their clients how to prepare American and Vietnamese-style meals on a limited budget, but their guidebook urged them to "remember the importance of fellowship," for cooking "brings people together for both learning and fellowship."[69]

Jill Nhu Hương Miller composed an English-language Vietnamese cookbook, first published in 1968, at the height of the Việt Nam War. She examines the historical and polycultural influences that characterize the buoyancy of Vietnamese gastronomy: "Vietnamese food has its own special character, as do most regional foods.

Though it has been much influenced by Chinese cooking through many centuries, it still retains its own individuality. Chinese and Japanese food especially are often darker in color because of the extensive use of soy sauce for seasoning. Since fish sauce is used for seasoning in Vietnam, the food retains more of its natural color. . . . Indian, Malay, and French cooking have also had some slight influence on Vietnamese regional recipes, and Buddhist vegetarian cookery has been well-known there for a long time. The combination makes for an endless variety of dishes."[70] Food, wine, and travel, and Houston-based journalist Mai Phạm (not to be confused with California chef, cookbook author, and restaurateur Mai Phạm) agrees that when the first wave of Vietnamese refugees resettled in the United States and made their secondary migration to Houston in the mid- and late 1970s, they brought with them the diverse traditions of Vietnamese gastronomy along with culinary elements of French, Chinese, and Southeast Asian influences.[71] Not surprisingly, Vietnamese food transformed preexisting cuisines in Texas and vice versa. A diverse culinary repertoire emerged, thanks to the influences of Tex-Mex, Cajun, and Southern cuisines. Mixing regional and international gastronomical influences to create new Vietnamese dishes is not uncommon at all in Vietnamese culinary history. The same could be said of Asian immigrant and refugee home cooks and chefs in the United States, who blend and combine the unique flavors and textures of their foods with the ever-changing, mosaic foodways that make up the American cuisine.

COMPLEXITIES, CHALLENGES, AND CREATIONS OF ASIAN FOODWAYS IN AMERICA

Asian American studies scholar Robert Ji-Song Ku asserts that "Asian Americans have always been and continue to be emblematic of the unassimilable American, not only in body politic but in gastronomic culture as well. Asian food is America's culinary stepchild, technically part of the family but never quite entirely. This, however, does not mean that it isn't good to think—or eat."[72] Donna R. Gabaccia has also written about immigrants and racial minorities and the importance they place on preserving their own food heritage; she reasons that "they mourned a different history from that of the mainstream, notably the losses—of culture, community and identity—they had experienced by voluntarily (or in some cases involuntarily) becoming part of the national group. For these new ethnics, the task at hand was to undo the cultural effects of three generations of assimilation. Not surprisingly, food became an integral part of that effort."[73] Similarly, Historian Yong Chen comments on how Chinese immigrants have created "home" in America: "In the minds of these early Chinese immigrants and others, home represented not only a physical location but the way things used to be in the pre-emigration world as well. While living in the United States, therefore, Chinese Americans also tried to re-create a physical and cultural space that they could call home. In doing so, they formed Chinatowns, transplanted and supported their cuisine, articulated the meaning of Chinese food, and affirmed their identity as Chinese Americans."[74]

Regarding Asian Americans cuisines, Martin F. Manalansan IV argues that "Asian Americans' relationship with the material and symbolic aspects of food is part of their continuing marginal and abject status in the American cultural imaginary."[75] He perceives the detrimental and reductive ways that Asian Americans are symbolically and stereotypically linked to food: "Media consumption of Asian American culinary alterity need not be seen only in terms of contemporary orientalist fantasies and desires. There is a need to better understand how the so-called objects of these desires are actually active agents in reading and interpreting these mass media cultural productions."[76]

Historically, Asian American chefs cooking their own respective ethnic cuisines often had to painstakingly "re-authenticate" their traditional meals to take control of their foodways and reclaim their culinary spaces by eschewing what was previously considered "their" cuisine—a cuisine that had been Americanized, marginalized, commodified, and appropriated over time to suit the mainstream palates of the day. Historian Mark Padoongpatt is astute in his assertion that "unlike white chefs, chefs of color do not have unbridled freedom to serve street-style or 'authentic' dishes with obscure ingredients for US consumers, because their food is, as it always has been, associated with their bodies. Due to the history of food and racialization in America, chefs of color must refine dishes (yet keep them exotic and different) to not only make them more palatable but to shield themselves and their communities from being labeled as disgusting, diseased, and not fully human. The kinds of dishes they serve have real consequences on how society views and treats them as people—not just as chefs."[77] Padoongpatt further argues, "Sensory experiences with cuisine are critical to processes of racialization in that they, in often visceral and emotional ways, draw boundaries around food and the people who cook and eat the food, distinguish between the foreign and the familiar, link cuisine and individuals to places, and inscribe relations of power onto plates and bodies."[78] Distinguished sociologist Linda Trinh Võ notes that this is changing as "a younger generation of Vietnamese American food entrepreneurs is transforming the industry using family recipes or knowledge acquired from commercial ventures but infusing them with their own creations and aesthetics and catering to a wide range of devoted fans."[79] Both Padoongpatt and Võ recognize that cuisines do not exist in a vacuum. In fact, they are constantly evolving, fusing the old flavors, textures, and tastes with the new. Home cooks, chefs, and restaurateurs may incorporate family recipes and utilize familiar tastes, but they also use their creativity and artistry to create not only new recipes and tastes but also expand foodways, especially those from marginalized populaces such as Thai, Vietnamese, and other Asian Pacific Americans.

Vietnamese American home gardeners, cooks, and chefs who tend and nurture their carefully cultivated herbs, fruits, and vegetables not only nourish themselves but also impose their own free will to dictate meaningful Vietnamese foodways that indelibly connect them to *their* Việt Nam. Empowered through gardening, Vietnamese diasporans control and leverage better terms (and healthier ingredients) for what they grow, cook, and consume, in addition to more elegantly defining who they are, where they are from, and why they are here. Thus, such gardening practices are democratic processes that help protect Vietnamese foodways in America, rendering the cultivation of familiar produce and the cooking of traditional Vietnamese dishes more readily available, accessible, affordable, and ubiquitous for Vietnamese diasporans. Home gardens and produce also help emancipate them from their past and present distresses of war, displacement, migration, ostracization, and racialization.

Sizable Vietnamese American populaces exist throughout Texas in cities such as Houston, Dallas, Austin, Amarillo, Arlington, Garland, and Haltom City, and in Gulf Coast communities like Port Arthur, Rockport, and Palacios. Not surprisingly, the hybridity of cultures and foods occur constantly and organically in these urban centers and commercial fishing towns. At the same time, such hybrid cultures and cuisines do not necessarily expunge foodways nor disrupt cultural continuities. Instead, the hybridity of cultures and gastronomies may lead to greater awareness, understanding, and enrichment of cultures and cuisines. Thus, we benefit from such intermingling of cultures and foods. Journalist Leah Binkovitz perceptively writes about the late, award-winning author, chef, and food and travel documentarian, Anthony Bourdain: "Food, as Bourdain understood, is thus an expression of survival and resistance, of adaptation and exchange. . . . In his visit here [in Houston], Bourdain didn't just marvel at the diversity but the unique products of it. The food scene here isn't just notable for its wide array of offerings but for its unique creations."[80] Food historian Mark Padoongpatt expands on Bourdain's assessment and asserts that "considering the role of food in struggles for a right to the global city offers a tangible entry point into the way people experience and perceived racialized spaces and a glimpse into the formation of metropolitan identity."[81]

He also rationalizes that food culture gives cities an identity and a sense of self, thanks to restaurants and festivals that act as "edible and sensory markers of multiculturalism, cosmopolitanism, provincialism, and 'All Americanism.'"[82]

Padoongpatt argues that food transcends beyond preserving our cultural heritage; food is also deeply rooted in the political economy.[83] Without a doubt, Vietnamese foodways have contributed to the political economies of Houston, the DFW metroplex, Port Arthur, and other urban areas, as well as small but significant fishing communities along the Texas Gulf Coast. More than preserving food heritage, Vietnamese American home gardeners have raised and produced a plethora of crops that sustain them with healthy food options and allow them to cook dishes that are familiar, comforting, and nurturing for them. Along with home gardeners, Vietnamese American home cooks, restaurateurs, chefs, food purveyors, and those who labor in the seafood industry all play an important role in preserving and expanding Vietnamese foodways. Not only is their labor essential, but they also claim their roots and rights to this American land as they reinforce the connections to both homelands via Vietnamese foodways. Cuisines and cultures are not static. Instead, they flourish and become vibrant, impactful, dynamic, and diversified. The intersections of food and culture are often the crossroads where we live, labor, and linger. The love for our food and culture are evident when we share and exchange them with others. In turn, new foodways are created, experimented with, and explored.

As for having Vietnamese food on the "Southern table," the preservation and expansion of Vietnamese cuisine in the US South must be determined by Vietnamese diasporic home cooks, chefs, restaurateurs, and gardeners themselves, or risk historical erasure and cultural appropriation. Regarding the significant history of African diasporic foodways in preserving, protecting, and expanding Black culture, Michael W. Twitty is clear: "The food is in many cases all we have, all we can go to in order to feel our way into the past. For others, we are an interesting note on the pages of a very different conversation. For African Americans and our allies, food is the gateway into larger conversations about individual and group survival."[84] Twitty perceptively writes about food, history, and race when he says, "It is a lie that food is just fuel. It has always had layers of meaning, and humans for the most part despise meaningless food. In America, and especially the American South, 'race' endures alongside the sociopolitics of food; it is not a stretch to say that race is both on and at the Southern table. But if it is on the table alone we have learned nothing; we continue to reduce each other to stereotypical essences."[85] He further asserts the importance of protecting, preserving, and promoting African cuisines that have been "Southernized" in the United States when he says, "The real history is not in the food, it's in the people. We are working against the loss of our cultural memory; against the consequences of institutional oppression; against indiscriminate and flagrant appropriation; and against courts of public opinion that question our authenticity, maturity, and motives in the revolutionary act of clarifying and owning our past. It is my belief that the very reason we are here in space and time is deliberately connected to our journey with food. The only question I've ever wanted to answer for myself was, 'How was my destiny shaped by the history of Southern food?'"[86] Twitty proposes a crucial, poignant, and valuable question: To what extent, in working against the loss of cultural memory, could African diasporic foodways be remembered and rescued? How can such foodways survive and expand as they work to overcome the destructive cultural genocide brought forth by the ongoing consequences of slavery, Jim Crowism, institutional racism, and cultural appropriation? Twitty's question must be recognized, addressed, and deliberated with meaningful action to combat and reverse the loss of cultural memory.

And how can Vietnamese diasporans prevent the further erosion of the cultural memory as time elapses? How can we preserve, protect, and extend our foodways with the historical baggage of war, refuge, displacement, and marginalization? How does Vietnamese cuisine fit in the rich history and pantheon of Southern food and vice versa? Will Vietnamese food be Southernized extensively as well, or could it be perceived as unique and individual to the US South, *and* as another exemplary gastronomy that can be exchanged, shaped, and shared with other Southern cuisines without being gastronomically homogenized or gentrified? Time will tell.

WHERE VIETNAMESE CUISINE "FITS" IN THE POST-MODERN SOUTH

Akin to Texas Mexican cuisine, Vietnamese food has also evolved over time and in new locales. Vietnamese gastronomy is not static but rather dynamic, and Vietnamese diasporans have brought forth their version of Vietnamese culinary traditions to new shores and elevated Vietnamese comfort food to new heights. Consequently, Vietnamese diasporans strongly influence and shape Vietnamese cuisine in the United States, while introducing their version of Vietnamese food to American palates. Along with rich culinary traditions in the US South, Vietnamese diasporans have added their own flavors, textures, smells, tastes, and garden produce to Southern foodways.

Food scholar Marcie Cohen Ferris writes, "Food stands at the center of Southern history and culture. From the prehistoric South, where Indigenous peoples discovered unparalleled food resources, to the contemporary South, where indus-trial agriculture and small farmers vie for the region's future, food had defined the region for over five centuries. . . . The lives of blacks, whites, and Native Americans intertwined with those of newcomers to the South, and nowhere is this more strongly expressed than in foodways."[87] Arguably, the US South and its people are more well-defined by their own brand of cuisine than in any other region in the country. The planting, kneading, boiling, and frying of Southern cuisine has been centuries in the making, first by the Indigenous peoples of the region, and then by imported African slaves, European colonists, Mexicans, and nineteenth century Southern and Eastern European immigrants and refugees. New ethnic groups have contributed significantly to the continued making and transformation of the ever-expansive Southern gastronomy. Yet, the assimilationist model does not accurately depict Vietnamese Americans and their foodways in Texas and the South.

Food historian Ted Ownby asserts, "Often the experience of immigrants in the midst of nonimmigrants helps establish something as identifiably ethnic food. Cer-tainly people did not eat in the South just as they had eaten somewhere else, but they could continue to contribute a few key ingredients or techniques or emphases, and those keys, identified both by the immigrants and by others, became the way to mark ethnic food."[88] Ownby provides an apt analysis of the culinary contributions of immigrants to Southern cuisine, but also notes that the ethnic cuisines of immi-grants continue to shape and evolve the US South and its gastronomic traditions, even while immigrants establish food sovereignty over their own respective ethnic dishes. Culinary traditions become malleable as they are invented and re-invented: what we eat, why we eat, and how we eat shape us and others. With the arrival of every new immigrant or refugee group and ethnic food introduced, Southern cui-sine changes even as it continues to be transformed from within by multigeneration and first-generation Southerners, further elevating the region's culinary options.

Naturally, as with other culinary traditions, Vietnamese cuisine changes over time. Việt food is dynamic, diverse, and resilient, adopting gastronomic elements from others, yet retaining its core tastes, textures, and scents. Vietnamese cooking traditions remain intact, even as Vietnamese American chefs and home cooks devise creative ways to prepare new Vietnamese dishes or transform them while maintain-ing the cuisine's unique, balanced flavors and essential ingredients. The hybridity of cuisines and cultures actually helps preserve Vietnamese food heritage as long as food praxis remain vibrant, pliable, and expansive for Vietnamese American home gardeners, cooks, chefs, and restaurateurs who experiment and get creative in their mixing of old and the new. Such experimentation and creativity are quite evident in

Texas, where the Global South of Vietnamese gastronomy meets the New(er) South of Southern cuisine. Both Vietnamese and Southern foodways are evolutionary and progressive, while remaining grounded in rich culinary traditions. Reflecting on the troubling history and myriad foodways of the US South, James Beard Award recipient and food scholar John T. Edge observes that "the dishes we have cooked and the meals we have staged have served the region and the nation as emblems of Southern struggles. Conversations about food have offered paths to grasp bigger truths about race and identity, gender and ethnicity, subjugation and creativity. Today, Southern food serves as an American lingua franca. Like the Black Power fist and the magnolia blossom, fried chicken discloses, cornbread suggests, potlikker tells."[89]

During their early resettlement years in the Houston metropolitan area, Vietnamese restaurateurs, chefs, and cooks had to make Vietnamese food more palatable to native-born Americans in order for their restaurant businesses to survive and succeed. Yet, they also needed to ensure that Vietnamese cuisine would not be overly compromised, much like the early Chinese immigrant restaurateurs had to do when they developed dishes such as chop suey, and later chow mein, egg foo yung, and General Tso's chicken for their economic survival.[90] After Vietnamese refugees were relocated throughout the contiguous United States, a large contingent made a secondary migration to Texas, especially Houston. In the first years of living in Houston, Vietnamese restaurateurs needed to make their Vietnamese food more palatable to Houstonians if they wanted to survive and succeed in the restaurant business. Trị La, owner of the historic Kim Son restaurant, rightfully proclaims that "we are proud to say that we were the first restaurant . . . to bring Vietnamese food to the main—to the 'Main Stream [*sic*] American.' So, you know, so that's what we [are] proud to say that."[91] Transforming traditional Vietnamese dishes into flavors, textures, and tastes that are more akin and receptive to non-Vietnamese palates is not a criticism of Kim Son restaurant, but rather it is a statement of perseverance, survival, adaptability, and ingenuity. For Trị La and his refugee family to create and operate a successful business that has remained open since the early 1980s in the highly competitive and labor-intensive restaurant industry is remarkable and nothing short of a miracle. True, most Vietnamese Houstonians may not dine at Kim Son for traditional meals that remind them of their homeland, but arguably Trị and his family have established a successful gateway restaurant that has introduced thousands of non-Vietnamese customers to "Americanized" Vietnamese food. In this way more people begin to learn to appreciate the textures, flavors, smells, herbs, fruits, and greens that come with traditional Vietnamese food.

Claudia Kolker deftly explains why some early Vietnamese restaurateurs took a more practical approach to ensure that their businesses would have a chance of survival. "Kim Son is a really good example," she says. "Kim Son is this entry level Vietnamese food restaurant for a lot of people who don't have contact with the Vietnamese community, and it's absolutely delicious and it was . . . it was strategized to be accessible to Americans. So sweeter, less fish sauce, less fire to it. And . . . I'm not sure if they've changed that, but many people adore that."[92] Kolker also discusses the growing changes in Houstonians' palates for more traditional Vietnamese entrées, condiments, and garnishes: "But then people became more and more foodies and connoisseurs and then . . . and a lot of people then branched out to their noodle shops. And they branched out places like Huỳnh [Restaurant], which is just . . . a little bit more . . . Vietnamese style I would say. Less designed for American palates, probably still as not as exactly what you would find in Vietnam. But Houstonians really love Vietnamese food, and . . . they have taken on an identity in the past twenty years as being an adventurous foodie city. So that's the other thing . . . the presence of all immigrants and refugees in Houston have changed Houstonians' perceptions of themselves."

Đại Huỳnh also perceives a pattern that emerged in Vietnamese restaurants by the early 2000s, especially with the emergence of Vietnamese American chefs, entrepreneurs, and restaurateurs from the 1.5 generation and second generation of refugees and immigrants. In the beginning of their resettlement in Houston, Vietnamese refugees opened restaurants as a vehicle to make a living here in America, as a means of postwar survival.[93] According to Huỳnh, many Vietnamese arrivals got their start in the restaurant business because it required very little English skills to run a Vietnamese restaurant. In the late 1970s and early 1980s, Vietnamese restaurateurs served a mostly Vietnamese clientele and therefore did not have to be fluent in English.[94] As they felt comfortable speaking in their native tongue, Vietnamese entrepreneurs also managed to attract a healthy number of customers because their restaurants tended to be inexpensive and have menus that included a diverse number of dishes to satisfy the palates of their fellow Vietnamese in addition to a new clientele.

However, in recent decades, the 1.5 generation and second generation of Vietnamese Houstonians are involved in the restaurant business because they see an economic *opportunity* and not an economic *necessity*, the way the previous generation of Vietnamese restaurateurs did. According to Huỳnh, the first generation of Vietnamese restaurant owners, if they had a choice, "probably would not open up a restaurant since many were not in the restaurant business in Viet Nam." However, the 1.5 generation and second generation of Vietnamese American chefs and home cooks look to the restaurant business as a career choice and vehicle for upward economic mobility.

Since the mid-1990s, a new generation of Vietnamese American entrepreneurs have built modern Vietnamese restaurants similar to those in New York and San Francisco where patrons are not hesitant to spend more of their disposable income on Vietnamese cuisine. In Texas, Vietnamese restaurants are no longer just places for cheap eats. The entrepreneurial maturation and clout of the 1.5 generation, second generation, and now emerging third generation of Vietnamese Texans has developed some restaurants into more upscale, modern, and expensive places to dine, where the clientele are willing to pay a little extra for Vietnamese dishes. Thus, more recent Vietnamese Texan restaurateurs have not only expanded their community's commercial presence, but they have also transformed their place-making means. Additionally, Vietnamese American restaurateurs, chefs, and entrepreneurs are more focused on commercial success than just opening up a business for their own economic survival. They have also constructed physical culinary contact zones where Vietnamese diasporans can gather to socialize and spend quality time with family and friends, network with business clients, and build community while having great food options to choose as they consume traditional or modern Vietnamese cuisine.

Reinvigorating the South: The Creolization of Vietnamese Food?

John T. Edge comments on the ever-changing, growing, and diversity of Southern cuisine when he says, "Southern food has never been static. Like all expressions of culture, from music to literature, foodways have been fluid reflections of time and place. Marriages of old ideas and new ethnicity defined a new creolized cuisine."[95] This does not necessarily mean the gradual assimilation or disappearance of Vietnamese cuisine. In fact, Vietnamese food itself is diverse, with the dishes, flavors, and tastes coming from different regions of the country. Interestingly, here in America, as certain Vietnamese dishes become more prevalent and gain greater reception in the mainstream, Vietnamese American home gardeners, cooks, chefs, and restaurateurs are finding inventive ways to expand or refashion Vietnamese culinary traditions.

With the arrival of Vietnamese gastronomy to Houston's culinary scene, as well as other major urban areas in Texas and the US South, phở and bánh mì are two of the more popular dishes. One can find a phở restaurant or a bánh mì shop in just about every neighborhood in the city; they are ubiquitous and growing in popularity.

David Leftwich thinks that "Vietnamese cuisine, at least in Houston and probably along the Gulf Coast and in New Orleans, has become of an accepted go-to cuisine just for everyday . . . like every neighborhood now has . . . a neighborhood Vietnamese restaurant . . . as these two [bánh mì and phở] may be really good but not the most adventurous. Like bánh mì and phở are like staples . . . for everybody, for almost all communities in Houston."[96] Concurrently, Vietnamese American restaurateurs, chefs, and home cooks are adding new ingredients, flavors, and textures borrowed from other cuisines. "You'll see, going both ways, Vietnamese restaurants adopting Southern cuisine to their stuff . . . like Việt-Cajun crawfish being probably the most primary example of it, where they've taken this . . . Cajun tradition of boiling crawfish and . . . put a Vietnamese spin on changing the spices and adding more butter," says Leftwich. "It's interesting, too, because it's a collusion of French from the Cajun and French from the Vietnamese."[97] In addition, Leftwich notes that local chefs like James Beard Award recipient Chris Shepherd infuse Vietnamese herbs, flavors, and cooking styles in their takes on Southern cuisine. He also believes that one day fish sauce, a commonly used ingredient and condiment in Vietnamese dishes, will become as ubiquitous as salsa. He also argues that despite the popular melting pot narrative, the United States is more of a mosaic nation where immigrants and refugees can, and should, retain their culture without it being diluted.

Traditional Vietnamese dishes such as phở remain popular in Việt Nam today and are arguably even more celebrated beyond the country's geographical borders. In fact, Vietnamese diasporic chefs have come up with creative ways to put a new spin on traditional phở. Food historian Vũ Hồng Liên notes that

> Over two millennia, Vietnamese traditional food has come a long way to become the version we know today. What is most remarkable, though, is that it is fast becoming a much-liked cuisine outside Việt Nam. It is a favorite for its lightness and freshness, as well as its taste. In many world cities, *banh mi* or *pho* shops have come to stay, and some are coming out of their ethnic enclaves to be warmly welcomed on high streets . . . The once humble filled lengths of French baguette, Vietnamese style, are now in serious competition with the traditional Western sandwiches. *Pho* is once again hailed in a Western accent, not by hungry soldiers in a faraway barrack but by the most sophisticated people in the most cosmopolitan cities of the world.[98]

Phở is certainly popular in Houston. Local food writer, Mai Phạm, makes the case for the omnipresent of phở. She asserts that over the years Houstonians have come to recognize, taste, and embrace phở, which is a centuries-old Vietnamese dish.[99] Phạm acknowledges that

> Comfort food takes different forms for different people. For me, a Vietnamese American whose parents immigrated to the US after the fall of Saigon in 1975, these are the smells of my childhood, my homeland. Pho is something I know by heart. I look around the eighteen-seat, hole-in-the-wall restaurant's [Phở Vễ Đêm on Bellaire] dining room. Patrons from an array of ethnic backgrounds are contentedly digging into their bowls, slurping up long strands of elastic rice noodles in between spoonfuls of rich, fragrant broth. The scene makes me proud—because as much as pho is an intrinsic part of me, it's finally gone mainstream . . . . A quick count of local establishments with the word "pho" in their name number well over one hundred. And that's not including traditional restaurants that simply serve the dish.[100]

Phạm also cites local chef Vincent Huỳnh, who proclaims that making phở in Houston would now be commonly equivalent to making gumbo in Louisiana. Chef Huỳnh believes that phở is a local dish that has become a part of Houston's culinary canon.

The produce cultivated and gathered from Vietnamese Texan home gardens helps build and expand a community of neighbors, relatives, friends, and fellow church congregants or temple-goers. As a result, Vietnamese greens, flavors, and style of cooking have gained traction in Texas. The blending of Vietnamese and Texan gastronomic tastes has expanded local foodways to form new and exciting flavors and hybrid cuisines. Furthermore, traditional Vietnamese culinary ingredients and flavors blend magically well with popular American dishes often thought of as comfort food. National Public Radio (NPR) reporter John Burnett sheds some light on Houston's Việt-Cajun phenomenon, describing the hybrid cuisine that is popular, prevalent, and gastronomically fitting with Houston's diverse food and restaurant scenes. Houstonians may find Việt-Cajun unsurprising (as Bryan Washington remarked), given the plethora of mixed cuisines in the nation's fourth largest city. Burnett reports on this thriving Việt-Cajun hybrid cuisine and interviews Mike Trịnh, owner of Mike's Seafood, in Houston's second iteration of Little Sài Gòn,[101] which sits along Bellaire Boulevard in southwest Houston.[102] After becoming a champion kickboxer, Trịnh decided to immerse himself in the burgeoning Vietnamese restaurant business and open Mike's Seafood.[103] Burnett explains that "Mike specializes in Vietnamese-Cajun seafood, an Asian-Southern fusion that has taken Houston by storm." Mike describes his Asian-Southern fusion cuisine: "We spice, we season everything. . . . Onions, garlic, everything. Vietnamese community we like a lot of flavor. Some people put ginger, some people put lemongrass. Everybody has their own twists of how to do things." From their cookbook, *Cook Like a Local*, chef Chris Shepherd and coauthor Kaitlyn Goalen also reflect on the still popular and growing Việt-Cajun cuisine in Houston: "The basic components of the dish are the same as what you might see in a Cajun crawfish boil, but with some untraditional ingredients, sometimes ginger or lemongrass, infusing the broth. The crawfish are then tossed in a ridiculously delicious spicy garlic butter and come to the table in a giant plastic bag."[104]

In addition, the ingredients and tastes in many Vietnamese dishes are also similar to Tex-Mex food. Claudia Kolker compares these two popular cuisines in Texas and their similarities: "I don't think Vietnamese restaurant owners knew how much Houstonians have fallen in love with their food and make it their own. The flavors are very Mexican—a lot of them—tamarind, chili, lime. The idea of something tart, the idea of something sweet and with chili on it. These are Mexican ideas, so they stumbled into an environment that really had the taste buds for their food anyway."[105] With shared tastes of blending the sweetness, tartness, and spiciness as the tripart culinary foundation of Mexican and Vietnamese gastronomies, unsurprisingly, Việt-Tex-Mex would be another inventive hybrid cuisine in Houston and offers to extend our gastronomical boundaries and help us explore new foodways. For example, the Houston chef and former owner of Saigon House,[106] Tony J. Nguyễn, has created some innovative Texan dishes of his own. Some of chef Nguyễn's notable hybrid dishes include "a hearty oxtail and smoked brisket pho, and the mini bánh xèo tacos (crispy Vietnamese egg pancakes stuffed with marinated pork belly, shrimp, lettuce, and herbs) that won him first place at the 2018 Gr8 Taco Challenge."[107]

The introductions, interactions, and intersections of other foods and cultures could also help preserve ethnic food cultures, including Vietnamese cuisine. Besides, no ethnic food exists in a complete vacuum. Donna R. Gabaccia asserts, "The American penchant to experiment with foods to combine and mix the foods of many cultural traditions into blended gumbos or stews, and to create 'smorgasbords' is scarcely new but is rather a recurring theme in our history as eaters."[108] John T. Edge describes the region's diverse Southern food heritage: "Food serves the region as a unifying symbol of the creolized culture we have forged, making explicit connections between the breads made from corn that Native Americans call pone and the breads made from corn that Mexican Americans call tortillas, bonding Louisiana Cajuns of French descent who boil crawfish in water spiked with Tabasco mash and Vietnamese Texans on the Gulf Coast who boil crawfish in pots that bob with lemongrass."[109] Edge also comments on the continuing complexity, diversity, and evolution of Southern cuisine into the twenty-first century. "A new kind of hybridized South emerged in the twenty-first century. . . . At strip mall charcuterie shops in Houston, Vietnamese artisans perfumed lunch meats with fish sauce and steamed bologna rolls in banana leaves. In Atlanta, Viet Cajun restaurants boiled crawfish in lemongrass broth and pressed sugarcane juice to order through wall-mounted rollers," explains Edge.[110]

Vietnamese Texan home gardeners continue to play a pivotal role in ensuring that their homegrown herbs, fruit trees, and vegetables are accessible and sustainable enough for home cooks, chefs, and restaurateurs to make, share, and consume Vietnamese dishes, old and new—whether they are eaten together with family and friends, or being shared for the first time with strangers. In other words, Vietnamese foodways must be traced back to homegrown produce of sả (lemongrass), rau muống, trái khổ qua, mướp, rau thơm, cà pháo, quả mít, cây quất, chuối nhỏ (small bananas), and much more. Such homegrown ingredients carefully cultivated by home gardeners represent the possibility of home-cooked Vietnamese meals, where raw ingredients are just a few feet away. Thus, Vietnamese cultural continuities exist and thrive thanks to Vietnamese Texan home gardeners and what raw ingredients they are able to produce and share. Instead of the creolization of Vietnamese food in Texas and the US South, what they bring to the dining table, literally and figuratively, helps expand Vietnamese foodways to non-Vietnamese people and cuisines, allowing home cooks, restaurateurs, and chefs to explore, incorporate, and expand Vietnamese gastronomy.

When the Global South meets the New(er) South, Vietnamese food intersects with Texan, Tex-Mex, Cajun, and Southern cuisines in many ways, particularly regarding the integration with some of the herbs, fruits, and vegetables. For example, đậu bắp is used in Vietnamese cooking to make several different dishes, including canh chua cá and đậu bắp xào (stir-fried okra). Other herbs, fruits, and vegetables include—but are not limited to—rau đắng (mustard greens), rau thơm, and ớt, which are commonly cultivated and consumed in Texas and the American South. Furthermore, not only has Vietnamese food been preserved, enhanced, and renewed, but it has also gained a more receptive audience and greater familiarity to Texans and Southerners, many of whom were unfamiliar with its cuisine not too long ago. Even more so, the introduction and impact of Vietnamese cuisine over the past forty-five-plus years has added to the historically rich culinary diversity of Texas and the US South. Consequently, but unsurprisingly, chefs and home cooks have come up with creative hybrid cuisines that are uniquely local (Texas), regional

(US South), and/or international (Mexico), all while preserving some of the essential Vietnamese ingredients, tastes, textures, and flavors. Hybrid cuisines have been celebrated with much fanfare and acclaim, further enriching Texas and Southern foodways, as Việt-Tex, Việt-Cajun, and Việt-Tex-Mex cuisines become more celebrated. The intersectionality of Texan, Southern, and Vietnamese gastronomies lie at the heart of sustainable praxis of growing greens and crops that are conducive to the local warm weather, rich soil, and extensive growing season. One important and sustainable practice is planting a home garden in the front and/or backyard, making fresh produce more accessible to the home gardener, and anyone fortunate enough to receive fresh herbs, vegetables, and fruits from the gardener. A new(er) South has arrived in the twenty-first century culinary world, thanks in part to the addition of Vietnamese cuisine, where home cooks, restaurant owners, and chefs embrace, elevate, and highlight the diverse gastronomy that makes up Texan, Cajun, Tex-Mex, and Southern cuisines, previously enriched, expanded, and diversified by Caribbean, West African, Creole, Chinese, Mexican, South Asian, Native American, Middle Eastern, Central American, and countless other cuisines.

Gabaccia argues that curiosity has fueled culinary exploration and accommodation in American foodways for centuries.[111] As she notes, "The foods we eat commemorate a long history of peaceful cultural interaction; our multi-ethnic eating daily proclaims our satisfied sense of affiliation with one another. The marketplace, and its consumer culture, may be a slim thread on which to build cross-cultural understanding. But given the depth of American fears about cultural diversity, it is better to have that thread than not."[112] Gabaccia is very clear about what this means for racial relations: "Rather than dismiss eating as a trivial consumer choice, Americans might do better to take our eating choices very seriously. Then we could recognize and celebrate that indeed we are what we eat—not a multi-ethnic nation, but a nation of multi-ethnics."[113]

Taking Gabaccia's cue, new culinary ventures abound for multi-ethnic America, advancing our palates and foodways. Cross-cultural gastronomic experiences allow people the opportunity to construct new intersections of food and culture. Food does that for us; and it democratizes us. By opening up our palates, we open new foodways and cast aside previous cultural, social, and language barriers, while surrendering ourselves to the natural fluidity between cultures. Culinary citizenship takes hold, where the confluences of profound intermingling of food and culture are rooted, constructed, forged, and bonded. Imagine, when we open up our minds as often as we do with our food, what other transformative wonders, possibilities, and advancements await us?

Food connects the immigrant/refugee "them" with the native/citizen "us" and, just as easily, vice versa. Food connects us, particularly when we share our meals, conversations, hospitality, and civility. Food is a portal that open previously closed doors and connect us all—the same could be said with art, film, dance, literature, theater, music, photography, fashion, sports, and so forth. Nothing is more American than to consume wholly new food experiences, like being invited to join an Iftar to breakfast during Ramadan. Such an invitation is a true, unique American experience, and one that can enhance our appreciation of being US culinary citizens. Furthermore, culinary citizenship offers us a greater sense of belonging to a land and to a people. Culinary citizenship is a social right of existence with direct relations to a nation-state via foodways, although I would acknowledge not lawfully in terms of legal status. Yet, the culinary citizen and the nation-state apparatus are not mutually exclusive; rather, they frequently intertwine in quotidian culinary contacts in our lives. After all, we should know in US history, and throughout our human history, what is considered legal is not always considered just. Culinary citizenship binds us with the food we cultivate and consume from the land, and therefore binds us to the transformed land as a birthright, if you will, to *jus soli*, law of the soil.

CHAPTER 5

Emancipatory Foodways

Food Sovereignty, Culinary Citizenship, and Homeland Duality

It is hot and dusty where we live. Some people think it's dirty but they don't know much about us. They haven't seen our gardens full of lemongrass, mint, cilantro, and basil. Driving by with their windows rolled up, they've only seen the pigeons pecking at day-old rice and the skinny cats and dogs sitting in the skinny shade of skinny trees. Have they seen the berries that we pick, that turn our lips and fingertips red?

—lê thi diem thúy, from *The Gangster We Are All Looking For*

Food culture is but one example of how practices of everyday life are often critical to how people make sense of the world around them, where they fit into that world, who should belong in that world, and how they imagine and remake new worlds.

—Mark Padoongpatt, from *Flavors of Empire*

The passage from lê thi diem thúy's novel, *The Gangster We Are All Looking For* juxtaposes the terrible reality and irony of a Vietnamese refugee family living in a neighborhood that treats and views them as perpetual strangers.[1] By doing so, their neighbors are blinded by prejudice, and do not (and cannot) see the beautiful, lush gardens of herbs and berries cultivated by the protagonist's family. The Vietnamese family's invisibility to their neighbors results in the readily accepted and flawed perception of the refugees' as dirty, filthy, and foreign, which further distances them from belonging and finding home here in the United States. It is the neighbors' failure (or refusal) to see the refugees' home garden that creates this widening chasm.

Mark Padoongpatt comments on the quotidian practices that shape reality, where food culture grants immigrants and refugees alike an opportunity to seek home and gain a level of belonging in a foreign United States on their own terms.[2] Immigrants and refugees mold their world by growing, producing, cooking, and consuming their own foods. They also create their own spaces of belonging with emancipatory foodways by cultivating home gardens replete with herbs, fruit trees, and vegetables. Through food sovereignty, immigrants and refugees in the United States not only regain some food security, but also their food heritage, resisting alternative food cultures and systems thrust upon them.

Food searches for our soul, and finds it. Food reminds us of what is good with the world—a world, for a refugee, that is fraught with so many awful wrongs. I was first introduced to the term "food sovereignty" after I had just finished presenting on Vietnamese Texans and their home gardens at an academic conference. During our panel's question and answer session at the Southwest Popular/American Culture Association conference, Dr. David Martinez, associate professor of American Indian Studies at Arizona State University, publicly declared that what Vietnamese Texan home gardeners practiced is considered a political act of food sovereignty. I listened to him and agreed wholeheartedly.

In this chapter, I hope to unpack the approaches that Vietnamese Texans use to gain emancipatory foodways and claim their own food sovereignty, culinary citizenship, and homeland duality. By establishing home gardens and cultivating fresh produce and thus, reclaiming their Vietnamese culture and identity, Vietnamese Texans demonstrate greater food security, resistance, and justice. Simultaneously, they construct their own American culture and identity through their food labor, produce, and consumption. As stated in the introduction, I assert that Vietnamese Texans demonstrate food resistance in specific ways: in the produce that Vietnamese plant, cultivate, water, and pluck in their yards; in where and how they prepare their meals; in what ingredients they incorporate into their meals; and in how they celebrate and consume their meals together. While Vietnamese Texans grow and work on their home gardens as a coping mechanism and a form of healing, the labor, time, effort, and consumption of produce also nurtures their physical and mental health, and offers cultural continuity that helps them construct an identity, build community, and resist the gradual marginalization of Vietnamese culture in the United States. From refuge to recovery to reclamation and finally redemption, home gardens provide Vietnamese Texan gardeners another roadmap to survive, live, and, in some cases, thrive while enduring, confronting, and living with the traumas of war, displacement, and racialization.

HOME GARDENS AS PLACES OF FOOD SOVEREIGNTY, RESISTANCE, AND JUSTICE

According to food scholars Hannah Wittman, Annette Aurélie Desmarais, and Nettie Wiebe, the term food sovereignty "was coined to recognize the political and economic power dimension inherent in the food and agriculture debate and to take a proactive stance by naming it."[3] They further elaborate on the concept, stating that "Food sovereignty, broadly defined as the right of nations and peoples to control their own food systems, including their own markets, production modes, food cultures and environments, has emerged as a critical alternative to the dominant neoliberal model for agriculture and trade."[4] Furthermore, they assert that food sovereignty is centered on local knowledge, closes the gap between food production and consumption, and seeks to democratize the food system and therefore, perceives food as vital to local cultures.[5]

Food sovereignty is a fitting and appropriate term to describe Vietnamese Texans and their cultivation of home gardens. Vietnamese Texan home gardeners seek and find some solace, healing, reclamation, and redemption via the home gardens that allow them to labor, live, and consume as Vietnamese. Home gardens become another way to live and express themselves as Vietnamese, where they have sovereignty over spaces—no matter how small—that allow them to plant, nurture, and grow crops. Through this emancipatory process of cultivating agriculture, they can express their creativity, resourcefulness, and resilience via home gardening. Thus, they are able to express themselves in a language they are fluent in: the language of gardening, farming their own land, and carving a place of their own. In addition,

Vietnamese Texan home gardeners forge acts of food resistance by challenging the complete assimilation to hegemonic American foodways, while protecting and preserving their food heritage.

Food scholars Robert Gottlieb and Anupama Joshi describe the new immigrant farmers in the United States, noting that "Some were war or political refugees from Cambodia, Vietnam, Somalia, Burundi, or Senegal. Others were immigrants, both legal and undocumented, including economic refugees from Mexico, Guatemala, Haiti, Togo, Ghana, Liberia, Nigeria, Ecuador, and the Dominican Republic. A connection to the land, whether as farmers or as backyard gardeners, was for many of them part of their cultural and economic heritage."[6] Gottlieb and Joshi further observe that "the relation of immigrants to food has long been a highly visible part of the American experience. . . . Immigrants have also been an important part of the urban gardening history in the United States . . . the presence of immigrant gardeners in the United States could be seen as part of the desire of immigrants displaced from their land, particularly those coming from rural communities where farming and gardening had been part of daily life, to recapture a connection back to the land."[7] Such performances of ingenuity, resourcefulness, and resolve demonstrate immigrant and refugee gardeners willingness to go to great lengths to gain food security and preserve their food heritage. Simultaneously, by maximizing tiny parcels of unused or abandoned land, they choose to *reengage* with the land, using gardening as an act of food resistance to survive and cultivate a healthy and affordable food option.

Such food resistance mirrors the ongoing struggles of immigrant and refugee gardeners to make better food choices where they can utilize their own skills, tools, and knowledge to grow the kinds of food they cherish and desire. They are taking back their food heritage and reclaiming it as their own. To correct the wrongs of the past, immigrant and refugee gardeners raise vegetables, herbs, and fruit trees, resorting to even renegade gardening on slivers of unused or abandoned land. They are enacting food justice to reject mainstream American foodways that are unsuitable and unhealthy to their nutritional needs and cultural preservation. Gottlieb and Joshi elaborate further, arguing that "Food justice includes immigrant farmers and gardeners who bring knowledge, skill, and passion to help reinvent and extend farming as a vocation. And perhaps most important, it includes farmworkers who seek to organize themselves to proclaim their own dignity, and to demonstrate their own value as food producers."[8] Such a description aptly summarizes and defines the refugee experience of Vietnamese Texans who are determined to retain their heritage while literally and figuratively planting the seeds of their food culture in America, asserting their own form of food justice in ways that counter their marginalization and racialization. While not explicitly about Vietnamese immigrants, anthropologist Ashanté M. Reese writes about the intersections of race and food when she says, "Food justice is fundamentally about racial justice, because in the United States, race and racism not only structure everyday experiences, but also influence the (under)development of neighborhoods and the implementation of policies that disproportionately disenfranchise Black communities."[9]

Vietnamese Texan home gardeners seek their own food justice by establishing ways to maintain and strengthen their Vietnamese culture, and home gardens provide them spaces to plant, control, and exhibit a part of their food heritage. Home gardens are spaces where Vietnamese Texans can cultivate their own culture and identity. Rau mùi (coriander), cây me chua (sorrel), húng quế (basil), tía tô, rau thơm, cà pháo, mướp, bí đao, ớt, quả mít, quất, đu đủ, trái khổ qua, đậu bắp, and other greens, vegetables, and fruits from their garden are spatial evidence and living proof of the smells, textures, and tastes that connect their senses with greater assurance and comfort, providing some stable roots to their lives as foreigners in a foreign land. These home gardens grant them a sense of normalcy, whether it be a brief respite or a long return home, after many years of struggle. The garden space and produce offer Vietnamese Texan home gardeners a reconnection to their homeland.

Despite challenges to gardening in the Texas heat, as well as the time and labor spent, Nguyễn Văn Nam, or Thầy Nam, believes that gardening helps the Vietnamese in the United States maintain a part of their tradition. "This is an effort to preserve and extend the traditions of our ancestors. The Vietnamese, when leaving their homeland, promise to themselves to preserve and to develop their traditions and culture," says Thầy Nam.[10] My father, Vũ Kiến An Quan, believes that gardening gives him "a greater sense of our mother country."[11] For Vietnamese Texan home gardeners, their home gardens serve as a creative space to remember, rebuild, and reconnect with their Vietnamese culture via the food cultivation of their favorite plants and fruits.

As stated before, home gardens give Vietnamese Texans some food sovereignty and therefore, a greater sense of food security and control over what they produce and consume. As food scholars Steve Ventura and Martin Bailkey note, "Activists use the term *food sovereignty* for 'rebuilding a new food system with new values.' For them, this includes building a new economy around food to alter 'a history of class struggle' and developing innovative ways to access and use the tens of thousands of acres of abandoned and vacant property within the city."[12] Professors Ventura and Bailkey also share their thoughts on food sovereignty. They argue that food sovereignty is tied to a community's self-determination, particularity a community with few resources, and creates an opportunity to gain control over food consumption.[13] They elaborate further, noting that "The primacy of food as a daily element of life— and the traditions and cultural practices around growing, preparing, and consuming it—means that community-based food system activism is a viable, proactive strategy for combating the effects of food injustice and outright racism."[14]

Ashanté Reese's brilliant ethnographic research on the predominantly African American Deanwood housing project, located in Ward Seven of the District of Columbia, advances critical food studies and conversations on the intersectionality of race, foodways, and gardens. Reese argues that the Deanwood community garden cultivated by local Black residents "was a product of the local grassroots organization's desire to address food insecurity in predominantly Black neighborhoods and residents' desires to do something meaningful in their community."[15] She asserts that gardening provided an opportunity to feed *and* beautify their community. Residents used vegetable gardens as an attempt to transform their community, exhibiting agency and active resistance to regain their own food sovereignty.[16] Reese observes that the "reflected tensions inherent in working to meet people's food needs under spatial and economic constraints . . . was a literal and symbolic spatial reflection of their commitment to building a healthy community."[17] She concludes that the Deanwood community gardeners "were not only part of a larger food justice system movement but also of a long-standing history of African Americans depending on self and community to address structural inequalities. . . . The gardeners' [*sic*] wished to feed more than bodies. They aimed to feed the soul a serving of hope with a side of self-reliance."[18]

Self-reliance for marginalized communities is an essential element in food justice. Sociologist Joshua Sbicca also suggests self-determination as another driving force behind community food justice and sovereignty, tracing this back to the Black Panther Party and other groups who valued self-determination as necessary to gain control over the means of food production and other decision-making spaces.[19] Sbicca argues that "food justice is the sine qua non that connects activists across a range of interests and stretches the frontiers of food politics precisely because of the resonance of food justice in broader social struggles."[20] He goes on to state that food justice leads to the just production and right to healthy food, while still recognizing the "diverse cultural foodways and historical traumas" inherent in a movement that "promotes equitable distribution of resources, democratic participation, and control over food systems."[21]

Food justice for marginalized populations, such as Vietnamese diasporans, can be established with home gardens that serve as transformed spaces of peace, remembrance, rebirth, and resistance. Vietnamese American home gardeners regain food sovereignty via the herbs, vegetables, and fruits they raise, share, and consume. Throughout US history, marginalized Asian Pacific American farmers have been stripped of their lands, human dignity, and freedom to cultivate crops on American soil. Even when the state passes well-intentioned legislation designed to protect labor unions and farm workers, refugee groups like the Hmong farmers in California can fall through the cracks and fail their farming inspections due to language and cultural barriers. In their study on Hmong farmers in California, coauthors Laura-Anne Minkoff-Zern, Nancy Peluso, Jennifer Sowerwine, and Christy Getz argue that "as the state regulates agricultural resources, it creates racial categories that separate lawful members of society from 'alien' outsiders. These designations then legitimate and are reinforced by everyday experiences of racial 'othering' or racial exclusion. We refer to the combined effects of these processes as *agricultural racial formations*."[22] The authors argue that, intentional or not, when laws, policies, or practices affect certain racial groups (especially in the case of the Hmong losing their land and agricultural rights) the dispossession becomes racialized.[23] They also conclude that "this push to protect both documented immigrant and unprotected family workers has inadvertently contributed to the construction of Hmong family farm labor as a 'problem' and thereby made Hmong farmers a 'problem population.' . . . Displaced by US interventions in their home country in the late twentieth century, Hmong are still being dispossessed of even the smallest gains they have achieved in their adoptive country. The terms are only subtler and more closely related to some relatively unexplored, racialized, dimensions of an agrarian question about the effects of capitalism on agriculture."[24]

The same could be stated about Vietnamese refugees and their food production and consumption practices. When Vietnamese diasporans resettled in the United States during the late 1970s, a majority of Americans did not welcome them. Not surprisingly, Vietnamese refugee food praxis was not embraced or well-received. Sociologist Fred R. von der Mehden studies the cultural disconnects and differences between native Houstonians and the arrivals of Vietnamese refugees, with the former marginalizing the latter. "Cultural differences are often a problem; other residents in densely populated hotels, housing projects, and low-cost housing areas complained about the refugees' living habits," says von der Mehden. "The most frequent complaints arise over issues of sanitation, the growing of vegetable gardens (and attendant flooding), strange smells from exotic cooking, drying fish, and noise standards."[25]

Another source describes the resilience, savviness, and ingenuity, albeit "illegal" practices, of cultivating gardens in public spaces: "Through unbearable hardships, many Vietnamese immigrants [and refugees] have attempted to maintain cultural connections to their homeland and even developed aquaculture farming techniques in hidden places, like Sims Bayou in southeast Houston. Behind crowded apartment complexes off of Park Place, the Asian tenants tried to establish rural living by the slow waterway. Evidenced by banana trees and cultivated bamboo, only remnants remain of the gardeners' efforts to sustain the lifeways of the Vietnamese people in their new city."[26] Unfortunately, not everyone appreciated and accepted the home gardens of St. Joseph nor was pleased with the horticultural astuteness and savviness of its village residents. Vietnamese Texan home gardeners endured some opposition from outsiders. Josh Harkinson reports one such case of protest against Vietnamese villagers at St. Joseph: "An entirely different set of problems sprouted in 2003 behind St. Joseph's [sic] Village, where residents were tending to a garden of Eden-like proportions along the banks of Sims Bayou. A nearby landowner threatened to sue the village for trespassing onto the waterway's public easement, says Niem Nguyen, a seventy-year-old resident [when the article was first published], and the greens, mints, and banana trees had to be plowed under. 'There's no land to grow the vegetables that I want,' she says."[27] Mrs. Nguyễn clearly expresses her frustration over the lack of available land for her and fellow villagers to cultivate the vegetables, herbs, and fruit trees that helped them survive their resettlement in a Houston working-class neighborhood.

By declaring such acts of unwelcomed cooking and renegade gardening as "alien" or "illegal" praxis of Vietnamese foodways, we further reduce the social acceptance of and alienate an already marginalized population. In precarious and uncertain times, newly arrived Vietnamese refugees and immigrants often feel compelled to use publicly shared or even city-managed (or neglected) lands to maximize what limited spaces they have surrounding their crowded living quarters. Especially when living in well-worn apartment complexes, Vietnamese diasporic residents make a concerted effort to raise home gardens in small, tight spaces, and even in restricted areas when necessary. Living in overcrowded, dense residences with limited land space, while enduring complaints stemming from cultural differences with non-Vietnamese neighbors, it is no wonder that Vietnamese villagers in Houston resort to finding open, unkept grounds and waterways and converting them into viable green gardens. In addition, they extend their green gardens to public lots, raising crops to subsist, survive, and remember their homeland by growing, selling, giving, and preparing the fresh herbs, fruits, and vegetables that they have carefully cultivated.

For the Vietnamese diaspora in Texas, home gardens provide small plots of land and spaces they can cultivate, nurture, and control. Vietnamese Texans regain some food sovereignty thanks to the vegetables, fruits, and herbs they raise. In addition, Vietnamese Texan home gardeners maintain cultural continuity and preserve their food heritage, especially because much of the produce grown serves as essential ingredients and garnishes in numerous Vietnamese dishes. As a result, personal home gardens and microfarms in community villages demonstrate the farm- or garden-to-table practices of Vietnamese Texans. Their home gardens and microfarms naturally lend themselves to a "farm-to-freedom" ethos, where Vietnamese Texans seek and gain refuge and liberation through the emancipatory foodways offered by food sovereignty, culinary citizenship, and homeland duality.

Other marginalized populations in the United States also continue to make a concerted effort to revive, retain, and expand their respective heritage foodways. For instance, Kristyn Leach, born in South Korea and adopted by an Irish Catholic family in New York, shares her remarkable story of farming crops that are essential in Korean food culture.[28] "I wanted to grow something distinctly Korean, and I sort of stumbled upon the seeds for perilla [deulkkae or ggaennip in Korean]," says Leach. "I didn't really know what it was, but I grew it and really loved it—it's an incredibly beautiful plant. It's a really tall broadleaf plant with purple undersides to the leaves. It's in the mint family and is related to *shiso*, a popular Japanese herb. Perilla is a staple Korean herb and subsequently after growing it, everyone Korean who has seen me growing it is blown away."[29] She reflects on the importance of maintaining her Korean food heritage: "It's interesting how it's turned out, having been adopted away from Korea and now coming back to my roots through food. It's very validating. I work for an older Korean lady who is a mushroom vendor here in San Francisco, and I brought her some perilla and she tried it and said to me, 'you are 100 percent Korean.' She would have me show it off to all her customers, and she was so proud that someone from my generation is growing perilla."[30] Leach says she loves how shared roots and deep connections between two people are made possible by food, in this case, plants such as perilla.[31]

Aileen Suzara, a Filipina American food educator, food justice activist, and chef residing in Berkeley shares her poignant farming history in California. "When I was farming, it just made me think about the fact that I was the first generation of my family born here on this land, but it also caused me to think about what took us off our own land. And what it means to now be on soil where other people have been oppressed. That all felt very physical for the first time," reflects Suzara.[32] Suzara makes an excellent distinction; she is able to acknowledge immigrants and refugees in the United States and how they must confront their own experiences of ostracization and racialization, but also recognizes that the resettled lands of the colonial settlers are the lands taken away from the Indigenous peoples. She further argues, "Race and history still matter and need to be understood, even with the rise of the 'new' good food movement. . . . It's about passing on that cultural tradition and honoring it . . . a space where cultural traditions can be renewed. . . . We have to renew who we are and how to live in a good way on this planet, and we need to keep having spaces for that. The kitchen, to me, is the perfect space."[33] Vietnamese diasporans are part of the colonial settler history, albeit as one of a continuing many Asian Pacific American refugees and immigrants who have experienced ostracization and racism as they resettled their lives in the United States. To add another layer of complexity to Vietnamese refugee history, Vietnamese diasporans must also be cognizant of rejecting the notion that their resettlement in America is solely a "gift" given by benevolent US policymakers of the Cold War era. We must understand how proxy wars, such as the Việt Nam War, disrupt lives, which was ultimately the reason for the mass exodus of Vietnamese refugees in the first place. This is the "you were there, so we are here" refrain of refugee experience so eloquently stated by notable scholar Yến Lê Espiritu, that connects US policymaking in the Cold War era to US refugee policies in the post–Việt Nam War years.

In Houston, Texas, microfarms and community gardens continue to be cultivated and harvested, a tradition of urban farming that harks back to African American migrants to Houston during the challenging and difficult days of Jim Crow. David Leftwich provides some details on Urban Harvest and one of the oldest community gardens in Texas, Alabama Community Garden, where locals address food desert issues and expand food sovereignty for African Americans. "Urban Harvest has . . . community gardens set up in food deserts with . . . the oldest raised bed community garden along the Gulf coast. . . . Urban Harvest kind of helps. But mostly they're running it on their own," says Leftwich.[34] He elaborates more on the Alabama Community Garden and its mission to serve food desert communities: "It's a pretty big community garden. It's primarily African American, but like there's a couple of schools have gardens there. Theirs is certainly a true community garden."[35] He discusses Urban Harvest's mission, saying that "Urban Harvest does a lot of work with the community gardens. Theirs is kind of overarching; they teach classes, provide logistic support and stuff."

To regain food sovereignty and justice, refugees, immigrants, and other marginalized populations in Houston often resort to collaborating with local, nonprofit agricultural organizations such as Urban Harvest and Plant It Forward Farms (the latter of which I will share more about in the Epilogue). Oftentimes, neighbors in marginalized communities rely on each other to ensure that they have adequate, diverse, and quality homegrown vegetables, herbs, and fruits in their community. Thus, community and home gardens play a tremendous role in producing enough healthy greens for their family, neighbors, and community. These community and home gardens give them opportunities to seek food justice, redeem themselves, and reclaim their food heritage. The community regains their food sovereignty, particularly in working-class, food desert neighborhoods. As a result, local residents root themselves in their respective neighborhoods and cultivate a part of their culinary citizenship to belong on this land, with and as Americans.

Cultivating Culinary Citizenship via Home Gardens

Home gardens are just one of many ways for Vietnamese diasporans to preserve their heritage and maintain cultural continuity. Holidays, festivals, memorials, flags, language schools, radio and television stations, restaurants, street signs, religious institutions, shopping malls, grocery stores, cultural and community centers, health fairs, and nonprofit organizations provide ample evidence of cultural continuity and resilience among Vietnamese Texans. From celebrating Tết (lunar new year) to community crawfish boils to the Tết Trung Thu (mid-autumn festival), Vietnamese food plays an integral and visible role at these celebrations. Notably, at every Tết celebration, bánh trung (sticky rice dish typically with pork or mung beans and wrapped in banana leaves) is omnipresent in Vietnamese diasporic communities and of course, in Việt Nam. Bánh trung is typically be made from scratch at home, with hours of meticulous labor, care, and love. Upon completion, bánh trung is cut and wrapped in large squares that are neatly tied with strings wrapped around the banana leaves that hold the sticky rice dish intact. Squares of bánh trung are then gifted to family members, relatives, and friends. Sometimes, squares of bánh trung are pan-fried are dipped in sugar as a snack. For Tết and other Vietnamese holidays, a family typically gathers together over a sumptuous and extravagant meal at home. Our biggest, most elaborate, and meaningful holidays are surrounded by the food we make, share, devour, and enjoy in the company of loved ones. Jacqueline An writes, "For me, cooking is about bringing people together. While we grew up eating together as a family, as we've now started families of our own, that precious time of gathering around the table to feast together is mostly reserved for special events and holidays."[36] For Vietnamese diasporans, Tết, Tết Trung Thu, and other holidays serve not only as significant community-building gatherings to celebrate together, but they also provide an opportunity for them to remember, embrace, and share their food heritage.

Vietnamese diasporans are not unique in this regard. Ahmed Afzal describes other ethnic holidays and festivals as symbolic yet significant cultural markers: "The origins of the Japanese Nisei Week Festival and the Mexican American Festival of Cinco de Mayo provide additional examples of the strategic use of festivals as a collective response in the face of the vulnerabilities experienced by minority communities in the United States."[37] Afzal references the historic and popular Nisei Week Festival where Japanese Americans in California organize as a practice of cultural citizenship; this practice both mitigates the fears and vulnerabilities that stem from racial animosity and celebrates their uniqueness as Japanese Americans.[38] As for the Pakistan Independence Day Festival in Houston, he asserts that "The Festival reveals a tremendous capacity for adapting to local developments as well as geopolitical contexts of subjectification that enable its characterization as a practice of cultural citizenship."[39]

Culinary citizenship, as a form of cultural citizenship, defines our social existence and right to foodways that cultivate our belonging to the homeland(s). In Texas, home gardens not only serve as a powerful and redeeming reminder of their homeland, but they also allow Vietnamese Texans to recapture what they lost from the war, soothing the memory and postmemory of generations of Vietnamese refugee families. For Vietnamese Texans, planting their home gardens restores a part of their culture and identity, and helps them wrestle some control over food production despite restrictive access to space. Yet, these home gardens are also liminal spaces where transitional and transformational experiences occur for the gardeners themselves. Home gardens demonstrate the resilience, recovery, and redemption of refugees from the traumatic wreckage of war and offer a counterpoint to their trauma, providing quiet, peaceful, and safe spaces for them to heal.

Loss of their homeland, more specifically South Việt Nam, has consequently led the Vietnamese diaspora to seek, express, and exhibit the cultivation of South Vietnamese citizenship by any possible means: flags, memorials, statues, and art, as well "Saigonizing" names of their restaurants, businesses, neighborhoods, and more. For Vietnamese refugees and immigrants who have experienced devastating personal loss and trauma, along with the loss of homeland, home gardens offer them the opportunity to cultivate a dual culinary citizenship through food production and consumption, and ultimately food sovereignty. This lends to homeland duality that reconnects them to their Việt Nam, while also allowing them to be rooted to their adopted home country. In this way, home gardens provide a healthy outlet, preserving and expanding Vietnamese foodways in the United States and beyond.

Vietnamese Texans define their culinary citizenship by cultivating home gardens—no matter the size or production—in the United States, and they do so of their own accord. They also prove and express their belonging to the US nation-state, in part by raising home gardens to reclaim Vietnamese foodways, but also by adding to the American mosaic of culinary traditions. Home gardens are one way they demonstrate the characteristics of what it is to be a good, model citizen on their terms: hard work, perseverance, ingenuity, resilience, community building, and improving and beautifying the land. In terms of improving and beautifying the land, Vietnamese Texan home gardeners transform the landscape of their yards and villages by planting and raising crops. They cultivate a model citizenship of their own definition, staking a claim and expressing their right to be here in the United States, not just as refugees, but also as citizens, as people who belong here, and who—by their hard labor, personal sacrifices, ingenuity, and contributions—have the right to remain here. They are indeed definitive, qualified citizens of a country that aspires to include all voices by virtue of its definition as a democracy. Hence, their home gardens are "victory" gardens—green spaces of recovery, redemption, and reclamation that show their success in overcoming the suffering they experienced during the war and postwar years.

Vietnamese Texan home gardeners take ownership and responsibility over a small plot of land that provides nutrients, outdoor exercise, time for contemplation, and an opportunity to improve their physical and mental health, while maintaining cultural continuity with design and purpose. Through determination, hard work, and savviness, Vietnamese Texan home gardeners produce fruits, herbs, and vegetables that invoke memories of their Việt Nam and establish their citizenship roots in the United States. Their home gardens are proof of their rootedness in America, and their willingness—through tremendous effort and persistence—to actively engage in the discourse of cultivating citizenship in the United States. They are not merely occupants of the bystander-victim bodies, but rather they embody the epitome of agency, acting of their own free will and determination to cultivate their hard-earned and deserved citizenship to be Americans in their adopted country. Such exemplary characteristics and contributions demonstrate the value and weight of American nonlegal citizenship versus legal US citizenship: in this case, the former defines the people who labored, toiled, and produced from the land, contributing and enhancing our American culture and thus, they helped refine and define the latter, the nation-state, by enriching our culinary traditions.

Home gardens grant the peace that many Vietnamese refugees and immigrants seek to find, giving them the chance to digest and overcome the visceral and violent experiences of war, exodus, resettlement, and racialization. Such green spaces transformed by Vietnamese Texans grant them the opportunity and hope to retain the citizenship to a Việt Nam—their South Việt Nam—they lost but dearly remember. Vietnamese Texan home gardeners often cultivate a citizenship to a South Việt Nam that no longer exists but a country that still remains alive in their hearts and souls. Just like the South Vietnamese stamps from the days of the Republic of Việt Nam, the fruits, vegetables, and greens depicted have been carefully planted, nurtured, plucked, and consumed here in Texas and throughout the United States. Mãng cầu (custard apple), trái bầu (gourd), trái khổ qua, and other fruits and vegetables help reconnect refugees to the place they grew up and lived in, and function as significant identifiers that bind them to their ghost country of South Việt Nam. Home gardens help Vietnamese diasporans cope with the trauma and violence of the Việt Nam War. University of Utah professor Paisley Rekdal writes perceptively about the distressing continuity of the Việt Nam War, and the traumas that continue long after the fighting has ended. She observes that "trauma and violence may not disconnect us from others but jolt us into an awareness of our intimate relationship with each other. Perhaps that is the ultimate value of recounting and listening to stories of trauma: to admit our emotional proximity to the past and to each other. To remember, when everything about our culture asks us to forget."[40] The Việt Nam War lives on in many ways. Yet, no matter how minuscule and insignificant home gardens may appear, they give Vietnamese Texan home gardeners safe spaces to resume their lives and reestablish their connections with community.

No doubt, home gardens offer Vietnamese Texans some peace, solace, comfort, security, and sovereignty over food production, not to mention, the more immediate and affordable access to a healthier consumption of organic produce. For them, home gardens are one avenue to greater food sovereignty, as well as a path to cultivate their Vietnamese American culinary citizenship. Vietnamese Texan home gardeners are remembering and recapturing a Việt Nam they left behind and temporarily lost. By digging into the soil of their backyards or communal spaces, their gardens and microfarms reveal their purposeful intentions of not only re-creating a plot of Việt Nam they loved and knew, but also reenacting the tastes, smells, and textures of their produce that are indelibly part of their food heritage. They are also holding onto a South Việt Nam that no longer exists on the global map. Nevertheless, home gardens offer a sliver of their homeland where they can cultivate and stake their citizenship to a ghost nation once home to them, and a nation that is their adopted homeland. Culinary citizenship is not limited by national borders; it is without boundaries.

FROM REFUGEES TO CITIZENS: RIGHT TO CULINARY CITIZENSHIP VIA VIETNAMESE FOODWAYS

Reflecting on the tremendous impact Anthony Bourdain had on food and travel writing, food journalist Dan Đào says, "It was truly Bourdain who showed so many like me that food writing could go beyond cookbook writing or restaurant reviewing—that it had the potential, as a form of travel journalism, to encapsulate hundreds of years of migration, trauma, and triumph into a single bite. Bourdain gave us a greater sense of obligation."[41] Đào pinpoints the importance of linking ethnic foodways through the threads of war, exile, displacement, resettlement, racialization, and exultation that bind and encapsulate the history of so many refugees. From the trauma to the euphoria, Vietnamese food heritage lives on, is renewed, and then evolves, thanks to Vietnamese American home cooks, chefs, gardeners, farmers, and restaurateurs.

Culinary citizenship falls under the purview of cultural citizenship, which refers to the right of a community to express their ethnicity without sacrificing their rights to participate in democratic processes. But the category and concept do not mandate nor condone the historical misapplication of cultural citizenship—especially during the World War II internment of Japanese Americans—when deployed by the US government as a means of restriction and oppression, as previously discussed in chapter 2. Rather, culinary citizenship here expresses the need and control by the oppressed to reenvision their suffering and misfortune by cultivating traditional foodways of creating, raising, procuring, consuming, and sharing their food with neighbors and strangers, whether they are friends or antagonists. Culinary citizenship is a close cousin of agrarian citizenship, but with an emphasis on the urban, suburban, and exilic places, not just the rural locales. However, not unlike agrarian citizenship, culinary citizenship also permits the oppressed to remember, recover, redeem, and expand their traditional foodways; it is the network of systemic praxis to grow food to live and live a dignified life of freedom from despair, hopelessness, poverty, and statelessness.

By cultivating their own food sovereignty and culinary citizenship, Vietnamese Texans navigate the boundaries of immigrant/refugee and citizenship dichotomy, and the barriers that are socially and racially constructed to drive a cultural wedge between the two, so that the citizen may discriminate against the immigrant/refugee. However, food opens the door for a citizen, or native resident, to traverse and enter the non-native resident's world. By tasting and consuming "foreign" or "exotic" food, the native takes the initial step to listen, reflect, understand, and relate to the non-native. For a moment, the native becomes the uninitiated, while the non-native steps into the role of expert and teacher. Lines between who is a native/citizen and who is a non-native/refugee in this food world start to blur. Social constructs of borders and barriers are temporarily, yet organically, removed. Journalist Leah Binkovitz says, "Food is a convenient way to learn the vocabulary of different places and people. It's an entry point. For food to tell its stories, however, you have to listen."[42] She describes the social dynamics of Houston while reflecting on Anthony Bourdain's 2018 visit to the fourth largest city in the nation:

> Because beneath the sometimes flattering rhetoric of a welcoming city are tangles of threads that tell our stories and articulate complicated, contested relationships to space in an ever-changing city that welcomes at the same time it seems to ask, where do you belong? . . . Food is a particularly powerful point of entry to these stories. For Bourdain, sitting at someone's table, eating their food, adjusts the scales in a meaningful way. They are performing labor, yes, but they are also setting the terms of the conversation. They are the experts. It stands in contrast to the settings of many "community engagement" meetings or the Technicolor renderings of new developments and green spaces with faceless people ambling about. What makes cities great are not the spaces within them, but the people who inhabit and alter them.[43]

Binkovitz could not be more truthful. She properly assesses the substance of food as an entry point for meaningful conversations and cultural connections between the cook and the dinner guests, who may be friends or strangers. Echoing Binkovitz, historian Donna R. Gabaccia explains, "We quite willingly 'eat the other'—or at least some parts of some others, some of the time. Eating habits like these suggest tolerance and curiosity, and a willingness to digest, and to make part of one's individual identity. . . . As food consumers, Americans seem as interested in idiosyncratic and individualistic affiliations to the foodways of their neighbors as they are in their own ethnic and regional roots."[44]

Sometimes, the nomenclature from another regional cuisine is utilized to better explain and express a certain dish whose name may sound and/or look too "foreign" for native-born American diners. Chef Chris Shepherd reflects on his experience eating "Vietnamese fajitas" at Mai's restaurant in Houston.[45]

> I first saw this dish on the menu at Mai's, that late-night spot where so many of my introductory experiences to Vietnamese food took place. . . . Even though I didn't know exactly what the dish was, the sense of the unknown was reduced by that cue: fajitas. Just that one familiar word gave me a context for what I'd be getting a dish of components that you build into a wrap. I'm sure this savvy name helped a lot of people order it; they might have passed if the dish were called say, bò nướng vĩ. But I suspect using that term is also a bit of a double-edged sword: it reinforces a watering-down of their own culture and kind of whitewashes their own stories, rituals, people, and places. This kind of catch-22 is something that immigrants face almost daily: How much of their own culture do they have to give up to put other people at ease around it?[46]

Chef Shepherd articulates an important question here, pointing out the slippery slope toward cultural appropriation *and* misrepresentation of foods, when immigrants and refugees must rename and/or remake one of their own dishes to make it more palatable and recognizable to the American masses, who otherwise might get lost in translation, not be discovered, or worse, viewed as too "foreign and exotic."

Yet, a social dynamic is transformed as well, when one is open to consuming a new cuisine. For instance, when one is invited by a friend or stranger for, say, a traditional Vietnamese four-course dinner, and is welcomed into the home, the dinner host represents the "other" for the guest, at first. The guest may momentarily pause and consider what he or she has experienced or consumed in the past that may be akin to what was about to be served for dinner, while knowingly—and maybe tepidly—treading into unfamiliar territory for such a meal. The Vietnamese meal cooked, presented, and offered by the host may appear strange and even a bit odd to the dinner guest. However, as the guest consumes traditional Vietnamese dishes, one morsel at a time, the guest gradually and acceptingly becomes the outsider or other being served by the host or cook who is more knowledgeable of the food consumed. The center of the meal, and thus, the center of the conversation, shifts to the host/cook, who takes over the insider or narrator role, and the guest occupies the periphery as the meal continues to be shared and eaten. The host/cook is the expert and occupies the central role over dinner, informing, educating, and enlightening the guest about what is being consumed. The roles have been transposed during this transformative culinary experience as the outsider/other listens, eats, and learns from the host/cook about the meal and the culture behind the meal: where the food comes from; how it was conceived, procured, prepped, and cooked; and why such food exists to satisfy their physical and spiritual appetites. By the meal's end, the guest hopefully gains a better understanding and appreciation of what was served, how it was served, and why it was served. Such a meal together may also provide an opportunity for the dinner guest and host/cook to share common culinary interests, as well as exchange gastronomic questions and ideas, leading to new possibilities of cooking and creating novel dishes. A new intersection of food and culture has been explored, planting new tastes into the evolving diversity of the American palate.

CULINARY RIGHT TO HEALTHY EATING: HOME GARDENS FOR WELLNESS

Home gardens give Vietnamese Texan planters a partial return to normalcy where they have control and sovereignty to cultivate, nurture, and redeem the memories of home that strengthen them. Not only do the fruit trees, vegetables, and herbs help repair their broken selves and memories, but they also nourish the physical and mental health of Vietnamese Texan home gardeners. In Texas, Vietnamese American planters partake the opportunity to raise produce for consumption and improve their overall health and wellness.

Scholar Michèle Companion claims that "cultivation and urban gardening are critical components of the food system around the globe. Food security studies in numerous countries find that urban food production increases resource access, coping mechanisms, and income-generation opportunities for new entrants into a wage economy, internal migrants, and marginalized groups, including female-headed households."[47] Companion describes the health benefits of gardening among low-income, urban Native Americans, noting, "In Indigenous cultures, traditional foods, medicines, and rituals are intertwined with health, spirituality, and lifeways.... Physiological pathologies are enhanced by the inability to access and consume fresh produce."[48] In her findings from the urban gardens pilot program, she discovered that Native American participants who cooked and raised plants together also created good opportunities to converse and share their bounties.[49] On the pilot program's significant health impact upon low-income urban Native Americans, Companion asserts that the findings reveal that gardens have proven to show emotional and spiritual healing qualities and thus support evidence gained from previous studies. Gardens meaningfully contribute to the positive overall impact, furnishing a sense of accomplishment and reinforcing personal and social empowerment for Native American gardeners.[50]

As mentioned in chapter 3, Son Hoàng's mother, Nguyễn Lan, enjoys thinking of these beautiful plants as the product of her hard work, and is grateful for the fresh produce that strengthens and improves their health.[51] His father, Quang, strongly believes that gardening helps him "remember the past," connecting them with their previous life in Việt Nam. They both find gardening to be a nurturing daily activity that not only reduces stress but provides a connection to nature. Quang explains, "Gardening makes you live close to nature and makes life more beautiful!" Lan adds, "It's also good for our relationship because it gives us things to do together."[52]

As for Trần Thị Lừng, a year after reuniting with her husband, Phạm Minh Thứ, she and her family relocated to a Duncanville home with a sizable backyard.[53] The spacious yard made Lừng happy because she could expand her garden and plant persimmon trees and more greens. In 2003, the family moved once more, relocating to a new subdivision in Grand Prairie, where Lừng and her husband now grow hẹ (chives), ngò (cilantro), rau mồng tơi (spinach), bầu (summer squash), mướp, trái khổ qua, ớt, rau thơm, tía tô, and sả.[54] In addition, she believes that "Gardening is for relaxation after a long day working or to see the new day with new things growing in the backyard."

For Vietnamese Texans, their home gardens give them a daily outdoor leisure activity to enjoy and improve their overall health. The benefits of home gardening extend beyond personal health and joy. Home gardens also provide the time and space for spouses to work on the soil together and help build community with their friends and relatives. Vietnamese Texan planters also seek solace, peace, cultural continuity, and food sovereignty with the herbs, vegetables, and fruits they produce from their labor of love.

CULTIVATING GENDERED, WORKING-CLASS FOODWAYS IN VIETNAMESE VILLAGES

Food cultivation in less-than-ideal residential spaces exemplifies and amplifies the independent nature of Vietnamese Texans. Such characteristics—a strong streak of independence, resourcefulness, and resilience—could be defined as indicative of their working-class ethos and identity. In addition, crops such as rau đắng, đậu bắp, and ớt are typically cultivated and consumed by native-born Texans as well as Vietnamese Texans. Plus, traditional and modern Vietnamese foodways, particularly where home gardens bloom in unexpected places and fresh produce are plucked and used in daily meals, carry gendered expectations as well, where

Vietnamese diasporic women play a prominent role, and also a preeminent one, in home gardening, food gathering, meal preparation, cooking, and passing their knowledge and practices of Vietnamese food traditions to the next generation.

Vietnamese American women continue to play an influential role in preserving, shaping, and expanding Vietnamese foodways in gardens, on farms, in restaurants, in the kitchens, in recipe books, and on dining tables. Not surprisingly, throughout US history, the monumental task of undertaking the preservation and transformation of American foodways, from the garden to the kitchen to the dining table, is led by women in their roles as gardeners, home cooks, and chefs. As notable food scholar Elizabeth S. D. Engelhardt explains, "While today my aunt and uncle share the labor of the garden supplying the meal, gardens in the late nineteenth century were often seen as the domain and responsibility of women. Gardens extended domestic spaces, and in a gender-divided society, they were quite different from farms. More than that, the responsibility of planning, directing, and coordinating meals from either the historical or present-day gardens fell mostly on women's shoulders."[55] She comments on this gender separation further, noting that "kitchen space, recipes, and conversations were very much women's domain at the family meal with my grandmother's slaw, biscuit, and fried chicken recipes, aunts bringing specialty desserts, and even my generation of female cousins hanging out in the kitchen while male cousins wandered outside."[56]

As for their working-class ethos, Vietnamese Texans share common traits with their fellow Tejanos. Growing up in the Mexican American working-class environment, Chef Adán Medrano recalls, "I spent my boyhood summers in the fields picking cotton, hoeing sugar beets and soybeans, picking tomatoes, watermelons, corn, okra, cherries, and apples. It was rough being economically poor, working long days, and being excluded from opportunity. Meals brought joy to our day. Cooking was an act of survival, creativity, and affirmation."[57] Here, Chef Medrano connects both the intrinsic and intangible values of cooking for the working-class culture, sensibilities, and ethos. He demonstrates how such an environment lends to the creation, preservation, and expansion of Texas-Mexican cuisine, which Chef Medrano differentiates from the anglicized Tex-Mex cuisine.

However, Chef Medrano is not dismissive of Tex-Mex cuisine, which remains ubiquitous, popular, appreciated, and ingrained in the Lone Star state culinary culture. As freelance writer and Houston native Melissa Hung notes, "Tex-Mex isn't some kind of fake Mexican food. It's a regional cuisine rooted in Tejano culture, going back to when Texas was part of Mexico. Yes, sometimes cuisines adapt to prevailing tastes.... But sometimes cuisines morph because of the ingredients at hand."[58] She reflects about her and her parents' longing for Tex-Mex food, and finding and reliving what they love about this wondrous cuisine: "My parents recently moved from the house where I spent my adolescence to a Houston suburb. . . . I was afraid I'd have to get my Tex-Mex fix at a mediocre chain restaurant. Silly me. Google revealed a family-run restaurant five minutes from their new home. My parents . . . were thrilled with this news. Though they don't eat Tex-Mex often, they crave it, too, sometimes. My mother lamented that it had been too long since she'd eaten tamales. That evening, they studied the vast menu online. . . . The next day, we went there together for lunch. We smiled as the waiter brought our meals out on a large tray—plates of comfort and abundance."[59] The transformative nature of Texas Mexican and Tex-Mex cuisines, arguably the pantheon of Texas cuisine, exemplify what the possible trajectory of Vietnamese and Viet-Cajun cuisines are to become in the Lone Star state.

Houston takes the claim as the most diverse city in the United States, and such a claim is validated and proven not only according to government census data, but also by the plethora of ethnic restaurants and grocery stores, hybrid ethnic restaurants with a diverse labor force, languages and accents spoken at any lunch rush gathering, and street signs, marquees, and store fronts advertising cuisines from around the globe. Simultaneously and unfortunately, Houston remains a heavily segregated city in terms of race, ethnicity, and income. Most low-income residential neighborhoods continue to be disproportionately occupied by people of color—both longtime residents and newcomers. Refugees and immigrants from different continents co-exist along with working-class, born-and-raised Houstonians. Even in low-income neighborhoods, one working-class ethnic or racial group typically is the predominant group residing in the neighborhood. With one ethnic or racial enclave neighborhood located next to another and another, the city has multiple ethnic and racial groups living in close proximity, yet in segregated apartment complexes and condo buildings within the same working-class ward or neighborhood. Despite their working-class struggles, Vietnamese diasporans currently residing in the six villages of southeast Houston manage to create a modest living in their humble abodes, which oftentimes are decorated in the vibrant cascades of various greens, fruit trees, and flowers. They retain their neighborhood community via cultural continuities of their Vietnamese food, language, religions, informal economy, and mutual aid associations. Vietnamese villagers have built, maintained, and strengthened their community, demonstrating their work ethic, resourcefulness, ingenuity, resolute will, and communal responsibility.

Vietnamese Houstonians are not alone in protecting and promoting their cultural continuities. Journalist Susan Rogers describes the St. Cloud apartment complex on

Hillcroft, located in one of Houston's "densest, poorest, and most diverse neighborhoods—Gulfton. But St. Cloud stands in stark defiance of expectations. Home to primarily ethnic Nepalese refugees from Bhutan, it is indescribably beautiful—it works like an 'urban village.' . . . On any day you can find men gathered in the courtyard playing the traditional board game carrom, children playing freely, mothers chatting on chairs moved outside to supervise, and pickling jars and container gardens dotting adjacent balconies and carports. In many ways the spatial definition of the courtyards has created a shared and safe space that is both central and watched over by all the residents."[60] Rogers describes the similar physical features of the urban enclave of Thái Xuân Village and how these define daily life:

> Today, Thai Xuan Village remains imperfect, but worth understanding. . . . Tenants grow vegetables and fruits in their small fenced yards or on the balconies, a small store occupying a former apartment serves residents' basic needs, and children play basketball on the slab of a demolished building. . . . The changes at Thai Xuan are entirely organic. The gradient from public to private space, a favorite mantra of designers and housing specialists alike, has been well defined, moving from the shared public courtyards to the semi-public fenced gardens and patios to the individual units. . . . St. Cloud and Thai Xuan Village illustrate the potentials of ground-up change in Houston's large multifamily complexes, but more needs to be done to ensure that affordable housing in dense and well-served neighborhoods is preserved.[61]

Rogers contends that much could be learned from both the Vietnamese residents of Thái Xuân Village and the Nepalese inhabitants of St. Cloud in terms of how they have organically transformed and retrofitted their dilapidated apartment and condo buildings into charter schools, places of worship, community centers, family-owned business, and youth programs. In addition, they have utilized their ingenuity and limited resources to convert small concrete spaces and grassy areas into vegetable gardens and microfarms. For Vietnamese villagers, protecting and preserving their urban living spaces and cultural continuities are imperative to their survival and success, particularly as many continue to live on the margins economically and remain largely segregated from other Houstonians. One method of making their urban living spaces more sustainable—and therefore, make their community more livable and substantial—is maintaining their home gardens, no matter the size.

The home gardens cultivated by Vietnamese village residents of Thái Xuân, Đà Lạt, Sài Gòn, Huế, Thanh Tâm, and St. Joseph demonstrate the importance of maintaining Vietnamese culture through foodways. These home gardens carefully planted in small spaces also prove the resilience of Vietnamese villagers living as part of the Texas' working-class. *Houston Chronicle* journalist and 2019 George Polk Award recipient, Lomi Kriel,[62] details the origins of Thái Xuân Village: "To help their community, some Vietnamese investors purchased rundown complexes in south Houston as a safe space for their compatriots. . . . The largest, Thai Xuan, still exists today near Hobby Airport. Its one thousand Vietnamese residents have transformed it into a token of the old country, renewing traditions and existing almost entirely in Vietnamese."[63] She reports how Thái Xuân Village's Vietnamese diasporic residents operate their informal economy. For instance, in the afternoons, Vietnamese village women gather and sit out in the parking lot to arrange their produce for sale; produce that they cultivated from their own small home gardens and microfarms.[64] Kriel further describes how "some wear *nón lás*, cream-colored cone-shaped hats made of straw and sell vegetables and fried egg rolls. . . . On hot days, they dole out *sam*, a sweet, iced herbal tea with natural cooling qualities, perfect for the oppressive humidity of the city they still call Saigon. On a stretch of Broadway Street in south Houston, these one thousand residents have over nearly three decades transformed the crumbling apartments they named Thai Xuan Village."[65]

What may appear humbling and crumbling on the facade of their apartment buildings is in reality a postwar resilient, innovative, celebrated, and even thriving Vietnamese culture in an urban setting where the language, social network, and home gardens are native to the Vietnamese refugees and immigrants. They have discovered, created, and preserved a home to be proud of, and a community that they could call their own. On the one hand, they are socially segregated and isolated. But on the other hand, they have built a safe and comfortable community to combat the daunting challenges for a traumatized and stigmatized diasporic population. Such home gardens help Vietnamese Texans build their sense of place, unity, and camaraderie. Their home gardens and familiar produce give them the opportunity to build a community and be better neighbors to one another. For Vietnamese Houstonians residing in working-class condominiums with limited space to cultivate gardens, they make the most of what they have and convert such restricted spaces into positive places of food sovereignty and culinary citizenship. It is no paradise, but the effort is evident. It is not the proverbial garden of Eden, but more. It is home.

HOMELAND DUALITY AND CULINARY CONTACT ZONES

Furthermore, their home gardens lead to a chosen path of homeland duality. With culinary citizenship, Vietnamese Texan home gardeners experience a homeland duality, as culinary citizens of both Việt Nam and the United States. By growing, nurturing, picking, cooking, and consuming the vegetables, herbs, and fruits from their home gardens, Vietnamese Texans establish a homeland duality, planting their culinary roots in the Texas soil with produce that reminds them of Việt Nam. Thus, homeland duality applies to the Vietnamese diasporic experience of rooting themselves here in the United States, by cultivating small plots of home gardens that are safe, positive spaces that, in turn, help them stay rooted to their old Việt Nam.

Here, I argue that Vietnamese Texan home gardeners practice culinary citizenship and embrace a homeland duality with the fresh ingredients plucked from their gardens to prepare and cook Vietnamese staples. Such meals are consumed communally with family and loved ones, and traditional Vietnamese dishes, flavors, textures, and smells are experimented with in order to expand Vietnamese foodways. This aids them in ascertaining a homeland duality, in the United States present, and in a transhistorical place that embodies the living evidence of a South Việt Nam past.

Home gardens provide a sliver of home away from their homeland. Hence, the term contains a distinctive double connotation. For Vietnamese Texans, home gardens give them the opportunity to root, carve, and shape their small plots of home here in the United States, while remembering and reviving their former spatial homeland of a ghost country that is South Việt Nam. Plus, Vietnamese Texan home gardeners have utilized the produce of their gardens to not only procure organic, healthy, and readily accessible herbs, fruits, and vegetables, but also to build a food community. Their home gardens have helped them transition them from being food insecure to reclaiming food sovereignty and justice. Coincidently, through the political and resolute act of home gardening, Vietnamese Texans are transformed from living as refugees to living in resistance; a resistance toward mainstream and dominant food processes and systems that are alien to them. Their food resistance lies in the labor put forth into the soil, where home gardens give birth to vegetables, herbs, and fruits essential to Vietnamese food culture. As explained in the previous chapter, home garden greens and crops are serve as indispensable ingredients to numerous traditional Vietnamese dishes, which are prepared and cooked at home, and become comforting and satisfying meals for Vietnamese Texan families to consume together. Therefore, cultivating home gardens serve as political acts of resistance to not only preserve a rich part of Vietnamese heritage, but to also challenge current mainstream US food processes and systems that lend to mass production and consumption of processed foods. Furthermore, Vietnamese Texan home gardeners create agency, directly defying what are considered US food culture norms and hegemony, and instead introduce Americans to the rich and diverse Vietnamese food culture that is vital to Vietnamese Texans' survival, wellness, and identity. In addition, their political act of home gardening helps them establish, secure, and define culinary citizenship on their terms.

Michael W. Twitty calls for culinary justice, which he identifies as "the idea that a people should be recognized for their gastronomic contributions and have a right to their inherent value, including the opportunity to derive empowerment from them."[66] He further expands on the importance of culinary justice and its growth as a form of food justice: "Today, this widens the lens of food justice, which centers around increasing access to healthy food and helps amplify how culture, food, and power interplay and amplifies the agents leading the revolution."[67] With the concept of culinary justice, Twitty has certainly advanced our philosophy on food—the production, procurement, preparation, sharing, consumption, and memory of food. I wish to add to culinary justice, that for the refugees, immigrants, enslaved, and marginalized populaces, they seek culinary citizenship as well—a right to belong and be a contributing member with valuable foodways, and not just reside here.

Environmental justice professor Monica M. White comments on this concept regarding African slaves remembering their homelands via foodways. She explains, "For those who were enslaved, this practice of growing food, especially foods from the motherland, and the social exchanges that went on in the marketplaces were also opportunities to enact freedom. Using food production, the enslaved were able to practice the cultural and ceremonial uses of land they had brought with them, as a way to celebrate their ancestors and the homeland they left behind."[68] White aptly recalibrates African slaves as freedom farmers who, despite the brutal oppression from slave captors, traders, and owners, offered daily resistance through foodways of their own cultivation, production, and consumption. African slaves were the original American freedom farmers in US history, not the plantation owners who signed the Declaration of Independence or led the Continental Army in the Revolutionary War against the British. Tracing the farm-to-freedom movement of African slaves to Black freedmen and freedwomen during Reconstruction and Jim Crow to African American farming cooperatives in the mid-twentieth century, White asserts, "Growing food was a life-affirming, collective strategy. Liberatory agriculture ignited the imagination of farmer-activists in African American farming cooperatives during the mid-twentieth century."[69] She also claims that self-determined agriculture continues into the twenty-first century as urban farmers and gardeners respond to the debilitating conditions of deindustrialization and economic downturn by learning lessons from past decades of successes and failures that offer them an opportunity to create successful Black farming cooperatives.[70]

As for Latinx immigrants who labored in the United States as migrant farmers, the desire to own a small farm and cultivate crops that remind them of home is palpable. Food scholar Laura-Anne Minkoff-Zern asserts, "For many immigrant farmers, establishing a farm is not only a survival strategy but also a way to create a new life in the United States—one where they are able to build on their culture as food producers to create a space of their own. Their nostalgia for home draws on both an idea of the past and dream for the future. . . . Looking forward to establishing a real home, they borrow from notions of an idealized one, ultimately creating a hybrid version of the place they remember combined with the realities of a new life."[71] She further says, "As many immigrants explained, they farm in the United States in part to re-create a *recuerdo*, or memory, of their former lifestyle in Mexico. These agricultural spaces are representative of a desire to for re-creating a home place, where farmers are able to define their own livelihoods and spaces."[72] The Mexican immigrant farmers Minkoff-Zern conversed with said repeatedly that they needed to grow food that connected them to familiar cultural practices they could associate with home. Purchasing healthy food for the family was not enough.[73] Here, liberatory agriculture is applicable to Mexican immigrant farmers and migrant workers and their strong aspirations to retain food practices that link them to their homeland. They seek to own land and manage a small farm that provides greater economic freedom and cultural liberation to preserve and expand their food practices. Fortunately, some have achieved land ownership. For Mexican immigrant farmers, such farm-to-freedom praxis serves as an essential counterweight to the consequences of late twentieth and early twenty-first century neoliberal global capitalism that has uprooted and created more displaced peoples on this planet than at any other time in human history.

Liberatory agriculture can also occur on a much smaller scale and apply to immigrant home gardeners digging and carving urban spaces to gain emancipatory foodways. Sociologist Pierrette Hondagneu-Sotelo argues that "gardens can serve as minizones of autonomy, as sites and practices of transcendence and restoration. Gardens offer compensation for lost worlds, bringing moments of pleasure, tranquility, and beauty, and they articulate future possibilities."[74] Hondagneu-Sotelo further asserts that "the cultivation of particular flowers, herbs, vegetables, and fruits forges critical connections to cultural memory and homeland . . . providing a narrative of home continuity and familiarity that is particularly meaningful for immigrants from rural preindustrial societies."[75] In her seminal work, *Paradise Transplanted*, she describes how undocumented immigrants living in Los Angeles are some of the poorest, most marginalized newcomer immigrants; they have been excluded from other urban spaces, but they have gathered together to cultivate homeland vegetables, share community ties, and construct new positive places of belonging. In fact, she argues that they have collectively transformed abandoned urban patches of ground into "oases of freedom, belonging, and homeland connection."[76] Hondagneu-Sotelo declares: "For new immigrants and refugees, community gardens provide thriving food-growing spaces and homeland connections."[77] She also states that community gardens give marginalized undocumented immigrants a chance to rebuild their lives and connect their past with the current disheartening realities. Thus, their community gardens "become linking objects to lessen the pain of lost social worlds."[78]

Hondagneu-Sotelo describes the important homeland connections made by recent Latinx immigrants in Los Angeles when they plant and raise community gardens. Such homeland connections are also made by diasporans when they cultivate home gardens in their front and backyards, on small parcels of land surrounding the aging condo buildings they reside in, or even in shared public spaces. No doubt, through homeland connections with their gardens and a collection of familiar crops grown, Vietnamese Texan planters unearth a homeland duality by their own agency. They are defining the conditions of belonging here in Texas, as well as reconnecting to their South Việt Nam by growing herbs, vegetables, and fruit trees familiar to them. Such gardens and produce also assist them in healing emotionally and physically from the terrors of war, abandonment, displacement, and racialization. With their gardens and produce, they are linking to an old homeland while simultaneously establishing a new place to call home.

These personal home gardens, as well as the microfarms and gardens of Vietnamese villagers, serve as physical culinary contact zones where they interact not only with nature, but also socialize with their fellow village residents or nearby neighbors to exchange seeds, planting tips, and produce while sharing their interests, stories, and latest news. Historian Mark Padoongpatt notes this tendency in immigrants from Thailand, observing that "physical culinary contact zones acted as central places for Thai Americans to form and express identity and build community and, in doing so, put forth a spatial imaginary based on public sociability, collective use of space, transnationalism, and liberal multiculturalism. . . . Thus, considering the role of food in struggles for a right to the global city offers a tangible entry point into the way people experience and perceive racialized spaces and a glimpse into the formation of metropolitan identity."[79] Here, I would add to Padoongpatt's observations and insightful scholarship and argue that these small plots of homeland and the crops planted and nurtured are individual (and communal) markers of physical culinary contact zones for Vietnamese Texan home gardeners. Therefore, the home gardens and microfarms cultivated by Vietnamese diasporans are physical evidence of how they wish to live a Vietnamese life in America—a life that was violently disrupted by war and relocation, but now is partially reclaimed and redeemed with their hands transforming the soil into their own treasured plot of homeland, one that also manifests as two homelands.

Scholars Alison Hope Alkon, Yuki Kato, and Joshua Sbicca remind us of the precarious nature of urban beautification and renewal for marginalized populations. "Urban gardens have historically served as a place for low-income people of color in the city to grow food that supplements their pantry, reminds them of home, and provides a place for ethnic or neighborhood solidarity," they explain.[80] Alkon, Kato, and Sbicca also remark that green spaces—such as community gardens originally created to provide food security and beautification in low-income neighborhoods—may unfortunately lead to urban gentrification that raises property values so high that displacement occurs in these neighborhoods. To enhance our study on the intersectionality of food and gentrification, Analena Hope Hassberg offers the term "citified sovereignty," which she calls "a theory that attempts to bridge food justice, which is largely a US-based concept applied to urban areas, with food sovereignty— an idea usually applied to rural settings in developing nations."[81] She states, "My theory of citified sovereignty posits that land ownership and autonomous community control of local foodways counters the potential negative impacts of redevelopment and revitalization efforts by preserving local spaces, identities, practices, and economies. . . . A thriving local food system that addresses the unique needs of the surrounding community contributes to a sense of place and belonging. It ensures that people who cannot easily leave the neighborhood due to lack of transportation, limited mobility, or disability are not stuck with meager options and low-quality food."[82] Here, Hassberg's citified sovereignty theory applies to Vietnamese Texan home gardeners, too, particularly for Vietnamese village residents living in deteriorating condominiums in the low-income, working-class neighborhoods of southeast Houston. These gardeners attempt to maximize their minimal garden spaces by utilizing the dilapidated infrastructure to cultivate herbs, fruit trees, and vegetables underneath stairways, along handrails, and on small balconies and patios. They are preserving Vietnamese foodways and keeping the past alive. Not only are they comfortable in the place-making of a village lifestyle, but they are also unlikely to be able to afford leaving their secluded village sanctuaries. Any urban planning and development (intentional or unintentional) toward the gentrification of these working-class neighborhoods and Vietnamese villages of southeast Houston would be disastrous and detrimental for the residents and their small yet unique urban gardens. It would result in yet another traumatized displacement for working-class Vietnamese diasporans and represent a "double" home loss. For now, Vietnamese Texan planters continue to cultivate their favorite greens and crops to gain better food security, remember their old homeland, and plant roots into their new home country.

With their home gardens, Vietnamese Texans construct spaces to help free themselves from the trauma of war, exile, relocation, and racialization, and consequently regain some food sovereignty and justice. They also contribute to local, regional, national, and international foodways, enriching the palates and tastes of our ever-evolving American food traditions. In *Eating Asian America*, food writer and activist Nina F. Ichikawa asserts that "Asian Americans were pioneering farmers, literally building soil that to this day forms the fertile foundation of arms that still exist."[83] Ichikawa goes on to say that "Asian American farmworkers today are more likely to be Hmong, Mien, Lao, Chinese, Filipino, or Vietnamese, and live in the upper Midwest, deep South, or anywhere along the rich growing area of the West Coast."[84] In microfarming and home gardening, Vietnamese Texans continue to make significant contributions to the United States' food culture and history. They also embrace and extend sustainable practices, as well as food sovereignty and justice by growing vegetables, fruit trees, and herbs that help maintain cultural continuity. Preserving Vietnamese food heritage via home gardening protects and enhances Vietnamese gastronomic traditions and praxis; strengthens the Vietnamese diasporic collective by gaining emancipatory foodways of food sovereignty, culinary citizenship, and homeland duality; improves, expands, and diversifies US food systems; and thus importantly, allows us to further advance food security and justice in America.

Award-winning and renowned Canadian visual artist, Liz Magor, was featured in a PBS documentary series called *Art21*. Aside from her amazing artwork over the years, Magor's philosophy on art and history struck me most. In the episode featuring Vancouver artists, Magor explains that her public art installation entitled *LightShed* (2005), was created in "keeping the past alive."[85] Home gardeners, in their own horticultural ways, are keeping the past alive by raising fruit trees, vegetables, and herbs that remind them of their past home. In their own ways, these Vietnamese Texan home gardeners are artists, too, using soil, seeds, water, and sunlight to create and preserve their produce so that generations may remember to keep the past—and themselves—alive by seeking, creating, and (re)claiming their own emancipatory foodways.

CHAPTER 6

Conclusion

From Refuge to Redemption

Quà

—Vietnamese word for fruit or gift

They have lost their countries of origin, either by choice or circumstance, and their hosts often see them as others. This sense of loss and otherness inflects their memories differently from the memories of majorities.

—Việt Thanh Nguyễn, from *Nothing Ever Dies*

Tall, wide trees in the forests of the Pacific Northwest serve as nurse logs to their seedlings after they fall, providing decades of water and nutrients as they slowly decay.

—Sir David Attenborough, from *The Private Life of Plants*

Analogous to a nurse log—a fallen tree that provides some of the essential ingredients for seedlings to grow—home gardens provide a necessary growing medium that is more sustainable for the Vietnamese diaspora to retain their

community and culture, strengthen an identity, and impart knowledge and an identity as their lives take root in the United States, which also roots the reimagined
homeland in memory and postmemory for generations of Vietnamese Americans.
For home gardeners and cooks like Trần Thi Lừng, they want to share their knowledge and expertise of cultivating produce and cooking traditional meals with their
children and grandchildren, preserving another slice of their homeland through
Vietnamese foodways.[1] In turn, the 1.5, second, and third generations will remember and retain an understanding of a bygone Việt Nam whether planting seeds to
grow đậu bắp, as tall as eye level; cutting fresh rau muống and rau thơm as garnishes
for phở bò for the entire family to eat for several days; incorporating hành lá (green
onions) and ngò as ingredients for comfort street eats like bánh xèo (sizzling savory
crepés); pickling cà pháo to nibble as a condiment; or consuming trái bưởi (pomelo) or đu đủ for dessert.

Wars never end, not for the victimized. For the victims who survived, both the war
and the dead haunt them and their descendants. To recover and heal, Vietnamese
refugees and immigrants transform their own negative spaces of war, exile, resettlement, and racialization. Such negative spaces have left them, and generations after,
traumatized and troubled by the Việt Nam War and bereft of a homeland. Yet many
have cultivated their own home gardens and microfarms, transforming negative
spaces into positive places where they rightfully earn their food justice and sovereignty despite their victimization and dehumanization during an atrocious, violent war.

In their postwar resettlement in the United States, Vietnamese Americans
have found a new home—once perceived as temporary, but now, for most, permanent. Yet, memories truly never die. What is practiced generation after generation
becomes habitual and ingrained as part of the culture—even when the homeland
of South Việt Nam is now a ghost nation. For Vietnamese refugees and immigrants, the common cultural praxis not only includes an anticommunist narrative,
but also comprises memories from the war, as well as before and after the war.
With these memories, fragments of their homeland are connected and jumbled
together, and they discover and recreate both a sanctuary and a piece of their old
homeland in the home gardens and communal microfarms of Vietnamese villages.
Vietnamese American home gardeners construct their own places of belonging and

cultural continuance, seeking emancipation through food sovereignty, culinary citizenship, and homeland duality that is centered in the food they produce, cook, consume, and share from the harvests of their home gardens.

Renowned sociologist Linda Võ asserts, "The argument that immigrants do not want to 'become Americans' because they organize themselves along ethnic lines or have maintained an attachment to their homeland is too simplistic; in fact, their participation in ethnic communities allows them to become integrated into their new homeland, and enables them to maintain components of their ethnic identities and history."[2] Independent and noted scholar Nhi T. Liễu argues, "Neither static nor pure, Vietnamese culture has always been in flux—an unstable process that is always in motion."[3] I could not agree with Võ and Liễu more. Vietnamese cuisine has always been in flux, where Vietnamese diasporic home cooks, chefs, gardeners, and restaurateurs constantly attempt to perfect old recipes while creating new ones to enhance, revive, and celebrate the flavors, textures, smells, and tastes that remind them of home and belonging. So long as they continue to seek and find these senses of home and belonging, Vietnamese gastronomy will remain in good hands with Vietnamese diasporic home cooks, chefs, gardeners, and restaurateurs.

In Texas, home gardens are instrumental in remembering, maintaining, and strengthening Vietnamese foodways, but for Vietnamese Texan home gardeners it offers so much more; it provides an avenue to gain strength, wellness, peace, solace, and some redemption. The herbs, vegetables, and fruit trees cultivated provide them an immediate access to such produce while preserving traditional Vietnamese cooking and cuisine. A plethora of herbs, fruits, and vegetables are utilized as essential ingredients for a variety of dishes and/or served as condiments and garnishes for meals. Vietnamese Texan home gardeners demonstrate their hard work and resilience to survive and succeed, while preserving and imparting their Vietnamese heritage via home gardening for current and future generations to build on. Furthermore, Vietnamese Texan home gardeners are part of a long, arduous history of the farm-to-freedom movement, where marginalized, oppressed, and subjugated populations seek freedom and liberation by fighting for and gaining their own food sovereignty and justice.

This book's chapters cover the gamut of the farm-to-freedom concept and of human longing and belonging: longing for freedom from war, tyranny, mass violence, oppression, and rootlessness, and belonging to a homeland of their own volition. For Vietnamese Texan planters, their gardens become a vital grounding connection to their lost homeland. Their homeland is not exclusively in Việt Nam nor the United States, but rather a homeland that exists in the historical ties and pulls between these two countries, where transnational linkages and foodways are established to remind them of home. Such transnational foodways become portals to past memories of taste, smell, sight, and touch—memories of not just the war, but much more—their own Việt Nam *and* now their United States. These fragmented memories of their homeland have been planted and nurtured in the Texas soil by Vietnamese diasporic home gardeners. When they harvest, share, and consume the bounty they produce in their home gardens, they share a portion of their homeland. They also discover and create both a sanctuary—from the distresses of war, evacuation, displacement, and racialization—and a new homeland. By replanting their roots here in the Texas soil, and raising bountiful and meaningful home gardens, Vietnamese Texans cultivate ties to a Việt Nam they remember, so that generations may enjoy the fruits of their labor. Whether purposefully or not, with their hands digging into the earth, they have cultivated a farm-to-freedom movement, liberating a part of themselves and others, by pursuing and achieving food sovereignty, culinary citizenship, and a homeland duality of their own free will and desire, while enabling and encouraging other Vietnamese Texans to do likewise.

Vietnamese Texan home gardeners and microfarmers broaden their farm-to-freedom movement by building community and an informal social network of sharing their produce and gardening tips with neighbors, friends, and relatives; by retaining foodways that are inherent yet dynamic in Vietnamese culture; by remembering and engaging in the cultural continuity of planting and producing herbs, fruits, and vegetables tailored to their diet and nutrition; and by cooking home meals that incorporate the home grown produce as essential ingredients to such traditional soups like canh rau đay (water spinach soup) and salads such as gỏi đu đủ (papaya salad). By tracing Vietnamese foodways from Việt Nam to refugee camps throughout Southeast Asia to diasporic communities in Texas, we witness how Vietnamese Texan home gardeners and microfarmers gain food security while sustaining their culinary heritage. The variety of produce from home gardens and microfarms allow Vietnamese diasporic home cooks to incorporate fresh greens and crops to make traditional Vietnamese meals or modern fusion dishes, and therefore retain and widen Vietnamese foodways for generations. The countless hours of gardening and farming and the fruits of such labor allow Vietnamese Texans to root out negative spaces and transform them into positive green places that also become transhistorical links to their ghost homeland of South Việt Nam. Vietnamese refugees and immigrants in Texas have shown incredible perseverance, strength, determination, innovation, and survival skills.

Vietnamese diasporans have suffered, survived, and succeeded in unearthing their very own existence through these home gardens, planting their future and freedom for current and future generations to remember, record, consume, share, and rejoice. From the produce they have grown in their yards to the Vietnamese gastronomy they have retained and reclaimed, Vietnamese Texan home gardeners and microfarmers have demonstrated acts of food sovereignty and culinary citizenship in search for a homeland duality that is theirs alone. Then perhaps, in their constructed homeland duality, they are finally emancipated from the shackles of the Việt Nam War.

Through kitchen and home gardens, historical patterns emerge in Vietnamese diasporic history. Vietnamese refugees and immigrants have made a concerted effort to regain food security, justice, and sovereignty, transforming negative spaces into positive places that redeem and preserve their homelands with gardens cultivated and the produce raised from their labor of joy. In addition, Vietnamese Texans plant their own version of victory gardens to survive and live a meaningful life, carving out an existence of reviving, preserving, expanding, and sharing their food heritage. Their victory gardens may not be referenced in history textbooks, or even classified as such, but for Vietnamese refugee and immigrant gardeners, they certainly deserve to reap the rewards. They have overcome daunting challenges and found the time, small spaces, and energy to plant gardens and an awesome array of produce, oftentimes under strenuous living conditions and terrible stress. By planting, raising, and consuming herbs, vegetables, and fruits that they nurture into existence with their own hands, they certainly have earned victory and liberation from the hostilities of war, exile, displacement, and racialization. For Vietnamese Texan home gardeners, such small victories are no doubt hard-fought triumphs to uphold cultural continuance through emancipatory foodways. In the home garden is where they spend countless hours toiling in the soil, processing the historical erasure and oblivion, and building their own food sovereignty, culinary citizenship, and homeland duality. Their home gardens and microfarms transform the little spaces available into astounding plots of greens and fruit trees. These home gardens and small farms function as places of religious and sacred observance, represent sustainable practices and cultural preservation, encourage physical health and spiritual well-being, build community and interpersonal relationships, and create food security, culinary freedom, and finally home.

Farm-to-Freedom for Congolese and Syrian Refugees

D uring my research in Houston, I stumbled upon a local nonprofit organization Plant It Forward (PIF) Farms thanks to mutual acquaintance and food journalist David Leftwich. Leftwich recommended that I contact Liz Vallette, then-president of PIF Farms. Once I started talking to Vallette, I quickly became drawn to their remarkable work with Congolese refugee farmers living and laboring in Houston. Clearly, I am no expert on African history, the Congolese diaspora, or even agricultural history. Nevertheless, my interest lies in the *whys* behind food heritage, food justice, and food sovereignty issues for marginalized communities. In addition, marginalized peoples occupy liminal or in-between spaces, and we often fail to see their interstitial lives among us. I am interested in writing about these invisible lives and hope that it will lead to greater visibility and appreciation for the marginalized. After all, history never ends until every story is told.

The powerful act of planting home gardens is also currently performed by Syrian refugees who have created beautiful food gardens in refugee camps strewn across the desert landscapes of Lebanon, Jordan, and Iraq. The vegetables, fruit trees, and herbs they plant and grow are small yet substantial reminders of their homeland that give them nourishment, hope, peace, and some sovereignty over the foods they consume. Syrian refugees in Domiz, northern Iraq, have named their communal garden the Azadi Garden, which means "liberation" in Kurdish.[1] In essence, Syrian refugees are cultivating their own farm-to-freedom experience, much like Vietnamese refugees.

The farm-to-freedom concept applies to the ongoing plight of Syrian refugees as they continue to endure daily struggles and the pains of a vicious civil war. Amid personal loss, persecution, and resettlement, Syrian refugees have cultivated beautiful gardens in refugee camps across the deserts of Iraq, Jordan, and Lebanon. Syrian

Figure E.1   Plant It Forward Farms at Westbury. Houston, Texas. (Photo by Ngọc Vũ.)

refugees at the Za'atari Camp in Jordan have established temporary, makeshift gardens. They grow fruit trees and vegetables for nourishment, maintain a part of their own identity, pass the time, and reject the notion of being invisible victims of war and displacement in spite a litany of mental and physical hurdles they must overcome as they live in chronic uncertainty with no home to return to. Akin to Vietnamese refugees of the late twentieth century, Syrian refugees are indeed active agents of history, visibly determined to survive and reestablish some control over their own food sovereignty in hopes of being free from war, destruction, destitution, and statelessness.

Congolese refugees from the Democratic Republic of the Congo (Congo-Kinshasa) and the Republic of the Congo (Congo-Brazzaville) have also experienced the troubles of war, displacement, refugee camp life, resettlement, and isolation. Many Congolese refugees have resettled in working-class neighborhoods in southwest Houston as they try to earn a modest living and adjust to life in a new country. Despite their overwhelming challenges, the Congolese diaspora in Houston continue to persevere as they develop their own community and retain much of their culture. Some have adopted the practice of urban farming and gardening to establish their own food sovereignty, culinary citizenship, and homeland duality via

Congolese foodways. These are just a few stories of the other victory gardens from marginalized, oppressed, and stateless peoples. The following stories of contemporary Syrian and Congolese refugees allow us to critically contextualize and historicize Vietnamese refugees and immigrants and their cultivation of victory gardens—a victory toward emancipatory foodways.

UNIVERSALITY OF HOME GARDENS: SYRIAN REFUGEE GARDENERS SEEKING HANEEN

Ever since 2011 when the civil war began to tear their country apart, Syrian refugees have demonstrated their political activism, resilience, and resistance by creating food gardens in the desert refugee camps of Lebanon, Jordan, and Iraq. They cultivate their own food gardens, growing vegetables, fruit trees, and herbs to sustain themselves, improve their overall health, survive, cope, rebuild community, and regain their food sovereignty. By regaining some food sovereignty, Syrian refugees maintain, remember, and strengthen their food heritage.

At the Domiz refugee camp in northern Iraq, National Public Radio (NPR) journalist Julia Travers reports: "Fig and pomegranate trees, grapes, carrots, and narcissus flowers are some of the plants that Aveen Ismail likes to grow in the Domiz refugee camp in northern Iraq where she lives. That's because these plants remind her of Syria and home." Travers explains that these gardens were not an immediate response: "At first, Ismail did not find the dry land welcoming. But she values greenery and gardening, so she cultivated a small patch of land next to the house her family built in the camp." She further describes the plight of Ismail and millions of Syrian refugees. "Ismail, her husband, and three children fled the Syrian Civil War in 2011," explains Travers. "They left their home in Damascus after several family members were killed in their neighborhood. More than eleven million Syrians have been displaced and more than 250,000 have died in the ongoing war. Ismail's family is among about 26,500 refugees in the Domiz camp, which covers approximately 710 square miles."[2]

Katie Dancey-Downs also covers the incredible gardens of Domiz. Dancey-Downs reports: "On a small plot of land, an organic demonstration garden has been set up. Fruit and vegetables grown in a polytunnel, whilst a women's and children's garden offers a place for children to play safely. From this small piece of land, people are harvesting broccoli, radishes, onions, and other seasonal vegetables."[3] She further states how, in Domiz, Syrian refugees need not only a communal space for some shade and respite, but they also need an activity to share and bond with each other. "This is not about imposing ideas, but about supporting people with what they already know how to do," analyzes Dancey-Downs. "Some people in the camp had even brought their own seeds on their journeys from Syria, others had gone to great lengths to source them. Whilst the charity brings the tools, seeds, and training, the rest is down to the very people who call this camp home. The project is refugee-run, and there are even employment opportunities. . . . Alongside food sovereignty and community building, there are other benefits to microgardening inside the camp; planting flowers beautifies the space; growing vegetables can provide a sense of purpose; and planting trees around homes create privacy, a sound barrier, and protection from the desert dust."[4] Dancey-Downs concludes that their microgardens help Syrian refugees deal with the traumas they endured while escaping their home country, and from adjusting to daily living in a challenging, new place.

Helen Briggs, a reporter for the BBC, pens a fascinating story on Syrian refugees living on the Domiz refugee camp in northern Iraq. Briggs also cites Aveen Ismail, who declares that "Creating a garden was a way for us to heal and remind us of home."[5] Briggs also explains that the camp gardeners would start with the seeds and plants brought to them from Syria by relatives. They would grow the seeds and plants to create a garden. The community would gather together and construct raised beds that are planted with vegetables and flowers.[6]

Helene Schulze of Food Tank sheds further light on the "greening of the desert" taking place in Domiz, Iraq.[7] While describing this transformation, Schulze provides a gendered analysis behind the fruition and success of refugee camp gardens: "Urban agriculture and greening can also support female empowerment within the camps. . . . Frequently, it is women who remain in the camp because husbands have found work elsewhere. Training women provides employment, activity, and food for the whole family."[8] Here, Schulze's argument is applicable to the social, economic, and political roles of refugee women when they cultivate and manage food gardens in camps. Refugee women make a tremendous and pivotal contribution to the refugee camp's food sovereignty, economy, and sustainable practices. Consequently, these home gardens that are mostly raised, nurtured, and managed by refugee women provide substantial moral and financial support for the entire camp community. Plus, home gardens empower refugee women, who are often relied upon for food sustainability and sovereignty to help retain, remember, and strengthen their Syrian heritage and homeland.

In Beirut, Lebanon, *Al Jazeera* journalist Olivia Alabaster reports of another Syrian refugee camp where home gardens are flourishing despite the overwhelming challenges faced by refugees. Alabaster describes the following scene: "Fatin Kazzi's sun-drenched balcony garden is a cluster of makeshift planters, some fashioned out of crates or the ends of two-liter plastic water bottles. . . . Already bursting with strawberries, mint, basil, peppers and celery, the garden is just a month old, but Kazzi—who is living in Beirut as a refugee having fled Aleppo five years ago [in 2011] amid Syria's civil war—eventually hopes to be able to make her own salad from the vegetables here." Alabaster notes how Kazzi's small balcony garden has impacted her mental health. In the article Kazzi says, "My spirit is relaxed when I'm out here. . . . It provides food and makes the terrace look nice."[9] Alabaster also quotes Gabi al-Halabi, another Syrian refugee who has cultivated a successful rooftop garden thanks to an initiative aimed at helping Syrian refugees in Lebanon grow their own food in rooftop gardens. Al-Halabi says, "What I like most about the project is that I'm eating healthy food, and enjoying my morning cup of coffee up here in my garden."[10] Al-Halabi's rooftop garden covers the terrace and is replete with herbs and vegetables, including coriander, mint, basil, celery, chili peppers, marjoram, thyme, onions, courgettes, and strawberries. Such a bountiful rooftop garden is a transformative and gratifying oasis of green surrounded by concrete jungle in congested Beirut.

Syrian refugees have cultivated a success story via gardening in dry, desert regions through their own volition, hard work, sheer ingenuity, and resilience. They preserve their food heritage by growing vegetables, fruit trees, and herbs that remind them of home. Syrian refugee gardeners seek food sovereignty and justice, demonstrating their creativity, resourcefulness, and perseverance. Even more, they craft their own victory gardens with their hands and determination; these small gardens mark a victory over their losses and traumas from a forced migration, which will affect them for a lifetime and for generations to come. Whether these victory gardens are as temporary as their refugee status or the refugee camps themselves, Syrian refugee gardeners have dug and carved out a piece of homeland for themselves, transforming dry desert spaces into lush gardens appropriately named "Azadi."[11]

Kimberly Meyer, freelance writer and author of *The Book of Wanderings: A Mother-Daughter Pilgrimage*, works with Amaanah Refugee Services and her current book project is about single mother refugees, particularly from Syria, Sudan, Iraq, and other Middle Eastern and African nations. The project is a concerted effort "to understand what was happening in their home countries; what this process of displacement was like for them."[12] In her latest work, she interviews and spends lots of time with an Iraqi single mother refugee, framing her story to follow five other single mother refugees, and writing about one of the most vulnerable populations in Houston.

In an interview, Meyer explained more about the project and her observations about Syrian refugees and their home garden in Houston: "Most of the other Syrians that I have met and written about, and just know, all seem to have gardens. Like this seems to have been part of life in Syria. Backyard gardens where they would grow different produce, fruit trees, pomegranate trees, lemon trees [and] olive trees . . . lots of herbs and fruits and vegetables that they would grow and then, of course, all of them seem to have these memories of leisurely afternoons with family in the garden, eating, drinking tea and coffee." During our conversation she also noted that "food seems huge to the Syrians. All of them, without fail. Entering a Syrian home, I am always offered cardamom coffee or tea, very sweet tea, and usually, depending on when in the day I'm visiting, it's a spread of nuts and fruit or some kind of sweet dessert, some kind of sweets."[13]

Meyer spoke about one particular Syrian single mother refugee she is following for her new book, and discussed how important cooking Syrian food is to her. "One of the women I'm writing about, her name is Zahara, and she is from a town called Hama in Syria. And she is just a cook at heart. Like this is what her soul is. She works in a restaurant here but her dream is to have her own catering business and to serve traditional Syrian foods. But you feel when you're with Zahara, and she's cooking, that she's . . . she's talked to me about how this act of cooking provokes in her this feeling of, the Arabic word is, حنين or 'haneen.'[14] It's longing. Longing. It's kind of a homesickness. It has different meanings, but it has all of those meanings: yearning, longing, a homesickness. Haneen."[15]

Meyer elaborates on Zahara's ways of recovering and retaining a part of her Syrian culture throughout resettlement: "It seems that there's this attempt to stay connected through their food to this culture. But, yeah, I mean, she's not cooking the Italian food that she cooks at her restaurant when she comes home. She's cooking the stuffed grape leaves and it seems very much that for Zahara, cooking is this way of maintaining connection, both with her immediate family and with the larger culture."[16]

For many Syrian refugees who have resettled in Texas, gardening and cooking provide them opportunities to reconnect with their culture and retain a part of their Syrian food heritage, as they seek a homeland to resettle in while not forgetting their birthplace. Haneen remains prominent in their hearts and minds as they continue to cultivate their own food sovereignty, culinary citizenship, and homeland duality in pursuit of emancipatory foodways here in the United States.

Congolese Refugee Farmers and Their Foodways

In recent decades, hundreds of thousands of Congolese refugees from the Democratic Republic of the Congo and the Republic of the Congo have experienced the traumas and difficulties of war, displacement, refugee camp life, resettlement, and marginalization. The more fortunate Congolese refugees were eventually granted political asylum to resettle in places such as Houston, Texas. In their brief resettlement history, they have worked tirelessly to earn a decent living wage while residing in the working-class neighborhoods of southwest Houston and adjust to living in a new country. Nevertheless, despite facing overwhelming challenges and odds, the Congolese diaspora in Houston continues to persevere and demonstrate resilience and agency as they develop their own community and retain their food heritage. Some have even turned to urban farming and home gardening, constructing their own homeland duality via Congolese foodways. PIF Farms assists Congolese refugee farmers in establishing sustainable, small-scale urban farms that sell fresh, organic, and locally grown produce, and also provides farmers an opportunity to earn a modest living.

Houstonian Liz Vallette was the President of PIF until October 2023. A West Point graduate and an Iraqi War veteran, Liz was very involved in PIF's collaboration with local refugees. She mentions some of the positive gains but also discusses their challenges, as well.

> It takes a while to get a farm up and running, and to many of the farmers, when they first start with us, are still learning English, and they are still learning to navigate the culture here. So, there's definitely . . . it's an uphill struggle. It does require a lot of work. As a growing organization, we're still going through some growing pains, and trying to make sure that we are able to support the training and enterprise programs fully. But ultimately, I do find the farmers seem at peace. They seem to enjoy—very much enjoy what they do for a living. They take a lot of pride in their farms and what they grow and what they produce and so I think in that sense, they're content. It is challenging. Sometimes, it takes a little while to get your income up to snuff. We did have one farmer who just bought a house though, and so there is, after three or four years of farming and saving money, we think that the farmers can get to a place of being able to tuck away a little bit of money and actually gain a little piece of the American dream.[17]

Regarding the successes for the farmers and what she is most proud of thus far, Liz says, "I was trying to think of mostly individual successes for the farmers. I guess that is sort of a success when you see the farmers being able to buy a home, or you're hearing that their kids are graduating at the top of their class from high school and heading on to go to college. So, sort of the second and third order effects of what the farmers are achieving through this income they're able to get. I think one of the most rewarding things to see, for me, is how confident they are in their abilities. So there's a lot of self-confidence that I think is . . . it's nice to see, particularly for folks having to start over, and maybe several steps down the rung of the ladder than they were back at home."[18]

One of PIF's refugee farmers is Constant Ngouala, a refugee from the Republic of the Congo, or Congo-Brazzaville.[19] In February 1999, Constant, his wife, and their children fled from the civil war that ravaged their native country. They fled to the neighboring country of Gabon and resettled in Tchibanga, along the Nyanga River. After making it safely to Tchibanga, Constant decided to return to farming for a living once more; for him it was a decision to return to some level of normalcy. He reflects on his ten years as a refugee farmer in Gabon: "At Gabon, when I get to Tchibanga, where I was living, I saw nobody was planting vegetables. Then, I start to plant vegetables and make my life over there. I love it. Because when I had my own farm in Tchibanga, that was around four hectares [almost ten acres]. And in very dry season, I was taking maybe twelve [up to fifteen] citizens to work with me. In the rainy season, maybe three or four people work with me."[20]

Constant and his family continued to work with United Nations High Commissioner for Refugees (UNHCR) officials, the US embassy, and other foreign embassies in hopes of resettling in another nation. After ten years of farming in Gabon, Constant and his family received approval through a US refugee program to resettle in the United States. On March 14, 2009, they left Tchibanga, Gabon and headed to America, arriving in Houston, Texas the very next day. Constant recalls their first few months of adjusting to Houston city life: "When I get here, it was not easy to start. It was very hard. I didn't know if I have some friends here. So, it's not easy. When I get here, maybe two months, I didn't find any Congolese. But in the same apartment we were living [in southwest Houston], there was many Congolese from my country. I didn't know that."[21]

Constant also remembers his first contacts with Urban Harvest and PIF: "Maybe one year [after arriving in Houston], I see there was a Westbury Farm [Westbury Community Garden]. I go to ask them I need to farm. They send me to

Figure E.2   Plant It Forward Farms at Westbury. Houston, Texas. (Photo by Ngọc Vũ.)

Urban Harvest. When I go to Urban Harvest, that was maybe April 2011, I was working [with them]. Almost one year later, they started Plant It [Forward]. They told me about that. I come to Plant It [Forward] and I start my training. I start after, maybe two months, they take me, took me to work with them. At the time I was taking my training, I was like a farm manager, after maybe one more year. After that, it's my small land to start farming by myself."[22]

Constant firmly believes there are many benefits to working with PIF, particularly when it comes to handling and completing the piles of paperwork that are required for a non-native, English-as-a-third-language speaker while working on an urban farm in Houston (figure E.3). When it comes to cultivating different types of crops in Houston, he says, "I plant all. Here, I plant . . . when I go to market, if somebody come to ask me a vegetable that I never plant, I ask, 'What is this?' Give me the benefit of the doubt. I'll see what I can get with seeds. Some people bring the seeds. I plant all, everything. Everything that I see, ike roselle. Now, many people want you to bring roselle when finished. And many farmers now start to plant it and sell to market, too. In my country, if you don't have roselle, it's no life." Ngouala also raises many other vegetables, herbs, and fruits, both familiar and unfamiliar to him.

Figure E.3　Constant Ngouala selling his organic produce at a Plant It Forward Farms market stall at the Houston Farmers' Market. Houston, Texas. (Photo by Ngọc Vũ.)

"Amaranth, emperor spinach, okra, eggplant, sorrel, cassava, water spinach, roquette arugula, fennel, parsnips, cilantro, chervil, papalo, dill, rosemary, tarragon, sage. My favorite is arugula. I like arugula a lot."[23]

Another refugee farmer who has raised and cultivated an urban farm with PIF is Toto Alimasi. He was born and raised in Uvira, Democratic Republic of the Congo, or Congo-Kinshasa, in 1960. Growing up, he learned farming from his mother, while his father operated a restaurant business in Uvira. Alimasi recalls, "My mother was a farmer all her life. From my mom, we mainly learned how to grow, how to prepare an area to do something. It was not for business but only for eating, for the family." He goes on to describe his family's farm: "It was a big farm. We planted corn, cassava, sweet potatoes, and different crops . . . black peas, peanuts, beans, eggplant—African eggplant."[24]

Unfortunately, Toto Alimasi's father passed away when he was young. When Toto turned twenty-one, he married Fatuma and became a teacher. He also became a pastor and a women's rights activist. At home, he cultivated a garden of crops for his family, not for business. As an outspoken pastor, it was his advocacy for women's rights, as well as coming to defense of one his fellow villagers over property rights, that his life was threatened by local authorities. In fact, Pastor Alimasi's secretary was shot and killed, and he was arrested, spending two terrifying nights in jail. [25] After his release, he gathered his family in preparation to leave their home country, and contacted UNHCR officials to seek political asylum in Uganda. In 2008, Pastor Alimasi, Fatuma, their children, and several nieces and nephews (seventeen people altogether), fled from their home country and trekked to south Uganda, where they eventually arrived at the Nakivale refugee camp, managed by UNHCR officials.[26] They spent nearly four years at the Ugandan refugee camp at Nakivale, but after receiving some necessary monthly provisions of beans and cooking oil, UNHCR officials gave him some land for his extended family of seventeen members, where Toto amazingly managed to cultivate a farm and plant some crops, such as corn, cassava, and sweet potatoes, growing more than enough food. Unfortunately, Pastor Alimasi's health began to deteriorate at the refugee camp.[27]

After three years and nine months at Nakivale, his case was finally approved for refugee resettlement by UNHCR officials. Alimasi and his family began their journey to the United States, arriving in Houston, Texas on September 20, 2011. He knew nothing about Houston. "What means Houston? I didn't know. When we came here, the weather here is like the weather in my country . . . and I like it."[28] After toiling in a few minimum wage jobs, including as a night security guard, Alimasi came in contact with PIF in 2014, thanks to his contact person with Houston's Associated Catholic Charities. After months of training with PIF personnel in their farming and entrepreneurial programs, he began working on his urban farm at the Westbury Community Garden in southwest Houston. There, he would cultivate crops according to the seasons: bok choy, collard greens, cauliflower, and okra. Alimasi also raises amaranth, African eggplant, sweet potatoes, and sugarcane—and all of them remind him of his homeland. Toto Alimasi says it makes a big difference: "When we eat this, we feel like home." At his small farm, he walks and guides me to his banana trees and points out the several bunches of small bananas, with each bunch carrying a dozen or more fruits. He proudly declares, "I grow . . . I grow these banana trees here. When we eat it [bananas], we remember Africa."[29]

Materanya "Pierre" Ruchinagiza is another West African refugee farmer currently working with PIF Farms. Born in Kutu, Democratic Republic of the Congo, Materanya's parents cultivated over two hundred acres of farmland and a two-acre garden. His parents also practiced animal husbandry, raising goats and rabbits. Materanya recalls his farming years back home, describing the rainy season and listing the vegetables, herbs, and fruit trees they grew: yams, beans, cassava, peanuts, sweet potatoes, sorghum, maize, cloves, cabbage, carrots, and beets, along with mandarin orange, lemon, and avocado trees.[30]

Both of Materanya's parents passed away years before he was forced to flee from his home country. In October 2010, due to the ongoing deadly civil war in the Democratic Republic of the Congo, Materanya, his wife, and their children made the decision to leave their home village of Kutu, and traveled three days by bus to Kenya, arriving at a UNHCR refugee camp. There, living alongside thousands of African refugees, Materanya and his family remained in the camp for approximately two years, during which he fell severely ill due to stress, malnourishment, and poor camp conditions. Eventually, with help from a friend, Materanya and his family were transferred to Nairobi, Kenya's capital, in May 2012. They stayed in Nairobi for four-and-a-half years, where his health improved and he was able to find a steady job, and his children returned to school. Yet, their status remained as refugees while they adjusted to life in a big city. Meanwhile, Materanya regularly made appointments to meet and interview with UNHCR officials in hopes of securing refugee resettlement approval for him and his family. Finally, in November 2016, his persistence paid off and they gained approval for refugee resettlement to the United States. He and his family were relocated to Houston in January 2017, and were assisted with housing and basic necessities by the Alliance for Multicultural Community Services, a local refugee resettlement nonprofit organization.[31]

That summer, Materanya discovered about PIF from another Congolese refugee: Pastor Alimasi. Pierre and his wife immediately applied for PIF's training program to be self-sufficient, urban farmers. They started training in August 2017 and completed the program in June 2018, where they were rewarded with a plot of land to farm in the Westbury Community Garden in southwest Houston. Materanya recollects how he became an urban farmer with PIF: "I was very interested and they make an application for me and my wife. So, from August [2017] to June [2018], we were trained here. Yeah, I was working at Pappa's Restaurant [while training with PIF]. I can say I was blessed to be chosen among our seventeen trained people. Me and my wife, we worked here to be . . . to get this place. This farm was for the demonstration of PIF. But they decided to give us this place."[32] Materanya and his wife continue to work hard and persevere, just like their fellow Congolese refugee farmers.

FARM-TO-FREEDOM GROWS

For the Congolese and Syrian diasporic communities, farming and gardening offer them freedom from a civil war, difficult refugee camp conditions, and rootlessness. Their small farms and gardens on the margins grow silently until they occupy and bloom in liminal spaces. For Congolese and Syrian refugees, they have suffered, survived, and succeeded in unearthing their very own existence, planting their emancipatory foodways for current and future generations; all to remember, record, consume, share, and rejoice the bounties of their harvests, newfound freedom, and sense of belonging here in the United States. Their produce reminds them of home. They use their homegrown, essential ingredients to cook and prepare Congolese and Syrian dishes, which in turn allow them to reclaim and expand their food sovereignty and make a living in their new home. In this way, Congolese and Syrian refugee farmers and gardeners demonstrate acts of culinary citizenship in search for a homeland duality that is theirs alone. Then perhaps, finally, their emancipatory foodways, which have helped them gain food sovereignty and culinary citizenship, can provide a path to healing while they plant new roots under the Texas sun.

Acknowledgments

First, I wish to thank the senior acquisitions editor at Texas A&M University (TAMU) Press, Marguerite Avery, for her indispensable advice and guidance. She is always quick to respond whenever I ask her questions, and patient with my submissions. Additionally, I want to thank Kelley A. Robbins, assistant project editor at TAMU Press, for her timely and prompt assistance. Many thanks to Katie Duelm, managing editor at TAMU Press, for overseeing our project in the "home stretch" as it nears the finish line. I also want to thank the other TAMU Press editors who witnessed the progress of this manuscript since its inception: Stacy Eisenstark, Emily Seyl, and Thom Lemmons. Furthermore, I am grateful for the tremendous assistance, guidance, and patience from Helen Wheeler, production editor at Westchester Publishing Services.

I also want to thank all the archivists who have helped me with my research over the years, particularly the incredible staff at the Special Collections and Southeast Asian Archive at the University of California at Irvine. Special thanks to Dr. Thúy Võ Đặng, Christina Woo, Audra Eagle Yun, Stephen McCloud, and Anne Frank at UC-Irvine. I am forever indebted to their expertise, assistance, and friendship. Additionally, my thanks to Emily Vinson, Vince Lee, and the wonderful archivists and librarians at the Special Collections of the M.D. Anderson Library at the University of Houston; Houston Metropolitan Research Center at the Houston Public Library; Gerald R. Ford Presidential Library and Museum at the University of Michigan; and the Vietnam Center and Sam Johnson Vietnam Archive at Texas Tech University. My special thanks to Dr. James M. Freeman for giving me permission to publish his photos. Dr. Freeman, thank you so much for documenting and preserving Vietnamese refugee history. I also wish to thank Rebekah June Née Cramer, administrative support coordinator for the Department Anthropology at San José State University, for connecting me with Dr. Freeman. Additionally, I want to thank Tim T. Hoàng for his time and effort to help me find the owner of a couple of photos.

I am grateful to the writers, scholars, farmers, home gardeners, friends, and family members whom I had the good fortune of meeting and sharing thoughtful conversations from different stages of the book project. I sincerely appreciate the assistance and support from the following: Đai Huỳnh, Tammy Đinh, Maurice Đinh, Nguyễn Văn Nam, Hồ Cap Xuân, Van Phạm, Son Hoàng, Hoàng Quang, Nguyễn Lan, Lê Đinh Qưới, Phạm Tuyết Bạch, Tina Đoàn, Trân Thi Lừng, Vũ Kiến An Quân, Trân Thị Diem, Dũng David Leftwich, Liz Vallette, Constant Ngouala, Materanya "Pierre" Ruchinagiza, Toto Alimasi, Claudia Kolker, and Kimberly Meyer. Thank you all for lending your time and sharing your stories. Plant It Forward Farms, Foodways Texas, and Urban Harvest have had a significant influence on my work. I am humbled and grateful to volunteer and learn from these exceptional non-profit organizations.

In addition, I am extremely thankful of my Dallas College colleagues and administrative leaders, particularly at the North Lake Campus, for their support, encouragement, scholarship, and friendship. They include Dr. Nathaniel Means, Dr. April Braden, Dr. Cody Smith, Katie Nisbet, Dr. Kristin Bocchine Dr. Darryl Howard, MaryAnn McGuirk, James Duran, Amanda Mello, June Charles, Shanee' Moore, Mara Dillman, Shani Suber, Neil Kaufman, Sherry Sherifian, Rebecca Escoto, Dr. Ivan Dole, Dr. LaQueta Wright, Dr. LaJuanda Bonham-Jones, Dr. Christa Slejko, Dr. Shawnda Floyd, Chancellor Dr. Justin Lonon, and countless others. Please forgive me for any omissions. Know that you all have made our workplace a family of joy and passion for learning. I am humbled to be awarded a sabbatical leave for fall 2019 to commence my writing of this manuscript. I send my sincere thanks to Chancellor Emeritus Dr. Joe May and the Dallas College Board of Trustees for approving my sabbatical.

I am indebted and grateful to my former Dallas College colleagues: Charlotte Rike, Dr. Elaine Cho, Lori Delacruz Lewis, Dr. Pamela Ice, Dr. Grady Cherry, Dr. Gabriel Bach, Dr. Beth Nikopolous, Dr. Zena Jackson, Tish Waters Hearne, Dr. Phyllis Elmore, Dr. Jerome Dotson, Enrique Otero, and so many others who have been influential in my academic career. My heartfelt thanks to Dr. Malcolm Frierson, whom I have the privilege and honor to befriend. You continue to inspire and amaze me with your scholarship, courage, resilience, humor, grit, and wisdom. Your beautiful wife, Nicole, and daughter, Eva, always make us smile and laugh when Ngọc and I visit. You all have certainly brightened our world.

I can never forget my colleagues who passed away all too soon, namely, Lynn Brink and Dr. Yolanda Romero. You both continue to live in our hearts and memories. Dr. Romero, you were my mentor, colleague, and dear friend. I could never forget your wise words and our friendship. Special thanks to Sammy Romero, a great friend I am eternally grateful to have known after Dr. Romero had moved on to another beautiful world.

To friends, scholars, and publishers that I have the good fortune to collaborate on academic projects, I am deeply appreciative to have the opportunity to work together and learn from you all. Hearty cheers to Dr. Thao Ha, whom I consider a great friend and scholar I admire, respect, and revere. To Dr. Linda Trịnh Võ, your wisdom and kindness are a gift and a treasure. Furthermore, I am thankful for Dr. Khyati Joshi, Dr. Jigna Desai, Dr. Joseph Pratt, Bethany Slaats, and David Leftwich for the opportunities to publish my scholarly works.

I would be remiss if I did not mention my University of Houston professors and graduate colleagues. I am extremely fortunate to study under the tutelage of Dr. Robert Buzzanco, Dr. Martin V. Melosi, Dr. Steven Mintz, Dr. Nestor Rodriguez, Dr. Jacqueline Hagan, Dr. Thomas O' Brien, Dr. Sarah Fishman-Boyd, Dr. Monica Perales, and many more. Thank you all for taking in a then-young, naive, and unknowledgeable graduate student with many miles to travel before becoming a worthy student to learn from you all. Special thanks to Dr. Robert Buzzanco, my graduate advisor, mentor, friend, and Sicilian savant. May we meet again in Italy! I also learned tremendously from my graduate colleagues, many of whom I continue to learn from and admire with prodigious awe: Dr. José Hernández, Dr. Ron Milam, Dr. Clayton Lust, Dr. Courtney Shah, Dr. Gregory Peek, and countless others.

My dearest friends, some of whom I have the honor to have known since the seventh grade and my miserable middle and high school years, I cannot thank you all enough in these pages. Tino and Anna Đình, Shatel and Pretty Bhakta, Chi-Chi and Samantha Le, Van Phạm, and Son Hoàng and Thanh, you are always near and dear in my heart. Thank you for saving me from the endless, desperate roads of despair. Your friendship will always be cherished and celebrated. I love you all.

Many thanks to my in-law siblings, Điệp and Shawn Besaw, Carlos Aillon, and Mike Ennis. Thank you for accepting and welcoming me as your little brother. To my incredible nieces and nephews: Aislinn, Donovan, and Sinead Ennis, Giselle Aillon, and Alexander and Nicholas Besaw, you all continue to amaze me with your talents, intellectual curiosity, diligence, and empathy. Sophia and Ian Ennis, we miss you dearly, but know that you will always remain in our hearts.

To my siblings I have the honor and privilege to grow up together in our humble abode: Margaret Ennis, Catherine Aillon, and Byron Vũ, I am endlessly grateful to all that you have given, shared, and taught. Know that your little brother will always look up to you. Thank you for all the storytelling, outdoor running and playing, TV watching, radio listening, and nurturing my love for reading, writing, and dreaming. I will never forget our latch-key years together. How we always dream to get away from our struggling, working-class ways, but only to realize now how such ways have shaped and helped us to where we are today.

My heartfelt thanks to my in-laws, Phạm Minh Thứ and Trần Thi Lừng and my grandmother-in-law, Nguyễn Nua. I also want to thank my parents, Vũ Kiến An Quân and Trần Thị Diem Dũng. I owe much of this book to all of them; not only for the wisdom they shared in their interviews and photos, but also teaching me so many of life's precious lessons. To my parents, you have raised me well, despite our family's meager means and difficult beginnings. May you finally find refuge and peace from the ghosts of war that will always haunt us.

Finally, I give thanks to Ngọc, my love, better half, best friend, and soulmate. I owe much of my happiness, joy, and peace to my wife. Without you, this book certainly would never have come to fruition. Thank you, my darling! You are my center, equilibrium, and horizon. Without you, I would not be here today.

Notes

INTRODUCTION

1. Throughout the manuscript, I will use the more colloquial and popular term among the Vietnamese diaspora, South Việt Nam. However, Southern Việt Nam would be the more appropriate term in accordance to the terminology utilized and terms agreed in the 1954 Geneva Accords. Nevertheless, I choose the former term, because it is most conveyed and accepted by Vietnamese Americans and their exilic communities throughout the world.
2. Thanks to Claudia Kolker for introducing me to this term and applying it to the Vietnamese diasporic experience.
3. Ngọc Pham Vũ, interview.
4. Aguilar-San Juan, *Little Saigons*, xxv.

CHAPTER 1

1. Nguyễn, *Nothing Ever Dies*, 39. Nguyễn describes these refugees as, "oceanic refugees, a term that lends more nobility to the sufferings and heroism of those whom the Western press called the 'boat people.'"
2. James A. Schill Collection of Photographs. MS-SEA064, Box 1, Folder 10. Special Collections and Archives, UC Irvine Libraries, Irvine, California.
3. Peters, *Appetites and Aspirations in Vietnam*, 31.
4. Ibid, 31–32.
5. South Việt Nam is sometimes referred to as Southern Việt Nam. Please see Buzzanco, *Masters of War*. His reference to South Việt Nam as Southern Việt Nam is to provide a clearer purpose behind the establishment of South Việt Nam as a created state mandated by the Geneva Accords and not the will of the southern Vietnamese populace. Thus, Southern Việt Nam was separated from the rest of Việt Nam, and based from that perspective, there was no such thing as a separate North and South Việt Nam but rather a single country and population that was divided by the geopolitics of the Cold War between the United States and Soviet Union. Although Buzzanco is correct, I choose to use the name South Viet Nam over Southern Viet Nam because it is the more commonly accepted and used vernacular, albeit an inaccurate one.
6. Collection of Vietnamese stamps and currency, UC Irvine Libraries.
7. Ibid.
8. Vũ, *Rice and Baguette*, 7.

9. Nguyễn, *Into the Vietnamese Kitchen*, 172.

10. Ibid.

11. Vũ, *Rice and Baguette*, 95.

12. Herring, *America's Longest War*, 5.

13. Duiker, *Sacred War*, 44.

14. Huỳnh, *Vietnamese Communism, 1925–1945*, 337.

15. Duiker, *Sacred War*, 51.

16. Also referred to as the Southern Republic. See recent scholarship by Nguyễn, "(Re)making the South Vietnamese."

17. Peters, *Appetites and Aspirations*, 22.

18. Ibid, 58.

19. Ibid.

20. Ibid, 59.

21. Ibid.

22. Buzzanco, *Masters of War*, 9.

23. FitzGerald, *Fire in the Lake*, 84.

24. Kolko, *Anatomy of a War*, 83.

25. FitzGerald, *Fire in the Lake*, 116.

26. Hickey, *Village in Vietnam*, 14.

27. Ibid, 26.

28. Ibid, 149.

29. Ibid, 153.

30. Ibid, 148.

31. Ibid, 149.

32. Ibid, 278.

33. Vang, *Hmong America*, 34–35.

34. Hickey, "Montagnard Refugee Problems," 1.

35. Ibid.

36. Ibid, 2.

37. Ibid, 3.

38. Ibid, 2.

39. Ibid, 4.

40. Ibid.

41. Nguyễn, "(Re)making the South Vietnamese."

42. Ibid.

43. Historian Jana K. Lipman asserts, "While the media, popular culture, government records, and the men and women themselves commonly and repeatedly referred to the Hungarians, Cubans, and Vietnamese as refugees, legally they were parolees." For more analysis, see Lipman, *In Camps*, 16–17.

44. Kolker, "Survival Essentials," 15.

45. Lipman, *In Camps*, 5.

46. Ibid, 11.

47. Ibid.

48. Ibid, 17.

49. Freeman, *Changing Identities*, 32.

50. Ibid, 33.

51. Ibid, 34.
52. Ibid.
53. Staats, "Indochinese Exodus," i.
54. Ibid, 1. These number break down as follows: "Thailand, about 147,000; Malaysia, about 51,000; other countries, including the Philippines, Hong Kong, Singapore, Japan, Indonesia, and areas on or near the Indochina peninsula, about 20,000."
55. Ibid, 31.
56. Ibid.
57. Boat People SOS Committee News Release, "Freedom or Death."
58. Ibid.
59. Boat People SOS News Bulletin, Issue 23, January 1993, 1.
60. Ibid.
61. Ibid, 4.
62. Boat People SOS News Bulletin, Issues 16–17, January–February 1992, 3.
63. Ibid.
64. Ibid, 2.
65. Boat People SOS News Bulletin, Issue 24, February–March 1993, 1.
66. Ibid.
67. Freeman, *Changing Identities*, 38.
68. Staats, "Indochinese Exodus," 29.
69. Congressional Delegation to Southeast Asia. "Refugees from Indochina," 7.
70. Staats, "Indochinese Exodus," 43.
71. Ibid, 34.
72. "Thailand Sikhiu 1992 Cooking Rice" and "Thailand Sikhiu 1992 Section of Camp," 1992, photos of Sikhiu Refugee Camp, Thailand, Special Collections and Archives, UC Irvine Libraries, Irvine, California.
73. Ibid, 39.
74. See "Pulau Bidong Refugee Camp 1978–1991, Malaysia," http://refugeecamps.net /images/bi28.jpg (photo courtesy of Tim T. Hoàng).
75. O'Brien, *Things They Carried*, 14–15.
76. Nguyễn, *Into the Vietnamese Kitchen*, 180.
77. An and An, *ăn: to eat*, 15–16.
78. Ibid, 22.
79. Ibid, 36.
80. Ibid, 79.
81. According to Vietnamese tradition, the person's last or family name is stated first, followed by the middle name, and finally the first name. To avoid confusion, names are quoted under Vietnamese formality throughout the text. However, the author has chosen to state Vietnamese names in accordance with American standards in the endnotes and bibliography.
82. Nam Văn Nguyễn, interview.
83. Ibid.
84. An Quân Kiến Vũ, interview.
85. Ibid.
86. Quang Hoàng and Ms. Lan Nguyễn, interview.
87. Ibid.

88. Son Hoàng, interview.
89. Bạch Tuyết Phạm, telephone interview.
90. Tammy Đình, interview.
91. Xu, "Diaspora, Transcendentalism, and Ethnic," 101.
92. Ibid, 104.
93. Vũ, *Rice and Baguette*, 226.
94. Lipman, *In Camps*, 91.
95. Ibid.
96. Ibid, 227–28.
97. Espiritu, "Vexed Solidarities." When referring to the Vietnamese resettlement in the United States and Texas, I will use the more appropriate term of "refugee settler" in settler colonial studies. "Refugee settler" acknowledges the colonization of Indigenous peoples in the Americas, and although Vietnamese newcomers may not play a direct role in colonization, they resettled upon lands violently taken from Indigenous peoples who (once) populated in Texas and the United States.

CHAPTER 2

1. Otsuka, *When the Emperor*, 66–67.
2. Cap Xuân Hồ, interview.
3. Matsumoto, *Farming the Home Place*, 204.
4. Nazarea, Rhoades, and Andrews-Swann, *Seeds of Resistance*, x.
5. Ibid.
6. Ibid, 12.
7. Matsumoto, *Farming the Home Place*, 7.
8. Coe, *Chop Suey*, 121–22.
9. Ibid, 123.
10. Ibid, 134–35.
11. Ibid, 136–37.
12. Zhu, *Chinaman's Chance*, 113.
13. Ibid.
14. Ibid, 113–14.
15. Ibid, 114.
16. Ibid, 75.
17. Tsu, *Garden of the World*, 5.
18. Gordon and Okihiro, *Impounded*, 67.
19. Ibid.
20. Daniels, *Prisoners Without Trial*, 67.
21. Phu, *Picturing Model Citizens*, 59.
22. Ibid, 69–70.
23. Ibid, 78.
24. Gordon and Okihiro, *Impounded*, 32.
25. Ibid, 32–33.
26. Ibid, 72.
27. Ibid.
28. Yoo, *Growing Up Nisei*, 103.

29. Ibid.
30. Ibid, 170.
31. Hikoji Takeuchi, interview.
32. Ibid.
33. Sue Kunitomi Embrey, interview.
34. Willie K. Ito, interview.
35. Rhoades, "When Seeds Are Scarce," 264.
36. Ibid, 271.
37. Ibid.
38. Đào, "How Asian Americans."
39. Ibid.
40. Medrano, *Truly Texas Mexican*, 11.
41. Ibid.
42. Gabaccia, *We Are What*, 110.
43. Steptoe, *Houston Bound*, 24.
44. Ibid.
45. Ibid, 6.
46. Binkovitz, "Is Houston's Food."
47. Ibid.
48. Leftwich, "Sowing the Grains."
49. Ibid.
50. Washington, "In Houston's Diverse."
51. Ibid.
52. Mejia, "How Houston Has Become."
53. Ibid.
54. Spiering, *Houston Cooks*, 7.
55. Ibid, 8.
56. Klineberg, *Prophetic America*.
57. Guerrero, *Nuevo South*, 182.
58. Ibid, 9.
59. Ibid, 5.
60. Ibid.
61. Ibid, 62.
62. Ibid, 12.
63. Ibid, 15.
64. Brief Profile of Yen Ngọc Huỳnh, UC Irvine Libraries.
65. Ibid.
66. Robinson, "'Vietnamization' Comes to Texas." I am indebted to Dr. Tom McKinney for providing this source.
67. Ibid, 1 and 6.
68. von der Mehden, *Ethnic Groups of Houston*, 87.
69. Ibid.
70. "The act defines a refugee as a person who is unable or unwilling to return to, and is unable or unwilling to avail himself of the protection of his country because of a well-founded fear of persecution on account of race, religion, nationality, membership in a particular group, or political action." Project Ngọc, *The Forgotten People*, 23.

71. Peranteau et al. *2004 Community Health Report*, 21.

72. Ibid.

73. Ibid. A refugee is classified by the United Nations Convention Relating to the Status of Refugees (1951). The definition of refugee can be found in Section 101(a) (42) of the Immigration and Nationality Act, as amended, and describes a refugee as "any person who is outside any country of such person's nationality . . . and is unable or unwilling to return to . . . that country because of persecution or a well-founded fear of persecution on account of race, religion, nationality, membership in a particular social group, or political opinion."

74. John S.D. Eisenhower, Memo to President Gerald R. Ford. "Presidential Advisory Committee on Refugees," 1.

75. Kelly, "Coping with America."

76. Migration and Refugee Services, "Amerasians Resettlement."

77. Gordon, "Settlement Patterns of Indochinese."

78. Hing, *Making and Remaking Asian*, 129.

79. Leba, *Vietnamese Entrepreneurs*, 174.

80. Nam Văn Nguyễn, interview.

81. Ibid.

82. Quang Hoàng and Lan Nguyễn, interview.

83. Ibid.

84. Son Hoàng, interview.

85. Ibid.

86. Tammy Đình, interview.

87. Ibid.

88. American Community Survey, United States Census Bureau, 2021: ACS 5-Year Estimates Selected Population Detailed Tables, https://data.census.gov/table/ACSDT5YS PT2021.B01003?q=vietnamese&g=310XX00US19100.

89. Lừng Thi Trần, interview.

90. Lừng Thi Trần, telephone interview.

91. Ibid.

92. Lừng Thi Trần, interview.

93. Ngọc Phạm Vũ, interview.

94. Shelton, *Power Moves*, 5.

CHAPTER 3

1. Phạm, *Pleasures of the Vietnamese*, 183.

2. An and An, *ăn: to eat*, 79.

3. Ibid.

4. Ibid, 259.

5. Rhoades, "When Seeds Are Scarce," 272.

6. Ibid, 273.

7. Ibid, 276.

8. Mazumdar and Mazumdar, "Immigrant Home Gardens."

9. Ibid.

10. The six current Vietnamese villages of southeast Houston are Thái Xuân, Đà Lạt, Sài Gòn, Huế, Thanh Tâm, and St. Joseph. At one time, there were reportedly at least eight Vietnamese villages throughout the city of Houston, including St. Mary Village and La Vang in southwest Houston. St. Mary Village and La Vang residents were evacuated in the mid-2000s and the villages were demolished. If we include Allen Parkway Village, which at one time had a sizeable population of Vietnamese residents, then we could count nine Vietnamese villages that have existed in Houston's history.

11. Nam Văn Nguyễn, interview.

12. Son Hoàng, interview.

13. Ibid.

14. Quang Hoàng and Lan Nguyễn, interview.

15. Ibid. After Hurricane Harvey, Son's parents decided to downsize their living space and sold their beloved Pearland home in 2018, moving to a smaller house in southwest Houston.

16. An Quan Kiến Vũ, interview.

17. Ibid.

18. Dũng Diem Thị Trần, interview.

19. Ibid.

20. Tammy Đình, interview.

21. Ibid.

22. Brettell and Reed-Danahay, *Civic Engagements*, 39.

23. Ibid.

24. Lừng Thi Trần, interview.

25. Ibid.

26. Bạch Tuyết Phạm, telephone interview.

27. Ibid.

28. Tina Mary Đoàn, interview.

29. Bullard, *Invisible Houston*, 43.

30. Ibid, 45.

31. Ibid.

32. Ibid, 46.

33. Wayne King, "Houston Housing Authority Accused."

34. Ibid.

35. Houston Institute for Culture, "Asian American Experience."

36. Ibid.

37. Historic Oaks of Allen Parkway Village (website), https://www.historicoaks.com.

38. Vietnamese residents referred to their condominiums as villages because, initially, they organized a social system where a village chief was appointed to run the daily activities of the condominium and was responsible for the safety and well-being of the residents. The residents became accustomed to such a social system because such a system was common practice in Việt Nam, and so they brought forth this village social structure to organize and maintain order. Furthermore, to preserve their Vietnamese identity and remember Việt Nam, each village was designated with a Vietnamese name, usually after a prominent city in Việt Nam or a Catholic patron saint. In addition, two Vietnamese villages used to exist in southwest Houston: St. Mary's and La Vang.

39. Kolker, "Gardens of Vietnam," 17.
40. Ibid.
41. Harkinson, "Tale of Two Cities."
42. Ibid.
43. Rogers, "Beautiful Projects."
44. Kolker "Gardens of Vietnam," 17.
45. Harkinson, "Tale of Two Cities."
46. Ibid.
47. Samuelson, "Thai Xuan Village."
48. Twitty, *Cooking Gene*, 59.

CHAPTER 4

1. Ngọc Phạm Vũ, interview.
2. Rhoades, "When Seeds Are Scarce," 271.
3. Ibid, 277.
4. Nguyễn, *Into the Vietnamese Kitchen*, 292.
5. Dũng Diem Thị Trần, interview.
6. Ibid.
7. Lừng Thị Trần, interview, October 8, 2019.
8. Ibid.
9. Bạch Tuyết Phạm, telephone interview.
10. Ibid.
11. Phillips, "Quieting Noisy Bellies."
12. Ibid.
13. Nguyễn, *Into the Vietnamese Kitchen*, 4.
14. Ibid, 4–5.
15. Ibid, 17.
16. Ibid, 172.
17. Ibid.
18. Phạm, *Pleasures of the Vietnamese*, 14.
19. Ibid, 183.
20. Phạm, "Bottle Gourds."
21. Ibid.
22. Fargione, "Food and Imagination."
23. Kinbacher, *Urban Villages*, 157.
24. Nguyễn, *Into the Vietnamese Kitchen*, 2.
25. Ibid, 5.
26. Dũng Diem Thị Trần, interview.
27. Nguyễn, *Into the Vietnamese Kitchen*, 11.
28. An and An, *ăn: to eat*, 11.
29. Ibid, 27.
30. Lê, *Little Saigon Cookbook*, 204.
31. Ha, *Recipes from My Home*, 53.
32. Dũng Diem Thị Trần, interview.

33. Lừng Thị Trần, interview, October 8, 2019.
34. Ibid.
35. Dũng Diem Thị Trần, interview.
36. Phạm, "Cooking Together Threads Past."
37. Ibid.
38. Vũ, *Rice and Baguette*, 206.
39. Kolker, *Immigrant Advantage*, 154.
40. Ibid, 160–61.
41. An and An, *ăn: to eat*, 27.
42. Phạm, *Pleasures of the Vietnamese*, 22.
43. Ibid, 10.
44. Ibid.
45. Phạm, "Herbs Inspire a Restaurant."
46. Nguyễn, *Into the Vietnamese Kitchen*, 313.
47. An and An, *ăn: to eat*, 231.
48. Lê, *Little Saigon Cookbook*, 4.
49. Ibid.
50. Trung Đoàn, interview.
51. Ibid.
52. Nhuận Phú Lê, interview.
53. Michelle Trần, interview.
54. Nguyễn, *Into the Vietnamese Kitchen*, 5.
55. Ibid.
56. Lê, *Little Saigon Cookbook*, 3.
57. Ibid, 7.
58. Lừng Thị Trần, interview, October 8, 2019.
59. Binkovitz, "Is Houston's Food."
60. Ibid.
61. I first came across the phrase "emancipatory foodways" through Dr. Lisa Rainwater. Many thanks to Dr. Rainwater for introducing me to this term.
62. An and An, *ăn: to eat*, 27.
63. Companion, "Lessons," 129.
64. Ibid, 137.
65. Ibid, 136.
66. Peters, *Appetites and Aspirations*, 6.
67. Origins of gà hộp lo, according to my older siblings, was first thought of by one of our gracious family sponsors, Mrs. Long, who suggested using chicken to replace the turkey for Thanksgiving. For my parents, chicken was more recognizable, familiar to taste, affordable, and manageable to cook. My father came up with the idea of using miến as the stuffing for our chicken.
68. Gabaccia, *We Are What We Eat*, 222.
69. Ibid.
70. Miller, *Vietnamese Cookery*, 8.
71. Phạm, "Beyond Pho."
72. Ku, *Dubious Gastronomy*, 13.

73. Gabaccia, *We Are What We Eat*, 176.
74. Chen, *Chop Suey, USA*, 174.
75. Manalansan IV, "Cooking Up the Senses," 180.
76. Ibid.
77. Padoongpatt, *Flavors of Empire*, 188.
78. Ibid, 4.
79. Võ, "Defiant Daughters," 210.
80. Binkovitz, "In Houston."
81. Padoongpatt, *Flavors of Empire*, 18.
82. Ibid, 183.
83. Ibid, 184.
84. Twitty, *Cooking Gene*, 21.
85. Ibid, 403.
86. Ibid, 404.
87. Ferris, *Edible South*, 333.
88. Ownby, "Conclusion: Go Forth," 367.
89. Edge, *Potlikker Papers*, 2.
90. Chen, *Chop Suey, USA*, 179.
91. Trị La, interview.
92. Ibid.
93. Dai Huỳnh, interview.
94. Ibid.
95. Edge, *Potlikker Papers*, 299.
96. David Leftwich, interview.
97. Ibid.
98. Vũ, *Rice and Baguette*, 229.
99. Phạm, "How Houstonians."
100. Ibid.
101. Houston's original Little Sài Gòn was established in Midtown, just south of downtown, during the 1980s and 1990s, before the commercial district became gentrified by the early 2000s.
102. Burnett, "Decades After Clashing."
103. Ibid.
104. Shepherd and Goalen, *Cook Like a Local*, 93.
105. Claudia Kolker, interview.
106. Unfortunately, Saigon House is yet another Midtown Vietnamese restaurant that has ceased its operations at the time of this writing, demonstrating the challenges of managing a restaurant business even with a great reputation and high-quality food.
107. Spiering, *Houston Cooks*, 182.
108. Gabaccia, *We Are What We Eat*, 3.
109. Edge, *Potlikker Papers*, 308–9.
110. Ibid, 298.
111. Gabaccia, *We Are What We Eat*, 225.
112. Ibid, 231.
113. Ibid, 232.

CHAPTER 5

1. lê, *Gangster*, 90.
2. Padoongpatt, *Flavors of Empire*, 179.
3. Wittman, Desmarais, and Wiebe, *Food Sovereignty*, 2.
4. Ibid.
5. Ibid, 7.
6. Gottlieb and Joshi, *Food Justice*, 135.
7. Ibid.
8. Ibid, 149.
9. Reese, *Black Food Geographies*, 11.
10. Nam Văn Nguyễn, interview.
11. An Quan Kiến Vũ, interview.
12. Ventura and Bailkey, "Food Justice," 9.
13. Ibid, 11.
14. Ibid, 13.
15. Reese, *Black Food Geographies*, 113.
16. Ibid, 122.
17. Ibid, 129.
18. Ibid, 130.
19. Sbicca, *Food Justice Now!*, 185–86.
20. Ibid, 1.
21. Ibid, 17.
22. Minkoff-Zern et al., "Race and Regulation," 66.
23. Ibid, 68.
24. Ibid, 81–82.
25. von der Mehden, *Ethnic Groups of Houston*.
26. Houston Institute for Culture, "Asian American Experience."
27. Harkinson, "Tale of Two Cities."
28. Bowens, *Color of Food*, 202.
29. Ibid.
30. Ibid, 203.
31. Ibid.
32. Ibid, 198.
33. Ibid, 199.
34. David Leftwich, interview.
35. Ibid.
36. An and An, *ăn: to eat*, 231.
37. Afzal, *Lone Star Muslims*, 211.
38. Ibid, 211–12.
39. Ibid, 176.
40. Rekdal, *Broken Country*, 108.
41. Đào, "Anthony Bourdain."
42. Binkovitz, "In Houston."
43. Ibid.
44. Gabaccia, *We Are What Eat*, 9.

45. Shepherd and Goalen, *Cook Like a Local*, 171.
46. Ibid.
47. Companion, "Lessons, 126.
48. Ibid, 127.
49. Ibid, 135–36.
50. Ibid, 137.
51. Son Hoàng, interview, September 6, 2015.
52. Ibid.
53. Lừng Thị Trần, interview, September 7, 2015.
54. Ibid.
55. Engelhardt, *A Mess of Greens*, 12–13.
56. Ibid, 13.
57. Medrano, *Truly Texas Mexican*, 3–4.
58. Hung, "When Authenticity."
59. Ibid.
60. Rogers, "Beautiful Projects."
61. Ibid.
62. Nielsen, "Houston Chronicle Reporter."
63. Kriel, "Vietnamese Refugees."
64. Kriel, "In South Houston."
65. Ibid.
66. Twitty, *Cooking Gene*, 409–10.
67. Ibid, 410.
68. White, *Freedom Farmers*, 13–14.
69. Ibid, 143.
70. Ibid, 143–44.
71. Minkoff-Zern, *New American Farmer*, 134.
72. Ibid, 104.
73. Ibid, 118.
74. Hondagneu-Sotelo, *Paradise Transplanted*, 4.
75. Ibid, 5.
76. Ibid, 23.
77. Ibid, 124.
78. Ibid, 135.
79. Padoongpatt, *Flavors of Empire*, 17–18.
80. Alkon, Kato, and Sbicca, *Recipe for Gentrification*, 12.
81. Hassberg, "Citified Sovereignty," 311.
82. Ibid, 312.
83. Ichikawa, "Giving Credit," 275.
84. Ibid, 283.
85. Wagner, "Liz Magor in 'Vancouver.'"

CHAPTER 6

1. Lừng Thị Trần, interview, November 14, 2019.
2. Võ, "Constructing," 102.
3. Liễu, *The American Dream in Vietnamese*, 134.

EPILOGUE

1. Travers, "Community and Vegetables."
2. Ibid.
3. Dancey-Downs, "Planting Seeds."
4. Ibid.
5. Briggs, "Seeds of Hope."
6. Ibid.
7. Schulze, "Urban Agriculture."
8. Ibid.
9. Alabaster, "Syrian Refugees Find Solace."
10. Ibid.
11. Travers, "Community and Vegetables."
12. Kimberly Meyer, interview.
13. Ibid.
14. حنين is the Arabic spelling for haneen.
15. Kimberly Meyer, interview.
16. Ibid.
17. Liz Vallette, interview.
18. Ibid.
19. Plant It Forward (website), https://plantitforward.farm/.
20. Constant Ngouala, interview.
21. Ibid.
22. Ibid.
23. Ibid.
24. Toto Alimasi, interview.
25. Ibid.
26. Gray, "This Refugee Family."
27. Toto Alimasi, interview.
28. Ibid.
29. Ibid.
30. Materanya "Pierre" Ruchinagiza, interview.
31. Ibid.
32. Ibid.

Bibliography

PRIMARY SOURCES

Alabaster, Olivia. "Syrian Refugees Find Solace in Rooftop Gardens." *Al Jazeera News*, September 2, 2016, https://www.aljazeera.com/news/2016/07/syrian-refugees-find-solace-rooftop-gardens-160726084911769.html

An, Helene, and Jacqueline An. *ăn: to eat: Recipes and Stories from a Vietnamese Family Kitchen*. Philadelphia: Running Press, 2016.

Attenborough, David. *The Private Life of Plants: A Natural History of Plant Behavior*. London: BBC Books, 1995. http://www.asknature.org/strategy/e0c8517027aa8edf4507a86244 25e89f

Binkovitz, Leah. "In Houston, What Can Urbanists Learn from Food?" *Urban Edge*, Kinder Institute for Urban Research at Rice University, June 21, 2018, https://kinder.rice.edu /2018/06/21/houston-what-can-urbanists-learn-food

———. "Is Houston's Food the Way to Understand Its Diversity?" *Houston Chronicle*, June 25, 2018. https://www.houstonchronicle.com/local/gray-matters/article/food -houston-bourdain-diversity-urbanism-13023556.php#

Boat People SOS. "Freedom or Death." Committee News Release. MS-SEA002, Box 14, Folder 9. Special Collections and Archives, UC Irvine Libraries, Irvine, California, date unknown.

———. News Bulletin. Issues 16–17, January–February 1992. MS-SEA002, Box 14, Folder 9. Special Collections and Archives, UC Irvine Libraries, Irvine, California, January–February 1992.

———. News Bulletin. Issue 23, January 1993. MS-SEA002, Box 14, Folder 9. Special Collections and Archives, UC Irvine Libraries, Irvine, California, January 1993.

———. News Bulletin. Issue 24, February and March 1993. MS-SEA002, Box 14, Folder 9. Special Collections and Archives, UC Irvine Libraries, Irvine, California, February–March 1993.

"Brief Profile of Yen Ngọc Huỳnh." James Ridgeway Collection, Box 2: Folder 6. Special Collections and Archives, UC Irvine Libraries, Irvine, California, date unknown.

Briggs, Helen. "Seeds of Hope: The Gardens Springing Up in Refugee Camps." BBC, May 21, 2018. https://www.bbc.com/news/science-environment-44174865

Burnett, John. "Decades After Clashing with the Klan, a Thriving Vietnamese Community in Texas." NPR, November 25, 2018. https://www.npr.org/2018/11/25/669857481 /decades-after-clashing-with-the-klan-a-thriving-vietnamese-community-in-texas

Congressional Delegation to Southeast Asia. "Refugees from Indochina: Current Problems and Prospects." MS-SEA056, Box 6, Folder 2. Special Collections and Archives, UC Irvine Libraries, Irvine, California, April 24, 1979.

Đào, Alana. "How Asian Americans Use Kitchen Gardens to Reclaim Their Heritage." *Huffington Post*, August 23, 2019. https://www.huffpost.com/entry/asian-american-kitchen-gardens_l_5d541892e4b05fa9df083eb5

Đào, Dan Q. "Anthony Bourdain Asked Us to Have a Greater Sense of Obligation—to Trauma, to Triumph, and to Food." *Esquire Magazine*, June 25, 2019. https://www.esquire.com/food-drink/a28166732/anthony-bourdain-legacy-next-generation-food-travel-writers/

Dancey-Downs, Katie. "Planting Seeds in Refugee Camps." *Regenerosity*, 2020. https://www.regenerosity.world/stories/planting-seeds-in-refugee-camps#:~:text=For%20the%2022.5%20million%20refugees,come%20as%20the%20gardens%20grow.

Eisenhower, John S. D. Memo to President Gerald R. Ford. "Presidential Advisory Committee on Refugees Visit to Ft. Chaffee, Arkansas, May 20, 1975." Folder: Trip to Ft. Smith, Ark., Box 78, Theodore C. Marrs Files, Gerald R. Ford Library, University of Michigan, Ann Arbor, Michigan, June 2, 1975.

Gordon, Linda W. "Settlement Patterns of Indochinese Refugees in the United States." INS Reporter/Spring 1980. Special Collections and Archives, UC Irvine Libraries, Irvine, California, 1980.

Gray, Lisa. "This Refugee Family Fled Congo. In Houston, They Grow Organic Vegetables." *Houston Chronicle*, January 11, 2020. https://www.houstonchronicle.com/life/article/This-refugee-family-fled-Congo-In-Houston-they-14968129.php#

Ha, Christine. *Recipes from My Home Kitchen: Asian and American Comfort Food*. New York: Rodale, 2013.

Harkinson, Josh. "Tale of Two Cities." *Houston Press*, December 15, 2005. https://www.houstonpress.com/news/tale-of-two-cities-6547193

Hickey, Gerald Cannon. "Montagnard Refugee Problems: The Bru and Hre of the Central Vietnamese Highlands." MS-SEA001, Box 22, Folder 2, Item 2. Special Collections and Archives, UC Irvine Libraries, Irvine, California, May 4, 1965.

"Hong Kong Shek Kong 1991 Garden at School." Photos of Shek Kong Detention Centre, Hong Kong. Special Collections and Archives, UC Irvine Libraries, Irvine, California, 1991.

Hung, Melissa. "When Authenticity Means a Heaping Plate of Tex-Mex." *Houston Chronicle*, January 6, 2020. https://www.houstonchronicle.com/life/food/article/When-authenticity-means-a-heaping-plate-of-Tex-Mex-14952827.php

Huỳnh, Dai. "Chef's Corner: Nicole Routhier." *Buzz Magazines*, January 1, 2017. https://thebuzzmagazines.com/articles/2017/01/chefs-corner-nicole-routhier

———. "Chef's Corner: Wayne Nguyen." *Buzz Magazines*, February 1, 2018. https://thebuzzmagazines.com/articles/2018/02/chefs-corner-wayne-nguyen

"Indonesia Galang 1992 Gardens." Photo of Galang Refugee Camp, Indonesia. Special Collections and Archives, UC Irvine Libraries, Irvine, California, 1992.

"Pocket Dairy of Southeast Asian Refugee." James A. Schill Collection of Photographs. MS-SEA064, Box 1, Folder 10. Special Collections and Archives, UC Irvine Libraries, Irvine, California.

King, Wayne. "Houston Housing Authority Accused of Racial Steering." *New York Times*, March 19, 1985. https://timesmachine.nytimes.com/timesmachine/1985/03/19/103508.html?pageNumber=16

Kolker, Claudia. "The Gardens of Vietnam." *Cité Magazine* (Spring 2001). Box 10, Claudia Kolker Papers. Special Collections, University of Houston Libraries, Houston, Texas, 2001.

———. "Survival Essentials." *Rice Business Magazine* (Fall 2017): 14–17.

Kriel, Lomi. "In South Houston Apartments, a Piece of Vietnam Flowers." *Houston Chronicle*, August 28, 2015. https://www.houstonchronicle.com/local/themillion/article/In-south-Houston-apartments-a-piece-of-Vietnam-6472465.php

———. "Vietnamese Refugees Broaden City's Culture." *Houston Chronicle*, September 10, 2016. https://www.chron.com/local/history/major-stories-events/article/Vietnamese-refugees-broaden-city-s-culture-9215281.php#photo-10906362

Lê, Ann. *The Little Saigon Cookbook: The Vietnamese Cuisine and Culture in Southern California's Little Saigon*. Guilford, CT: Globe Pequot Press, 2011.

Leftwich, David. "Sowing the Grains of Change: How a Japanese Immigrant Stirred the Pot in a Creole City." *Edible Houston*, October 27, 2017. https://ediblehouston.ediblecommunities.com/food-thought/sowing-grains-change

Medrano, Adán. *Truly Texas Mexican: A Native Culinary Heritage in Recipes*. Lubbock: Texas Tech University Press, 2014.

Mejia, Brittny. "How Houston Has Become the Most Diverse Place in America." *Los Angeles Times*, May 9, 2017. https://www.latimes.com/nation/la-na-houston-diversity-2017-htmlstory.html

Migration and Refugee Services. "Amerasians Resettlement by United States Catholic Conference." United States Catholic Conference. February 5, 1988. Sam Johnson Vietnam Archive, Texas Tech University, Lubbock, Texas, 1988.

Miller, Jill Nhu Hương. *Vietnamese Cookery*, 6th ed. Rutland, VT: Charles E. Tuttle Company, Inc., 1986.

Morago, Greg. "Le Colonial." *Houston Chronicle*, August 15, 2016. https://www.houstonchronicle.com/life/food/article/Vietnamese-chef-Nicole-Routhier-comes-full-circle-9144212.php

Nguyễn, Andrea. *Into the Vietnamese Kitchen: Treasured Foodways, Modern Flavors*. Berkeley, CA: Ten Speed Press, 2006.

Nielsen, James. "Houston Chronicle Reporter Wins Prestigious George Polk Award for Exposing Family Separation at Border." *Houston Chronicle*, February 19, 2020. https://www.houstonchronicle.com/news/houston-texas/houston/article/Chronicle-reporter-wins-award-border-separation-15068132.php

Peranteau, Jane et al. *2004 Community Health Report: Houston's Alief and Park Place Super Neighborhood*. Houston: St. Luke's Episcopal Health Charities, 2004.

Phạm, Mai (journalist). "Beyond Pho: 10 Vietnamese Noodle Soups to Discover in Houston (and Where to Find Them)." *Houston Chronicle*, January 10, 2018. https://www.houstonchronicle.com/life/food/article/Beyond-pho-10-Vietnamese-noodle-soups-to-12488437.php

———. "How Houstonians are Shaping the Future of the Vietnamese Soup." *Houston Chronicle*, December 26, 2019. https://www.houstonchronicle.com/life/food/article/Houston-The-best-city-for-pho-in-the-United-10819292.php

Phạm, Mai (chef). "Bottle Gourds by Any Name Would Be as Sweet," *Houston Chronicle*, January 8, 2003. https://www.houstonchronicle.com/recipes/article/Bottle-gourds-by-any-name-would-be-as-sweet-2642455.php

———. "Cooking Together Threads Past with Present, Grief with Joy." *Houston Chronicle*, February 20, 2002. https://www.houstonchronicle.com/recipes/article/Family-comforts-Cooking-together-threads-past-2871941.php

———."Herbs Inspire a Restaurant Career." *Houston Chronicle*, September 7, 2005. https://www.houstonchronicle.com/recipes/article/Herbs-inspire-a-restaurant-career-2610486.php

———. *Pleasures of the Vietnamese Table: Recipes and Reminiscences from Vietnam's Best Market Kitchens, Street Cafés, and Home Cooks.* New York: HarperCollins Publishers, 2001.

"Philippines Palawan 1991 Camp Gardens." Photos of Palawan Refugee Camp, Philippines. Special Collections and Archives, UC Irvine Libraries, Irvine, California, 1991.

Pfeifer, Mark E. "Vietnamese American Populations by Metro Area, 2010 Census." https://vacoc.org/wp-content/uploads/2018/05/The-Vietnamese-Population-2010_July-2.2011.pdf

Project Ngọc. *The Forgotten People: Vietnamese Refugees in Hong Kong.* Special Collections and Archives, UC Irvine Libraries, Irvine, California.

Robinson, Douglas. "'Vietnamization' Comes to Texas: Number of Allies Training in U.S. Being Tripled." *Houston Chronicle* 69, no. 67, section 1. December 19, 1969.

Rogers, Susan. "The Beautiful Projects: Contradiction and Complexity in Houston's Multifamily Housing." *Cité Magazine*, July 11, 2014. http://offcite.org/the-beautiful-projects-contradiction-and-complexity-in-houstons-multifamily-housing/

Samuelson, Ruth. "Thai Xuan Village." *Houston Press*, March 29, 2007. https://www.houstonpress.com/news/thai-xuan-village-6577374

Samuelsson, Marcus. *No Passport Required.* Season 2, aired January 27, 2020 on PBS.

Schulze, Helene. "Urban Agriculture and Forced Displacement in Iraq: 'This Garden Is My Kingdom.'" *foodtank*, January 15, 2018. https://foodtank.com/news/2018/01/greening-iraqs-refugee-camps-urban-agriculture/

Shepherd, Chris, and Kaitlyn Goalen. *Cook Like a Local: Flavors That Can Change How You Cook and See the World.* New York: Clarkson Potter Publishers, 2019.

Spiering, Francine. *Houston Cooks: Recipes from the City's Favorite Restaurants and Chefs.* Vancouver, BC: Figure 1 Publishing Inc., 2019.

Staats, Elmer B. "The Indochinese Exodus: A Humanitarian Dilemma." Report to the Congress by the Comptroller General of the United States. MS-SEA056, Box 5, Folder 2. Special Collections and Archives, UC Irvine Libraries, Irvine, California, April 24, 1979.

Trần, Dũng Diem Thị. Recipe Book, Houston, TX. Accessed December 27, 2018.

Travers, Julia. "Community and Vegetables Grow Side-By-Side in Syrian Refugee Camp Gardens." NPR, February 22, 2018. https://www.npr.org/sections/thesalt/2018/02/22/587708405/community-and-vegetables-grow-side-by-side-in-syrian-refugee-camp-gardens

Wagner, Pamela Mason, dir. "Liz Magor in 'Vancouver.'" *Art21*, PBS, aired September 23, 2016. https://art21.org/watch/art-in-the-twenty-first-century/s8/liz-magor-in-vancouver-segment/.

Washington, Bryan. "In Houston's Diverse Culinary Landscapes, Who Cooks, Who Eats, and Who Gets to Stay?" *Catapult Magazine*, February 20, 2018. https://catapult.co/stories/column-bayou-diaries-food-as-culture-in-houston

INTERVIEWS

Alimasi, Toto. Interviewed by author, Houston, TX, October 12, 2019.

Đình, Tammy. Interviewed by author, Houston, TX, August 18, 2019.

Đoàn, Tina Mary. Online interview conducted by author, April 12, 2021.

Đoàn, Trung. Interviewed by Catherine Yuh and Isabelle Soifer, Houston, TX, April 6, 2012. Houston Asian American Archive Chao Center for Asian Studies, Rice University.

Embrey, Sue Kunitom. Interviewed by John Allen, November 6, 2002. Courtesy of the Manzanar National Historic Site Collection. www.ddr.densho.org

Hồ, Cap Xuân. Interviewed by author, Houston, TX, August 18, 2000.

Hoàng, Quang, and Lan Nguyễn. Interview surveyed by Son Hoàng, Houston, TX, September 6, 2015.

Hoàng, Son. Interview surveyed by author, Houston, TX, September 6, 2015.

———. Interviewed by author, Houston, TX, February 21, 2016.

Huỳnh, Dai. Interviewed by author, Houston, TX, December 2003.

Ito, Willie K. Interviewed by Kristen Leutkemeier, December 5, 2013. Courtesy of the Manzanar National Historic Site Collection. www.ddr.densho.org

Kolker, Claudia. Interviewed by author, Houston, TX, July 16, 2019.

La, Trị. Interviewed by Sherri Sheu, Houston, TX, January 19, 2019. Foodways Texas Greater Oral History Project, Iconic Restaurant Project, Kim Son Restaurant, Part Two.

Lê, Nhuận Phú. Interviewed by Tiffany Sloan and AnhThu Dang, Houston, TX, June 28, 2019. Houston Asian American Archive Chao Center for Asian Studies, Rice University.

Leftwich, David. Interviewed by author, Houston, TX, December 2, 2018.

Meyer, Kimberly. Interviewed by author, Houston, TX, July 15, 2019.

Ngouala, Constant. Interviewed by author, Houston, Texas, August 15, 2019.

Nguyễn, Nam Văn. Interviewed by author, Houston, TX, September 20, 2015.

Phạm, Bạch Tuyết. Telephone interview conducted by Lừng Thi Trân, Grand Prairie, TX, December 17, 2020.

Ruchinagiza, Pierre Materanya. Interviewed by author, Houston, Texas, December 14, 2019.

Takeuchi, Hikoji. Interviewed by John Allen, November 7, 2002. Courtesy of the Manzanar National Historic Site Collection. www.ddr.densho.org

Trần, Dũng Diem Thị. Interviewed by author, Houston, TX, September 7, 2019.

Trần, Lừng Thi. Interview surveyed by author, Grand Prairie, TX, September 7, 2015.

———. Interviewed by author, Grand Prairie, TX, October 8, 2019.

———. Interviewed by author, Grand Prairie, TX, November 14, 2019.

———. Telephone interview conducted by Ngọc Phạm Vũ, Irving, TX, January 3, 2021.

Trần, Michelle. Interviewed by Jocelyn Monroy and Emily Hughes (assistant), Houston, TX, March 27, 2012. Houston Asian American Archive Chao Center for Asian Studies, Rice University.

Vallette, Liz. Interviewed by author, Houston, TX, June 8, 2019.

Vũ, An Quan Kiến. Interview surveyed by author, Houston, TX, September 27, 2015.

Vũ, Ngọc Pham. Interviewed by author, Irving, TX, August 8, 2018.

SECONDARY SOURCES

Afzal, Ahmed. *Lone Star Muslims: Transnational Lives and the South Asian Experience in Texas.* New York: New York University Press, 2015.

Aguilar-San Juan, Karin. *Little Saigons: Staying Vietnamese in America.* Minneapolis: University of Minnesota Press, 2009.

Alkon, Alison Hope, Yuki Kato, and Joshua Sbicca, eds., *A Recipe for Gentrification: Food, Power, and Resistance in the City.* New York: New York University Press, 2020.

Bowens, Natasha. *The Color of Food: Stories of Race, Resilience and Farming.* Gabriola Island, BC: New Society Publishers, 2015.

Brettell, Caroline B., and Deborah Reed-Danahay. *Civic Engagements: The Citizenship Practices of Indian and Vietnamese Immigrants.* Stanford, CA: Stanford University Press, 2012.

Bullard, Robert D. *Invisible Houston: The Black Experience in Boom and Bust.* College Station: Texas A&M University Press, 1987.

Buzzanco, Robert. *Masters of War: Military Dissent and Politics in the Vietnam Era.* Cambridge: Cambridge University Press, 1997.

Chen, Yong. *Chop Suey, USA: The Story of Chinese Food in America.* New York: Columbia University Press, 2014.

Chew, Jessica. "Vietnamese and Chinese American Cultures: Destination Houston." *Houston History* 13, no. 1 (October 28, 2015). https://houstonhistorymagazine.org/2015/10/vietnamese-and-chinese-american-cultures-destination-houston/

Coe, Andrew. *Chop Suey: A Cultural History of Chinese Food in the United States.* New York: Oxford University Press, 2009.

Companion, Michéle. "Lessons from 'The Bucket Brigade': The Role of Urban Gardening in Native American Cultural Continuance." *Cities of Farmers: Urban Agricultural Practices and Processes*, edited by Julie C. Dawson and Alfonso Morales. Iowa City: University of Iowa Press, 2016, 126–140.

Daniels, Roger. *Prisoners Without Trial: Japanese Americans in World War II.* New York: Hill and Wang, 1993.

Donnelly, Nancy D. *Changing Lives of Refugee Hmong Women.* Seattle: University of Washington Press, 1997.

Duiker, William. *Sacred War: Nationalism and Revolution in a Divided Vietnam.* New York: McGraw-Hill, Inc., 1994.

Edge, John T. *The Potlikker Papers: A Food History of the Modern South.* New York: Penguin Books, 2017.

Engelhardt, Elizabeth S. D. *A Mess of Greens: Southern Gender and Southern Food.* Athens: University of Georgia Press, 2012.

Espiritu, Evyn Lê. "Vexed Solidarities: Vietnamese Israelis and the Question of Palestine." *Lit: Literature Interpretation Theory* 29, no. 1 (2018): 8–28.

Fargione, Daniela. "Food and Imagination: An Interview with Monique Trường." *Gastronomica* 16, no. 4 (Winter 2016): 1–7. University of California Press, JSTOR. https://www.jstor.org/stable/10.2307/26362389

Ferris, Marcie Cohen. *The Edible South: The Power of Food and the Making of an American Region.* Chapel Hill: University of North Carolina Press, 2014.

Fisher, MFK. *How to Cook a Wolf.* New York: North Point Press, 1954.

FitzGerald, Frances. *Fire in the Lake: The Vietnamese and the Americans in Vietnam.* New York: Little, Brown and Company, 1972.

Freeman, James M. *Changing Identities: Vietnamese Americans, 1975–1995.* Boston: Allyn and Bacon, 1995.

Gabaccia, Donna R. *We Are What We Eat: Ethnic Food and the Making of Americans.* Cambridge, MA: Harvard University Press, 1998.

Gordon, Linda, and Gary Y. Okihiro, eds. *Impounded: Dorothea Lange and the Censored Images of Japanese American Internment.* New York: Norton, 2006.

Gottlieb, Robert, and Anupama Joshi. *Food Justice.* Cambridge, MA: MIT Press, 2013.

Guerrero, Perla M. *Nuevo South: Latinas/os, Asians, and the Remaking of Place.* Austin: University of Texas Press, 2017.

Hassberg, Analena Hope. "Citified Sovereignty: Cultivating Autonomy in South Los Angeles." In *A Recipe for Gentrification,* edited by Alison Hope Alkon, Yuki Kato, and Joshua Sbicca. New York: New York University Press, 2020.

Herring, George C. *America's Longest War: The United States and Vietnam, 1950–1975,* 3d ed. New York: McGraw-Hill, Inc., 1996.

Hickey, Gerald Cannon. *Village in Vietnam.* New Haven, CT: Yale University Press, 1964.

Hing, Bill Ong. *Making and Remaking Asian America Through Immigration Policy, 1850–1990.* Palo Alto, CA: Stanford University Press, 1994.

Hondagneu-Sotelo, Pierrette. *Paradise Transplanted: Migration and the Making of California Gardens.* Oakland: University of California Press, 2014.

Houston Institute for Culture, "The Asian American Experience: Building New Saigon." http://www.houstonculture.org/cultures/viet.html

Huỳnh, Khánh Kim. *Vietnamese Communism, 1925–1945.* Ithaca, NY: Cornell University Press, 1982.

Ichikawa, Nina F. "Giving Credit Where It Is Due: Asian American Farmers and Retailers as Food System Pioneers." In *Eating Asian America: A Food Studies Reader,* edited by Robert Ji-Song Ku, Martin F. Manalansan IV, and Anita Mannur, 274–87. New York: New York University Press, 2013.

Kelly, Gail P. "Coping with America: Refugees from Vietnam, Cambodia, and Laos in the 1970s and 1980s." *Annals of the American Academy of Political and Social Science* 487 (September 1986). Special Collections and Archives, UC Irvine Libraries, Irvine, California, 1986.

Kinbacher, Kurt E. *Urban Villages and Local Identities: Germans from Russia, Omaha Indians, and Vietnamese in Lincoln, Nebraska.* Lubbock: Texas Tech University Press, 2015.

Klineberg, Stephen L. *Prophetic America: Houston on the Cusp of a Changing America.* New York: Avid Reader Press, 2020.

Kolker, Claudia. *The Immigrant Advantage: What We Can Learn from Newcomers to America about Health, Happiness, and Hope.* New York: Free Press, 2014.

Kolko, Gabriel. *Anatomy of a War: Vietnam, the United States, and the Modern Historical Experience.* New York: New Press, 1994.

Ku, Robert Ji-Song. *Dubious Gastronomy: The Cultural Politics of Eating Asian in the USA.* Honolulu: University of Hawai'i Press, 2014.

Lai, Thanhha. *Inside Out and Back Again.* New York: HarperCollins Children's Books, 2013.

Lê, Thi Diem Thúy. Author prefers her full name to be in lowercase. *The Gangster We Are All Looking For.* New York: First Anchor Books, 2004.

Leba, John Kong. *The Vietnamese Entrepreneurs in the U.S.A.: The First Decade.* Houston: Zieleks Company, 1985.

Liễu, Nhi T. *The American Dream in Vietnamese.* Minneapolis: University of Minnesota Press, 2011.

Lipman, Jana K. *In Camps: Vietnamese Refugees, Asylum Seekers, and Repatriates.* Oakland: University of California Press, 2020.

Manalansan IV, Martin F. "Cooking Up the Senses: A Critical Embodied Approach to the Study of Food and Asian American Television Audiences." In *Alien Encounters: Popular Culture in Asian America,* edited by Mimi Thi Nguyen and Thuy Linh Nguyen Tu, 179–93. Durham, NC: Duke University Press, 2007.

Matsumoto, Valerie J. *Farming the Home Place: A Japanese American Community in California, 1919–1982.* Ithaca, NY: Cornell University Press, 1993.

Mazumdar, Shampa, and Sanjoy Mazumdar. "Immigrant Home Gardens: Places of Religion, Culture, Ecology and Family." *Landscape and Urban Planning,* January 4, 2012.

McNamee, Gregory. *Tortillas, Tiswin, and T-Bones: A Food History of the Southwest.* Albuquerque: University of New Mexico Press, 2017.

Minkoff-Zern, Laura-Anne. *The New American Farmer: Immigration, Race, and the Struggle for Sustainability.* Cambridge, MA: MIT University Press, 2019.

Minkoff-Zern, Laura-Anne, Nancy Peluso, Jennifer Sowerwine, and Christy Getz. "Race and Regulation: Asian Immigrants in California Agriculture." In *Cultivating Food Justice: Race, Class, and Sustainability,* edited by Alison Hope Alkon and Julia Agyeman, 65–85. Cambridge, MA: MIT Press, 2011.

Nazarea, Virginia D., Robert E. Rhoades, and Jenna E. Andrews-Swann, eds., *Seeds of Resistance, Seeds of Hope: Place and Agency in the Conservation of Biodiversity.* Tucson: University Arizona Press, 2013.

Nguyễn, Việt Thanh. *Nothing Ever Dies: Vietnam and the Memory of War.* Cambridge, MA: Harvard University Press, 2017.

Nguyễn, Y Thiên. "(Re)making the South Vietnamese Past in America." *Journal of Asian American Studies* 21, no. 1 (2018): 65–103.

O'Brien, Tim. *The Things They Carried.* Boston: Mariner Books, 2009.

Oliver, Mary. *Upstream: Selected Essays.* New York: Penguin Books, 2019.

Ownby, Ted. "Conclusion: Go Forth with Method." In *The Larder: Food Studies Methods from the American South,* edited by John T. Edge, Elizabeth Engelhardt, and Ted Ownby. Athens: University of Georgia Press, 2013.

Otsuka, Julie. *When the Emperor Was Divine.* New York: Anchor Books, 2003.

Padoongpatt, Mark. *Flavors of Empire: Food and the Making of Thai America.* Oakland: University of California Press, 2017.

Peters, Erica J. *Appetites and Aspirations in Vietnam: Food and Drink in the Long Nineteenth Century.* Lanham, MD: AltaMira Press, 2012.

Phillips, Delores B. "Quieting Noisy Bellies: Moving, Eating, and Being in the Vietnamese Diaspora." *Cultural Critique* 73 (Fall 2009): 47–87. University of Minnesota Press, JSTOR. https://www.jstor.org/stable/25619837

Phu, Thy. *Picturing Model Citizens: Civility in Asian American Visual Culture.* Philadelphia: Temple University Press, 2012.

Reese, Ashanté M. *Black Food Geographies: Race, Self-Reliance, and Food Access in Washington, D.C.* Chapel Hill: University of North Carolina Press, 2019.

Rekdal, Paisley. *The Broken Country: On Trauma, a Crime, and the Continuing Legacy of Vietnam*. Athens: University of Georgia Press, 2017.

Rhoades, Robert E. "When Seeds Are Scarce: Globalization and the Response of Three Cultures." In *Seeds of Hope, Seeds of Resistance: Place and Agency in the Conservation of Biodiversity*, edited by Virginia D. Nazarea, Robert E. Rhoades, and Jenna E. Andrews-Swann, 262–86. Tucson: University of Arizona Press, 2013.

Sbicca, Joshua. *Food Justice Now! Deepening the Roots of Social Struggle*. Minneapolis: University of Minnesota Press, 2018.

Shelton, Kyle. *Power Moves: Transportation, Politics, and Development in Houston*. Austin: University of Texas Press, 2017.

Steptoe, Tyina. *Houston Bound: Culture and Color in a Jim Crow City*. Oakland: University of California Press, 2016.

Tsu, Cecilia M. *Garden of the World: Asian Immigrants and the Making of Agriculture in California's Santa Clara Valley*. Oxford, UK: Oxford University Press, 2013.

Twitty, Michael W. *The Cooking Gene: A Journey Through African American Culinary History in the Old South*. New York: Amistad, 2018.

Vang, Chia Youyee. *Hmong America: Reconstructing Community in Diaspora*. Urbana–Champaign: University of Illinois Press, 2010.

Ventura, Steve, and Martin Bailkey, eds. "Food Justice and Food Sovereignty." *Good Food, Strong Communities: Promoting Social Justice through Local and Regional Food Systems*. Iowa City: University of Iowa Press, 2017.

Võ, Linda Trịnh. "Constructing a Vietnamese American Community: Economic and Political Transformation in Little Saigon, Orange County." *Amerasia Journal* 34, no. 3: 84–109.

———. "Defiant Daughters: The Resilience and Resistance of 1.5-Generation Vietnamese American Women." In *Our Voices, Our Histories: Asian American and Pacific Islander Women*, edited by Shirley Hune and Gail M. Nomura. New York: New York University Press, 2020.

von der Mehden, Fred R., ed. *The Ethnic Groups of Houston*. Houston: Rice University Studies, 1984.

Vũ, Hồng Liên. *Rice and Baguette: A History of Food in Vietnam*. London: Reaktion Books, 2016.

White, Monica M. *Freedom Farmers: Agricultural Resistance and the Black Freedom Movement*. Chapel Hill: University of North Carolina Press, 2018.

Wittman, Hannah. "Reconnecting Agriculture and the Environment: Food Sovereignty and the Agrarian Basis of Ecological Citizenship." In *Food Sovereignty: Reconnecting Food, Nature and Community*, edited by Hannah Wittman, Annette Aurélie Desmarais, and Nettie Wiebe, 91–105. Oakland, CA: Food First Books, 2010.

Wittman, Hannah, Annette Aurélie Desmarais, and Nettie Wiebe, eds. *Food Sovereignty: Reconnecting Food, Nature and Community*. Oakland, CA: Food First Books, 2010.

Xu, Wenying. "Diaspora, Transcendentalism, and Ethnic Gastronomy in the Works of Li-Young Lee." In *Eating Identities: Reading Food in Asian American Literature*. Honolulu: University of Hawai'i Press, 2008.

Yoo, David K. *Growing Up Nisei: Race, Generation, and Culture among Japanese Americans of California, 1924–49*. Urbana–Champaign: University of Illinois Press, 2000.

Zhu, Liping. *A Chinaman's Chance: The Chinese on the Rocky Mountain Mining Frontier*. Boulder: University Press of Colorado, 1997.

ARCHIVES

Foodways Texas Greater Oral History Project, Iconic Restaurant Project, https://www
  .foodwaystexas.org/oral-history (online archive).
Gerald R. Ford Presidential Library, University of Michigan, Ann Arbor, Michigan.
Houston Asian American Archive Chao Center for Asian Studies, Rice University, Houston,
  Texas, https://haaa.rice.edu/ (online archive).
Houston Metropolitan Research Center, Houston, Texas.
Manzanar National Historic Site Collection, www.ddr.densho.org (online archive).
Sam Johnson Vietnam Archive, Southwest Collection, Texas Tech University, Lubbock,
  Texas.
Special Collections and Archives, the University of California–Irvine Libraries, Irvine,
  California.
Special Collections, University of Houston Libraries, Houston, Texas.

Index

Page numbers in italics refer to illustrations.